TEN HOURS' LABOR

Ten Hours' Labor

Religion, Reform, and Gender in Early New England

Teresa Anne Murphy

Cornell University Press

Ithaca and London

For Joel and for Max

Contents

Preface

The artisans and operatives of New England who fought for a ten-hour day in the 1830s and 1840s sought access to a world of leisure that would bring time not only for salvation and moral reform, but for intellectual development. As early industrial workers, they confronted a workplace in which the physical activities of wage-earning were increasingly divorced from the intellectual excitement of learning. Without the chance to think, they argued, they would be less than human.

Reading through their newspapers and speeches, I have felt acutely the privilege of my own work in writing this book. I could not have done so without the generous support of numerous individuals and institutions. At an early stage I received fellowships from the American Association of University Women and the Charlotte Newcomb Foundation. Support from a National Endowment for the Humanities Fellowship for College Teachers, as well as subsequent grants from the Charles Warren Center at Harvard and the office of the vice-president at the University of Rhode Island, allowed me much-needed time to expand and rewrite. This process was further aided by the hospitality of the Princeton History Department, which welcomed me as a visitor for two years, and by an NEH Summer Seminar program at the State University of New York at Binghamton.

I have also benefited from the help provided by the staffs at many libraries and historical societies, including the Sterling

Memorial Library at Yale, the Firestone Library at Princeton, the Houghton, Baker, and the Divinity School libraries at Harvard, the John Hay and Rockefeller libraries at Brown, the SUNY Binghamton Library, the University of Rhode Island Library, the Library of Congress, the Manchester Public Library, the Woonsocket Public Library, the New York Public Library, the Boston Public Library, the Massachusetts State Archives, the Rhode Island State Archives, the Archives of the Superior Court of Rhode Island, the American Antiquarian Society, the Rhode Island Historical Society, the Worcester Historical Society, the Lynn Historical Society, the Andover Historical Society, the New Hampshire Historical Society, the Fitchburg Historical Society, the Vermont Historical Society, the Museum of American Textile History, the Essex Institute, the First Baptist Church of Fall River, and, in particular, the Fall River Historical Society and its director, Florence Brigham. Scott Navitsky provided invaluable help as a research assistant in tracing the ten-hour petition signers.

During the many drafts of these pages, friends and colleagues provided crucial support. Sydney Ahlstrom was a patient adviser, and Paul Johnson gave a helpful reading. David Davis and David Montgomery provided important suggestions for shaping this work and have continued to support my efforts to expand and redirect my thinking over the years. I have tried out ideas on many of my colleagues and received valuable advice in return. For this I am particularly grateful to Sarah Blank, Mary Blewett, Deborah van Broekhoven, Frank Costigliola, Ileen DeVault, Lori Ginzberg, Karen Halttunen, Shaun Marmon, Louis Masur, Susan Porter, Nick Salvatore, Kathryn Kish Sklar, Barbara Smith, Michael Smith, Susan Smulyan, Sharon Strom, Cindy Taft, Marta Wagner, Sean Wilentz, Chris Wilson, and the participants in the NEH Summer Seminar at SUNY Binghamton. Others who read parts of this manuscript and provided important suggestions for revision include Joel Bernard, John Brooke, Gary Cross, Ann Fabian, Bruce Laurie, Howard Rock, and David Zonderman. Tom Dublin, Tony Fels, David Jaffee, and Joel Kuipers have read the manuscript in its entirety, saving me from critical mistakes and pushing me in new directions. Peggy Hoover provided many important improvements during her copy editing. Peter Agree has cheered me on throughout. From all these people I learned to appreciate the importance of intellectual community. I could not have completed this book without them.

My son, Max Kuipers, has given up a lot of time with me so that I could complete this book. I know my absences were painful and I apologize. My husband, Joel Kuipers, has not only provided intellectual companionship, he has shouldered extra family responsibilities without complaining about either the professional or emotional price he has paid. I cannot thank him enough.

TERESA ANNE MURPHY

Kingston, Rhode Island

Abbreviations

AAS   American Antiquarian Society, Worcester, Massachusetts

AHS   Andover Historical Society, Andover, Massachusetts

FRHS   Fall River Historical Society, Fall River, Massachusetts

HBS   Special Collections Department, Baker Library, Harvard University Graduate School of Business Administration, Boston

MATH   Museum of American Textile History, North Andover, Massachusetts

MSA   Massachusetts State Archives, Boston

NHHS   New Hampshire Historical Society, Concord

RIHS   Rhode Island Historical Society, Providence

TEN HOURS' LABOR

Introduction

In the fall of 1840, John Hunt, president of the Journeymen Bootmakers' Society in Boston, stood trial in Municipal Court. He and the other officers of the Bootmakers' Society faced several counts of conspiracy because the rules of their organization forbade members from working in a shop where men who were not in the society were employed. As a result, they had demanded that master bootmaker Isaac Waitt fire a journeyman who had refused to join the organization. Waitt complied rather than face a walkout by the rest of the men in his shop. As far as the Commonwealth of Massachusetts was concerned, Waitt had acted against his will; he had been compelled to fire one of his employees. Furthermore, the state charged, this compulsion grew out of a conspiracy of the Bootmakers' Society to impoverish uncooperative journeymen and masters.

Unfortunately for the state's case, Waitt found the rules of the society quite reasonable, and several other masters agreed. One argued, "The work had been better of late; twenty-five percent better than in 1835." Another added, "The men were more temperate now than formerly. The society had put an end to 'blue Monday.'"[1]

Peter Thatcher, the judge who heard the case in Municipal

---

1. Peter Thatcher, *Thatcher's Criminal Cases*, October term, 1840, pp. 615–620.

1

Court, was not impressed by these arguments and directed the jury to convict Hunt and his companions of conspiracy, advice the jury followed. But Chief Justice Lemuel Shaw, who heard the case on appeal, disagreed. His decision in *Commonwealth v. Hunt*, handed down in the spring of 1842, would become one of the most famous in the history of American labor law. In effect, Shaw upheld both the legitimacy of the union and its demand for a closed shop.[2]

The significance of Shaw's opinion, and the extent of its influence on the evolution of labor law, have been widely debated.[3] But largely overlooked has been the analogy Shaw used in analyzing the Journeymen Bootmakers' Society: he compared it to a temperance organization. What if workingmen agreed among themselves "not to work in a shop in which ardent spirit was furnished, or not to work in a shop with any one who used it, or not to work for an employer, who should, after notice, employ a journeyman who habitually used it." Such a resolve would make it difficult for intemperate journeymen to find work and inconvenient for masters who would like to do things differently, but Shaw saw nothing illegal in either the means or the ends employed.[4] As long as workingmen were not bound by a preexisting contract, they could follow their consciences collectively in choosing with whom and for whom to work. Shaw was, in effect, using moral terms to legitimize a new and potentially antagonistic relationship between master and journeymen.

Shaw's comparison of the union to a moral reform society was no accident. Witnesses for the journeymen had played up the elements of self-improvement in their descriptions of the Bootmakers' Society. But their testimony represented more than a canny defense strategy. Moral reform had been central to New England

2. *Massachusetts Reports* 45 Metcalf 4 (1842), pp. 111–137.
3. Christopher L. Tomlins, "Criminal Conspiracy and Early Labor Combinations: Massachusetts, 1824–1840," *Labor History* 28 (1987): 370–385; Victoria Hattam, "Unions and Politics: The Courts and American Labor, 1806–1896" (Ph.D. diss., M.I.T., 1987), esp. pp. 62–72; Marta Wagner, "The Limits of Criminal Conspiracy: *Commonwealth v. Hunt* in Its Historical Context" (Paper, Harvard Law School, 1990).
4. *Massachusetts Reports* 45, p. 130.

labor-organizing in the 1830s and would grow in importance during the 1840s, buttressed by additional appeals to Protestant religious beliefs. Religion and reform structured the discourse of labor activism in antebellum New England and distinguished it from labor movements elsewhere. How and why they did so are the focus of this book.

Two important labor-reform organizations were created during this period in the moral reform tradition: the New England Association of Farmers, Mechanics, and Other Workingmen, which operated during the early 1830s, and the New England Workingmen's Association, which flourished during the mid-1840s. Unlike the Bootmakers' Society, these regional organizations focused on the demand for a shorter workday rather than on higher wages or a closed shop. Both movements were concentrated in the mill villages of New England, though many of the leaders were skilled craftsmen from such traditional trades as carpentry. And unlike emerging trade unions, these organizations were not limited to wage earners; anyone of good moral character could join. Indeed, organizing took place by community rather than by trade, except in the large cities of Providence and Boston. Thus, these labor associations looked very much like the temperance and antislavery societies with which they coexisted. And by the 1840s, the concerns of Protestant religion suffused labor rhetoric.

The structure of these organizations is somewhat surprising, because labor historians have generally associated evangelicalism and moral reform with the values of the middle class and interpreted the influence of religion on workingmen as a drain on labor militancy. Paul Johnson argues effectively that evangelical Protestantism in the early nineteenth century, with its emphasis on free moral agency, legitimated the economic domination of capitalists who employed wage labor. Workshop relationships of earlier years may have been based on assumptions of moral dependency in which masters assumed responsibility for their journeymen, but those of the antebellum period were not. Workingmen who joined churches in later revivals, Johnson suggests, probably did so under pressure from their employers. Anthony Wallace, in a study of mills outside Philadelphia, contends that evangelicalism led manufacturers to acts of benevolence (including passage of a weak ten-hour law) that had the effect of pacifying employees in their mills.[5] From such perspectives, nineteenth-century Protestantism subdued unruly workers and became a defining characteristic of the bourgeois mentality.

A few historians have felt less comfortable ceding Protestantism solely to the middle class. Both Bruce Laurie and Sean Wilentz, studying antebellum working people in Philadelphia and New York, note that during the 1840s evangelical workers incorporated criticism of working conditions into their religious perspectives. Those who demanded a shorter workday in Philadelphia might be deferential to their employers, but they were also vigilant parents concerned about the plight of their children in the mills. In New York, the Order of United American Mechanics, a Protestant (and nativist) labor organization that rose to prominence after 1845, and the Mechanics Mutual Protection Association, which established a branch in New York City in 1846, were more than outposts of ethnic bigotry or religious enthusiasm. The Order of United American Mechanics opposed immigration because it drove down wages, and the Mechanics Mutual championed higher wages for artisans and a ten-hour day for factory workers as critical for a Christian republic.[6]

But Wilentz and Laurie acknowledge the limits of religious inspiration and the close connection between Protestantism and middle-class hegemony. Wilentz prefaces his discussion of the mechanics' movements by pointing out that, until 1845, Protes-

5. Paul Johnson, *A Shopkeeper's Millennium: Society and Revivals in Rochester, New York, 1815–1837* (New York, 1978), pp. 137, 121; Anthony Wallace, *Rockdale: The Growth of an American Village in the Early Industrial Revolution* (New York, 1978), pp. 388–394. Paul Faler's study of shoemakers in Lynn makes a similar assertion: conflict between masters and journeymen was undermined by shared participation in the Methodist church. See Paul G. Faler, *Mechanics and Manufacturers in the Early Industrial Revolution, Lynn, Massachusetts, 1780–1860* (Albany, N.Y., 1981), pp. 102–106, 137.

6. Bruce Laurie, *The Working People of Philadelphia, 1800–1850* (Philadelphia, 1980), p. 143; and Sean Wilentz, *Chants Democratic: New York City and the Rise of the American Working Class, 1788–1850* (New York, 1984), pp. 344–349. For an important discussion of the way religion could be used to criticize employers, see Jama Lazerow, "Religion and Labor Reform in Antebellum America: The World of William Field Young," *American Quarterly* 38 (Summer 1986): 265–286.

tantism was "an article of entrepreneurial faith" that "dulled class antagonisms" with assertions of cultural superiority. Despite their economic critiques, the nativism of the American Mechanics and the opposition of the Mechanics Mutual to strikes and unions undercut the class consciousness of the 1830s. In fact, the importance of these groups lies in their function as a bridge to the future, a bridge that evangelical workers traveled to reunite with radical workers from whom they had been estranged during previous decades.

Laurie's workers appear even less militant than those in New York. He notes that while religiously inspired workers might petition for a ten-hour day, they would not strike for one, for that "was tantamount to acknowledging class polarities and denying the social fluidity that was the ideological keystone of revivalism."[7] We are left to wonder whether these ten-hour advocates in Philadelphia were simply subscribing to the philosophy of the middle class. Did religion provide them with any kind of language to describe themselves as workers in opposition to employers, or was it a language that denied such opposition? Were working people asserting certain values that they did not share with their employers, especially when it came to issues of time?

My argument in this book is that many working people were unwilling to cede control of religion and moral reform to the middle class. In part, their perspective arose out of the popular evangelicalism of factory towns which challenged the authority of educated elites. Moral reform movements, such as the Washingtonians, did the same, inverting traditional hierarchies and critiquing the pretensions of middle-class piety. Labor activists further elaborated these cultural conflicts as they moved beyond criticism, appropriating middle-class prerogatives in dictating moral standards, and attacking the social relations of paternalism that were so central to New England labor practices.

Many of the labor activists were evangelically inspired and committed to a broad range of reform activities. But religion and reform provided more than ideological commitment for partici-

7. Wilentz, *Chants Democratic*, p. 343; Laurie, *Working People of Philadelphia*, p. 146.

pants; they also provided a common linguistic currency for the largely Protestant working people of New England. There were differences, however. The language of labor protest was far more historically situated than the language of religion and reform, and it was more attuned to differences of economic circumstance and industrial development. This in itself made labor reform far more threatening to the social order than revivals and temperance meetings.

The fact that religion and reform were shared languages rather than shared ideologies is an important point. The same language can be common to a large group of people, but the words can be given different meanings depending on who says them, how they are spoken, and under what circumstances. In this way the words are given different "accents." It is a process that allows for both communication and conflict as different groups struggle to control the meaning of the words.[8]

Religion and reform provided not only a way for working people to confront their employers, but also the means for working people from different backgrounds to communicate and engage in collective struggle. Still, it was not an easy process. Building trades workers, shoemakers, and textile operatives, for example, existed in very distinctive social and economic environments, which they had to explain to one another. Carpenters from Fall River with a strong base in institutional religion would have to confront cordwainers from Lynn, a town that was

8. V. N. Volosinov uses the term "accents" to describe the way in which different social classes compete to impart their own meanings to particular signs, resulting in their multi-accentuality. Particularly pertinent for the discussion which follows is Volosinov's observation that "a sign that has been withdrawn from the pressures of social struggle—which, so to speak, crosses beyond the pale of the class struggle—inevitably loses force, degenerating into allegory and becoming the object not of live social intelligibility but of philological comprehension." *Marxism and the Philosophy of Language* (Cambridge, Mass., 1973), 22–25. For further elaboration on the way in which this theory of multi-accentuality can be applied, see Stuart Hall, "Deconstructing the Popular," in *People's History and Social Theory,* ed. Raphael Samuel (London, 1981); Michael Denning, *Mechanic Accents: Dime Novels and Working-Class Culture in America* (New York, 1987), pp. 82–84; and Mary Kupiec Cayton, "The Making of an American Prophet: Emerson, His Audiences, and the Rise of the Culture Industry in Nineteenth-Century America," *American Historical Review* 92 (June 1987): 597–620.

the epicenter of "come-outerism." Local patterns of industrial-ization and religious expression were different, and labor activ-ists were attempting to unify the skilled and the unskilled, a distinction strongly influenced by differences of gender.

Although the New England Association of Farmers, Mechan-ics, and Other Workingmen was exclusively male and the New England Workingmen's Association was predominantly male, gender was a critical component in their evolution. The attack on moral dependency, which the bootmakers used to legitimate their labor-organizing, affected households as well as workshops. The same popular evangelicalism that challenged the authority of elites also undermined the authority of workingmen within their own families as wives and children flocked to religious services, creating considerable tension in many cases. This spir-itual antagonism mirrored the economic transformation taking place in many mill villages as family contract labor gave way to individual wage-earning and a voluntary family wage economy replaced an involuntary one. From this perspective, Washingto-nianism takes on additional significance as a temperance move-ment that not only criticized the authority of elites but also morally rehabilitated husbands and fathers, men who had been displaced both economically and spiritually in their households and whose very failures became the basis for their leadership.

The kinds of moral rehabilitation that Washingtonianism en-couraged facilitated the transformation of an all-male labor movement in the 1830s into a coalition of both men and women in the 1840s. Morality was transformed from a public and secu-lar concept into a more personal and religious one, dependent on spiritual progress as much as on intellectual accomplishment. As a result, men from such towns as Fall River and Lynn sought female support to legitimate their activities as undertakings in moral reform. Some women responded, particularly if they were related to the men, but female participation in the labor move-ment was always problematic and was incessantly being re-negotiated. This was particularly the case when women from Lowell entered the fray as fellow wage earners rather than sup-portive relatives. Lowell women used the rhetoric of religion and reform to legitimate their participation in the labor movement and their growing leadership, in ways that the men had not anticipated.

This final point is particularly important in light of recent scholarship on the protests of workingwomen. Christine Stansell, writing about workingwomen in New York, argues that morally based visions of universal womanhood undercut a class-based gender identity as propriety conflicted with labor militance. Mary Blewett suggests that male shoemakers in Lynn were ambivalent in their appeals to female shoebinders for moral support precisely because the men associated moral influence with middle-class values.[9] What these historians fail to recognize, however, is not only the subversive nature of working-class religion, but also the fact that religious language, far more than any political language of republicanism, allowed women access to the public arena and thus facilitated the development of a labor movement of men and women working together.

Paternalism in New England structured both gender and class relationships, affecting factories, families, and labor-organizing. The entrepreneurial elite may have appropriated both religion and reform during this period to justify their position, but that does not mean they controlled these arenas completely. Religion and reform provided working people with a language of autonomy that was fundamentally at odds with the assumptions of paternalism, thus producing a critical site of conflict.

9. Christine Stansell, *City of Women: Sex and Class in New York, 1789–1860* (Urbana, Ill., 1987), pp. 147–149; Mary Blewett, *Men, Women, and Work: Class, Gender, and Protest in the New England Shoe Industry, 1780–1910* (Urbana, Ill., 1990), pp. 79–80.

Chapter 1

Family, Work, and Authority:
The Parameters of
New England Paternalism

On July 3, 1832, sixteen-year-old Paulina Brown allowed a leather to get off her top roller in the spinning room of Samuel Slater's factory in Smithfield, Rhode Island. The young woman might have been tired, or perhaps goofing off (after all, it was almost Independence Day), but to Parris Richmond, her overseer, it was a clear case of disobedience that required punishment.

First Richmond placed a torn hat on the young woman's head and marched her through the aisles of the spinning frames for about half an hour, exposing her to the ridicule of her co-workers. Next he shook her and forced her to stand on the stove for almost two hours. Paulina cried and tried to cover her face, but Richmond pulled her hands away—"*struck* them down," as one witness would later recall. After her public humiliation, Richmond took Paulina into the oil room (better known to the factory workers as the whipping room) and closed the door. Paulina claimed he whipped her with a leather strap, leaving her hands black and blue for a week so that her brother had to take over piecing ends for her.

Although Richmond believed he was well within his rights as an overseer, Paulina's father, Walter Brown, disagreed. He charged Richmond with trespass, assault, and battery before George L. Barnes, a local justice of the peace. The warrant issued for Richmond's arrest claimed that he did "beat bruise, pinch, choak and push about and their & then with great vio-

lence did thrust the Plaintiff against the wall and other enor-
mities." Barnes found Richmond guilty but did not attach too
much significance to the offense; Richmond was ordered to pay
$2.96 to cover court costs and 10 cents in damages to Paulina.
Walter Brown was outraged, and he decided to appeal the case
before the Court of Common Pleas in Providence. This was not
easy, for it required him to guarantee $50 to cover court costs if
his suit failed (a guarantee he could make only with the help of
his friend Ira Burlingame).

The plaintiff, defendant, lawyers, and witnesses assembled in
Providence during February 1833 for the trial. Several of Paulina's co-workers came to testify, including Miranda and Diana
Hume, Abigail Win, Sephtha Brown, and Caleb Logee. Richmond claimed that Paulina was a servant in his establishment,
that she had willfully disobeyed him, and that he had laid his
hands on her "gently." Apparently the testimony of the other
young women who worked in the factory refuted his story. The
jury, more sympathetic than the justice of the peace had been,
awarded Paulina $20 in damages, the highest award they were
allowed to make, and charged the defendant $36.18 in court
costs. Their disapproval of Richmond's acts was apparent also on
the following day, when they awarded one of the Hume girls $10
in damages and charged Richmond court costs for his assaults on
her.[1]

This was not the first case in New England involving a conflict
of parental and factory authority. For example, Gary Kulik notes
a similar attack in Pawtucket a decade earlier, when charges
were brought against an overseer by the Commonwealth of Massachusetts instead of by the parents. In this particular case, the
jury was asked to decide whether authority to inflict corporal
punishment on a child had been delegated to the overseer by the
parent, because, as the court pointed out, "the owner or overseer,
as such, had no right to inflict corporal punishment on those

1. Reported in the *Providence Republican Herald*, February 20, 1833, and
Working Man's Advocate (New York), March 2, 1833. Specific testimony in the
court records of the Providence Court of Common Pleas, November term, 1832,
Richmond v. Brown.

employed by him . . . [unless] that authority had been so delegated by the father." In this earlier case the jury found in favor of
the overseer.[2]

The contrast between the two cases is important, for it suggests
the way in which changing attitudes toward family, work, and
factory paternalism were interrelated. The revulsion the jury felt
at Parris Richmond's behavior reflected broader changes taking
place in attitudes toward discipline. By the 1830s, the emphasis
was on emotional rather than physical forms of discipline in
childrearing. Internalized restraints, rather than external coercion, were at the center of new theories of family government, as
the cultivation of conscience through love and persuasion was
promoted as an alternative to physical punishment. A brutal
whipping, like that administered by Richmond, was unacceptable in this scheme. Equally unacceptable was the public humiliation built into this punishment. Punishment for any misdeed,
even the most violent of crimes, was becoming increasingly privatized in nineteenth-century America. Discipline that had been
tolerated at Slater's factories in the 1820s was criticized in the
next decade.[3]

Related to the question of discipline was the jury's rejection of
the factory as a type of household. Richmond had argued that
Paulina was a "servant" who should be disciplined as any other
member of a family. His defense relied on the rapidly disappearing phenomenon of a workplace united with the home, in which
employer and father were one and the same. In the emerging
world of separate spheres, factory and family were distinct. Indeed, the term "servant" had taken on class rather than domestic

2. *Manufacturers' and Farmers' Journal* (Providence), September 22, 1823;
Gary Kulik, "The Beginnings of the Industrial Revolution in America: Pawtucket,
Rhode Island, 1672–1829" (Ph.D. diss., Brown University, 1980). Records for this
trial cannot be found in the recordbooks of the Court of Common Pleas in Massachusetts.

3. On childrearing, see Elizabeth Pleck, *Domestic Tyranny: The Making of
Social Policy against Family Violence from Colonial Times to the Present* (New York,
1987); Bernard Wishy, *The Child and the Republic: The Dawn of Modern American
Child Nurture* (Philadelphia, 1968). On changing attitudes toward criminal punishment, see Louis Masur, *Rites of Execution* (New York, 1988).

connotations, and the press attacked Richmond for his aristocratic pretensions.[4]

The issues this trial raises are ones we generally associate with
the emerging middle class of this period. Mary Ryan, for example, argues that evangelical mothers instilled internalized restraints in their children and constructed voluntary, affective
relationships to replace the failing economic and external con-
trols of a crumbling patriarchal society, most visible in the inability of fathers to pass down land or a viable trade to their sons.
This privatized world of the family embodied values that the
middle class would use both to define itself and to dominate others who did not share their sensibilities. Thus Richard Brodhead
describes this new regime as "discipline through love" and argues that within this context corporal punishment became the
"sign of insufficiency" in other cultures, whether they be those of
the old New England patriarchy or recent Irish immigrants.[5]

The trial of Parris Richmond raises issues that make sense
within the context of emerging middle-class values, but because
these issues were raised by people who were part of an emerging
working class, they suggest that factory brutality was a sign of
multiple meanings, both potent and volatile. And precisely because this sign was so central to middle-class domination, it was
also highly contested. Continuing litigation and reports of factory brutality suggest that working people gave corporal punishment a different accent in order to challenge the authority of
their employers. At a time when both labor and the laborer were
becoming commodities, certain aspects of parental authority

4. *Providence Republican Herald*, February 20, 1833.
5. Mary Ryan, *Cradle of the Middle Class: The Family in Oneida County, New
York, 1790–1860* (New York, 1981); Richard Brodhead, "Sparing the Rod: Discipline and Fiction in Antebellum America," *Representations* 21 (Winter 1988): 76.
The literature on this subject is vast, but for further discussion of the ways in
which these values were used in a middle-class context, see Kathryn Kish Sklar,
Catharine Beecher: A Study in American Domesticity (New York, 1976); Paul Johnson, *A Shopkeeper's Millennium: Society and Revivals in Rochester, New York,
1815–1837* (New York, 1976); Karen Halttunen, *Confidence Men and Painted
Women: A Study of Middle-Class Culture in America, 1830–1870* (New Haven,
Conn., 1982).

were becoming inalienable, inescapable by-products of "disciplinary intimacy."

Thus the *Pawtucket Chronicle* reported in 1837 that an eleven-year-old factory boy in Kensington, Pennsylvania, had been brutally beaten by an overseer. The newspaper was careful to report the court's charge to the jury that "the parent of a child had not, in law, the power to hire his child to another, delegating to the employer the right to chastise—nor had he the power himself to exceed the bounds of moderate salutary correction."[6]

In 1844, "Fearnobody" wrote to *The Mechanic* in Fall River complaining that the overseer at a local woolen factory had far too passionate a temper to be placed in charge of the boys who worked there. Worse yet, "a man called a father authorized this human volcano of wrath, to do as he pleased with his boy. The monster of an overseer has beaten him most cruelly at his pleasure, and has kicked him so badly, that the boy is full of wounds, and bruises especially on his lower extremities." Fearnobody attributed this abuse not so much to the failings of a particular individual as to a larger problem of policy: "We affirm that none but parents ought to be permitted to correct children. If boys will not obey the overseers, let the parents be informed of it. If they will not do any better, let them be expelled [from] the works."[7]

In 1846, a new overseer in the carding room at the James mill in Newburyport was charged with assault in the local police court for forcibly ejecting a young female worker who did not conform to his ideas of discipline: "He laid hold of her to hurry her along, thereby tearing her clothes." The court's judgment was not reported in the *Voice of Industry*, which ran the story, but public reaction was: "Considerable feeling was manifested by people living in the vicinity of the mill, so much so, that the overseer was pelted with snowballs in the street."[8]

6. *Pawtucket Chronicle*, June 2, 1837.
7. *The Mechanic* (Fall River), November 23, 1844.
8. *Voice of Industry* (Fitchburg and Lowell), February 6, 1846, reporting from the *Newburyport Advertiser*, January 23, 1846. The conflict may have arisen over clothing, for the newspaper also reported: "We have been informed that a man named Glidden was discharged from the same card room for wearing a paper cap

These reports of assault often emerged in the labor press of New England as part of a larger attack on the paternalistic policies of New England factory owners, an attack that coalesced in the 1830s and 1840s around the demand for a ten-hour day. The control of time, like that of corporal punishment, was tied to issues of internalized restraint and separate spheres of home and work, as working people demanded time for self-improvement, spiritual growth, and domestic felicity. Their focus on their own families was played off against the familial metaphors, hierarchical organization, and feigned protection of New England paternalism. At the same time, however, their own family relations were changing dramatically. It was a struggle rooted partly in changes that were taking place among families of the emerging working class, families whose experiences would converge with but not replicate that of middle-class families, so that issues of voluntary emotional ties, for example, took on different meanings. It was also a struggle in which the nature of New England paternalism was a crucial element. As they radically transformed the economic relations of the region, New England capitalists legitimated their activities with the rhetoric of moral uplift and traditional community values.

New England Paternalism

Paternalism suffused a variety of economic and social relationships in nineteenth-century America, from slavery to workshop to factory, taking on different shapes in different contexts. Economic protection and moral uplift were cornerstones of paternalistic ideologies in almost all cases, but as Philip Scranton notes in laying out a typology of paternalism, there were at least three ways in which these relations could be constructed in textile factories: formally, familially, and fraternally. And as Jonathan Prude argues with respect to New England, the paternalis-

---

such as is often worn by mechanics for the purpose of keeping the head and hair clean; and we believe our informant stated that the difficulty with the girls was in some measure owing to a similar cause."

tic arguments put forward in the southern part of the region were predicated on assumptions about a lack of morality among the factory population, in contrast to a concern for preserving the morality of factory workers in the large mills of northern New England.[9] Despite these differences—differences that had to be negotiated at crucial points in the labor movement—regionally distinctive features of the way industrialization unfolded in New England provided an important context for the exercise of paternalism.

First, the merchant class was actively involved in the reorganization of production. This class provided a level of capital which was absent elsewhere and a physical embodiment of the process of industrial transformation which did not exist in such cities as New York and Philadelphia. Workshops expanded in Boston and Providence, just as they did in cities of the Middle Atlantic region; inside contracting, and a division of labor undermined the craft processes in both areas. But the context of production was different. Boston and Providence were not the manufacturing centers that New York and Philadelphia were, nor were they centers of trade. The New England cities were financial and commercial centers in which *some* master artisans were expanding their workshops. Dominating the industrialization of the area were the wealthy capitalists, the economic elite of these towns. Many had directed their capital away from trade during the War of 1812 and continued that reorientation in later years, while Philadelphia and New York eclipsed Boston as the major trading ports on the East Coast. New England capitalists funneled their money into textile industries in the countryside, though they kept their eye on activities in the city as well. A recent study of textile investors in Boston reveals that more than two-thirds of them were active in commerce, half of them also held investments in banks and insurance companies, and one-

9. Philip Scranton, "Varieties of Paternalism: Industrial Structures and the Social Relations of Production in American Textiles," *American Quarterly* 36 (Summer 1984): 235–257; Jonathan Prude, *The Coming of the Industrial Order: Town and Factory Life in Rural Massachusetts, 1810–1860* (New York, 1983), pp. 110–116.

third had invested in wharves and railroads. More than 50 percent of these investors were worth $50,000 or more.[10]

In the Middle Atlantic cities, master artisans were primarily responsible for transforming the relations of production, particularly in the way they organized their labor force. Often they were men of humble origin.[11] In New England a visible body of merchant capitalists controlled the economic strings to which masters and journeymen, as well as foremen and operatives, jumped. Where these capitalists did not exert direct control, they set a tone for aspiring manufacturers.

The differences among New England textile factories have been well documented, but by the 1830s those differences were disappearing, as some textile mills in southern New England adopted the management structure of those to the north, integrated their factories with the use of the power loom, and sought incorporation for their larger ventures. Another important similarity was that, regardless of individual variations, these mills often dominated the economic landscape of the surrounding area, not only because of the textiles they produced but also because of the auxiliary economic enterprises they controlled. Of key importance here were the banks, land development companies, iron works, and machine shops. Sometimes they were owned outright by a mill corporation; in other cases they simply were controlled or owned by the same men who ran the corporations. Either way, it gave a few men tremendous power over the economic lives of people in these communities.

In Fall River, two entrepreneurial clusters that had begun mill operations at the beginning of the nineteenth century developed important auxiliary enterprises. The group that created the Fall

10. On workshop transformation, see Gary John Kornblith, "From Artisans to Businessmen: Master Mechanics in New England, 1789–1850," 2 vols. (Ph.D. diss., Princeton University, 1983); and William H. Pease and Jane H. Pease, *Web of Progress: Private Values and Public Styles in Boston and Charleston, 1828–1843* (New York, 1985), p. 27. Lisa Lubow describes the growing impact of real-estate speculation on the building trades of Boston in "Artisans in Transition: Early Capitalist Development and the Carpenters of Boston, 1781–1837" (Ph.D. diss., University of California at Los Angeles, 1987), esp. pp. 26–307.

11. Sean Wilentz, *Chants Democratic: New York City and the Rise of the American Working Class, 1788–1850* (New York, 1984), pp. 35–42; Bruce Laurie, *Working People of Philadelphia, 1800–1850* (Philadelphia, 1980), pp. 16–17.

River Manufactory for the production of textiles also started the Fall River Iron Works in 1820 (and incorporated it in 1825). The Iron Works employed twenty-four hands in 1827, but by 1840 the work force had grown to 250. The Iron Works, which became a quite successful venture, provided important capital and contacts for the textile mills this group would continue to develop in the nineteenth century.[12]

Textile manufacturers often created machine shops to supply their own mills. This was the case for the Waltham and Lowell mills, where a large machine shop evolved, primarily to service the needs of the extensive mill network in those towns. In Saco and Biddeford, Maine, a machine shop was set up for the York Manufacturing Company; in Manchester and Nashua, a similar pattern was followed for the Amoskeag Mills and the Nashua Manufacturing Company. When the Taunton Manufacturing Company acquired several textile mills in Taunton it acquired their machine shops as well. And Samuel Slater set up the Providence Machine Company in 1827 on the first floor of his Steam Cotton Manufacturing Company to supply the Slater factories with equipment. Slater's control of the production process was further increased by having the machine shop purchase most of the iron for machinery construction from the Providence Iron Foundry, of which he was part owner.[13]

There were independent machine shops as well. At its inception, the Fall River Manufactory set up a machine shop and was selling pickers by 1814, but most of the machine shops in Fall River remained independent of mill ownership.[14] In 1842, Wil-

---

12. Robert K. Lamb, "The Development of Entrepreneurship in Fall River, 1813–1859" (Ph.D. diss., Harvard University, 1935), chap. 9.

13. George Sweet Gibb, *The Saco-Lowell Shops: Textile Machinery Building in New England, 1813–1949* (New York, 1950); John Lozier, *Taunton and Mason: Cotton Machinery and Locomotive Manufacture in Taunton, Massachusetts, 1811–1861* (New York, 1986), pp. 47, 141–142; Barbara Tucker, *Samuel Slater and the Origins of the American Textile Industry, 1790–1860* (Ithaca, N.Y., 1984), pp. 189–202.

14. Lozier, *Taunton and Mason*, pp. 31–32. The first meeting of the Troy stockholders included an agreement to build a machine shop and a blacksmith's shop to be rented to John Borden (who had worked in the Waltham machine shop), but this venture does not seem to have prospered. Lamb, "Development of Entrepreneurship in Fall River," pp. v–16, vi–40.

liam Mason purchased the machine shop that had belonged to the Taunton Manufacturing Company, but with money provided by Boston commission merchant James K. Mills.[15]

In some cases, independent machine shops even grew strong enough to take over textile works. In Newton Upper Falls, a machine shop was set up for the Elliot Manufacturing Company, but under the dynamic leadership of the machine shop's boss, Otis Pettee, it developed a national and international clientele, primarily located in the southern states and in Mexico. In 1840, Pettee and his machine shop took over the textile mill. A similar situation developed in Andover. Smith, Dove & Company, a machine shop headed by several Scotch machinists, set up a flax mill during the 1830s and eventually abandoned machinery production for the expanded production of flax, which they facilitated by taking over the woolen mills in Abbot Village which had failed in 1837.[16] In these cases, as in those where textile factories owned the machine shops, a powerful set of owners emerged to control the economic destinies of a wide variety of workers in their local area.

In some of these towns, such power was further augmented by land development. Early in Lowell's history, mill investors revived the Locks and Canals Company to handle the real estate, water rights, and general building of the town. When this plan was carried out in 1825, the Locks and Canals Company also took over management of the machine shop. The machine shop was responsible not only for building textile machinery but also for constructing mills and boardinghouses for operatives, a hotel, streets, locks, and canals. By 1835, three hundred men were employed in the machine shop. This pattern of combining the machine shop with the land development company would be followed in other mill towns too.[17] The records of the repair shop at the Blackstone Manufacturing Company, for example, grouped machinists and mechanics together. Mill construction, house

15. Lozier, *Taunton and Mason*, pp. 197, 282–283.
16. Gibb, *The Saco-Lowell Shops*, p. 162; Sarah Loring Bailey, *Historical Sketches of Andover (Comprising the Present Towns of North Andover and Andover)* (Boston, 1880), pp. 574–605.
17. Gibb, *The Saco-Lowell Shops*, pp. 67–74.

painting, machinery repair, and farm labor were part of the same administrative unit.[18] As a result, the same management structure was in charge of a large number of carpenters as well as machinists in mill towns, and both were intimately involved in mill work. The skills of male textile operatives, machinists, and carpenters might be dramatically different, but in many of these factory towns their ultimate employers were the same.

The powerful legal mechanism of incorporation also contributed to the growing influence of a few. While few corporations existed in the United States before the Civil War, those that did were concentrated in textiles. Unlike the corporations of later years, however, shares in these early corporations were usually tightly controlled by a few men and their families, and that practice contributed to their popular image as bastions of special privilege.[19] Struggles to limit the liability of shareholders further fueled corporate strength. In a time of burgeoning individualism, corporations—capable of manipulating their fictional legal status as persons for the benefit of shareholders—emerged as the most powerful of "individuals."

With such legal instruments as incorporation, the power of the industrial elite in New England grew. This was not by any means a completely unified or homogeneous elite. Boston Brahmins kept their distance from country upstarts, Quakers and Congregationalists would continue to regard one another with some suspicion, and in a few towns (such as Lynn) new manufacturers and old merchants constituted distinct and rival classes. This was still, however, a much more uniform elite than one would find in other areas, such as the Middle Atlantic states, where mercantile and manufacturing pursuits remained more distinct. Reinforcing this uniformity would be strong elements of ethnic and religious homogeneity and a history of corporate hierarchy that had characterized New England towns of the colonial period and that still informed the ideals of many in the upper echelons of society (albeit in a somewhat transmuted form).

18. "Mechanics Time Book," Blackstone Manufacturing Company, Mss. 9, Subgroup 1, Series D, vol. 517 (1847–1853), RIHS Manuscripts Collection.
19. Alfred D. Chandler Jr., *The Visible Hand: The Managerial Revolution in American Business* (Cambridge, Mass., 1977), p. 60.

This outlook was particularly evident in Boston. Frederic Jaher argues: "Multi-dimensional hegemony made the Brahmins an upper-class, and thus distinguished the enclave from more narrowly based political, economic, or social elites that characterized the fragmented power structure of other cities."[20] Although some old-guard shipping families resisted at first, the mercantile elite quickly entered the field of manufacturing and absorbed into its ranks the few men, such as Nathan Appleton and the Lawrences, who were not of mercantile background.[21] Thus there was no split in the Boston elite, as there was in the elites of such cities as New York and Philadelphia, where mercantile money continued to flow into trade, land, finance, and transportation. In the lives of New England working people, capitalists were a far more visible and potent presence than they were elsewhere.

Robert Dalzell notes that many of the Boston Associates actually came from small towns outside Boston in which their families, formerly prominent, were faced with decline. The Associates had come to Boston in part to find (or create) new economic opportunities for themselves, because the old ones no longer existed. But, Dalzell maintains, their economic vision was tempered by the desire to recreate the traditional communities of their childhood, communities in which corporate hierarchy and deference, as well as neighborliness, were valued.[22] Although Dalzell stresses the importance of these values in the Boston community, it is not difficult to detect their presence in the mill villages as well. In particular, the boardinghouse system was designed to maintain the bonds of paternalistic order in which young women felt bound by family rules and community morality.[23]

The Boston Associates were not the only ones intent on assert-

20. Frederic Cople Jaher, "The Politics of the Boston Brahmins: 1800–1860," in *Boston, 1700–1980: The Evolution of Urban Politics*, ed. Ronald P. Formisano and Constance K. Burns (Westport, Conn., 1980), p. 60.

21. Frederic Cople Jaher, *The Urban Establishment* (Urbana, Ill., 1982), pp. 48–49.

22. Robert F. Dalzell Jr., *Enterprising Elite: The Boston Associates and the World They Made* (Cambridge, Mass., 1987), pp. 115–129.

23. Thomas Bender, *Toward an Urban Vision: Ideas and Institutions in Nineteenth-Century America* (Lexington, Ky., 1975), pp. 110–111.

ing "traditional community values" in their mill ventures. According to Barbara Tucker, this was also the intention of Samuel Slater in his smaller mill villages. Tucker argues that Slater adopted "the traditional rural village as a blueprint for the design of his factory colonies." In support of this, she points to the maintenance of the family system of labor, support of the church for religious discipline, and even the physical pattern of the town.[24]

Such communities, and the paternalism embedded in them, were created to maintain a fixed hierarchy. Mill owners expected the young women and families who worked in these factories to maintain their dependent status as wage earners. Philip Scranton argues that these paternalistic expectations differed from those of the textile manufacturers in Philadelphia, where upward mobility among workers into positions of management and ownership was a possibility. In part, the difference in expectations was gender-based. The overwhelming majority of the textile workers in New England were women. In Philadelphia, on the other hand, skilled male workers constituted a significant part of the textile work force, and some of them could and did establish or take over factories. No one expected a woman to do the same. Implicit in this distinction, moreover, were the differences of a paternalism rooted in craft traditions of hierarchy rather than a community tradition; the former assumed upward mobility, the latter did not. Thus, while a certain degree of camaraderie characterized the paternalism of textile factories in Philadelphia, deference and distance were more important in New England.[25]

The moral dimensions of these different relationships were equally significant. Whether mill owners saw themselves as providing moral uplift to the family workers of southern New England, or protecting the moral virtue of single female workers in northern New England, they assumed the permanent moral de-

24. Tucker, *Samuel Slater*, 26–29, 125–162. For a discussion of the architectural and landscape implications of this policy, see John R. Stilgoe, *Common Landscape of America, 1580–1845* (New Haven, Conn., 1982), pp. 324–333.
25. Philip Scranton, "Varieties of Paternalism," 236–257.

pendence of their work force. The construction of moral autonomy was thus a critical component in the challenges working
people made to New England paternalism.

The New England Work Force

The attempt of New England industrialists to create a "traditional community order" was aided by the rural New England
background of the work force during this period. Workers in
New England were far more ethnically homogeneous during the
1830s and 1840s than workers in New York and Philadelphia.
While impoverished English and Irish immigrants were stream-
ing into New York and Philadelphia at the end of the eighteenth
century and the beginning of the nineteenth, relatively few found
their way into the ports of Providence and Boston. Oscar Handlin
has stated that annually, before 1840 less than 4,000 Irish arrived
in Boston, and less than 2,000 before 1830. As a result, New England towns, even cities and new industrial centers, remained
overwhelmingly Yankee before 1850. In Waltham, for example,
only eight Irish households were recorded in the census of 1840,
although by 1850 there were 163 Irish households, constituting one-quarter of the town's population. In Manchester, New
Hampshire, 85 percent of the population was native-born in
1850, as was 88 percent of the Amoskeag work force in 1860. In
1850, only 10.5 percent of the Lynn population was foreign-born,
and the population remained overwhelmingly native throughout
the nineteenth century.[26]

This is not to deny that immigrants were a part of the work
force in New England or that ethnicity was a factor in community life. The largest population of Irish in New England before

26. Paul G. Faler, *Mechanics and Manufacturers in the Early Industrial Revolution* (New York, 1978), pp. 144–145; Cynthia Shelton, *The Mills of Manayunk:
Industrialization and Social Conflict in the Philadelphia Region, 1787–1837* (Baltimore, 1986), pp. 34–35, 48–49; Howard M. Gitelman, *Workingmen of Waltham:
Mobility in American Urban Industrial Development, 1850–1890* (Baltimore, 1974),
p. 15; Thomas Dublin, "Rural-Urban Migrants in Industrial New England: The
Case of Lynn, Massachusetts, in the Mid-Nineteenth Century," *Journal of American History* 73 (December 1986): 625; James P. Hanlan, *The Working Population of
Manchester, New Hampshire, 1840–1886* (Ann Arbor, Mich., 1981), pp. 81–83.

1850 was in Boston, but the second largest community was in Lowell, where large numbers of Irish had found jobs as day laborers in the construction of canals and mill buildings. One estimate put Lowell's Irish population in 1843 at 20 percent of the entire community. Most of them, however, remained outside the occupational structure of the mills. An analysis of the records of the Hamilton Manufacturing Company there revealed that in the 1830s, 96 percent of the operatives were from the United States, as were 92 percent in the middle of the 1840s.[27]

English and Scotch immigrants were also to be found in cities and mill villages, sometimes in surprising numbers. In Andover, where many of the small mills were owned and operated by Scotch or English immigrants, the labor force reflected a similar diversity. In Fall River, Irish and British immigrants also found employment. And according to an 1846 survey, almost 25 percent of the population in Woonsocket was foreign-born.

Ethnic segregation and discrimination, not to mention eruptions of more overt hostility, accompanied immigration. But to a surprising extent, despite these many problems, immigrants and Yankees lived together more harmoniously in New England than they did in New York and Philadelphia, at least before the arrival of the famine Irish in the late 1840s. Certainly there was nothing to compare with the Kensington riots of 1844. Brian Mitchell argues that in Lowell a small but important group of shopkeepers and foremen set a tone for the larger Irish community with values that were consonant with those of resident Yankees in the years before large waves of pauperized Irish flooded the town as a result of the potato blight. A similar relationship may well have existed in Andover among British textile workers and the immigrants who owned small factories there.

But even where there was not an overlapping of values, the fact that immigrants were a relatively small part of the population had to have had an impact. While other parts of the nation confronted ethnic and racial heterogeneity as one of the most

27. Thomas Dublin, *Women at Work: The Transformation of Work and Community in Lowell, Massachusetts, 1826–1860* (New York, 1979), p. 26; Robert G. Layer, *Earnings of Cotton Mill Operatives, 1825–1914* (Cambridge, Mass., 1955), p. 70; Brian C. Mitchell, *The Paddy Camps: The Irish of Lowell, 1821–1861* (Urbana, Ill., 1988), pp. 85–86.

important features of community change and as major characteristics of an emerging working class, New England did not. If
20 percent Irish in Lowell in 1843, and 25 percent foreign-born in
Woonsocket in 1846, represent the high end of immigrants for
New England, keep in mind that 35 percent of New York City's
population in 1845 was immigrant, up from 9 percent in 1830.[28]
Cynthia Shelton argues that by 1825 large numbers of English
and Irish immigrants began filling the mills of Pennsylvania and
New Jersey.[29] Because immigrants came nowhere near to constituting a majority in any of these New England towns, their
values were far less threatening to Yankee hegemony.

As a result, ethnicity would not have the same class overtones
evident in the big cities of the Middle Atlantic region, where a
predominant part of the work force was immigrant while the
middle class remained overwhelmingly Yankee. In New England,
the work force, as well as the emerging middle class and the capitalist upper class, was predominantly Yankee. As James Russell
Lowell wrote, master and servant were of the same background,
thus engendering a "becoming respect" for "decent authority"—
and, as others pointed out, creating a standard of morals which
could not exist elsewhere.[30] Lowell's assumptions were the basis
of New England paternalism, for they required a shared culture
and a shared history. The conflict that emerged in New England
between working people and employers would be rooted not in
different cultures but in a struggle for control over a culture they
shared.

The Voluntary Family

If the family was a metaphor for factory organization, it was
also a reality in the daily lives of people who worked in them. The

28. Christine Stansell, *City of Women: Sex and Class in New York, 1789–1860*
(Urbana, Ill., 1987), p. 44.
29. Shelton, *Mills of Manayunk*, p. 63. For an important discussion of the way
ethnicity shaped the development of working-class life outside New England, see
Richard B. Stott, *Workers in the Metropolis: Class, Ethnicity, and Youth in Antebellum New York City* (Ithaca, N.Y., 1990).
30. Jaher, *The Urban Establishment*, p. 69.

paternalism of New England capitalists was rooted in a metaphor of family organization which they themselves were, in fact,
subverting. It was not a process industrialists had initiated. Several historians have demonstrated that the decline in available
land in New England had been undermining patriarchal authority for several generations.[31] But factories also challenged the
claim of male heads of household to provide protection and
support.

The case of Paulina Brown suggests one of these problems.
Described in the trial documents as "an infant," her father was
no doubt collecting her wages, and therefore her income was
probably important to the family economy. This would have
been typical during the 1830s in Slater's mills, where heads of
household contracted with agents for their children's labor. Parents did not work alongside their children in these situations,
though why that was the case has been the subject of some
dispute. Barbara Tucker argues that adult men preferred outdoor labor, but Jonathan Prude attributes the situation to management discrimination that sought to avoid parental challenges
to the discipline of overseers in the factory. Walter Brown's outrage over the way his daughter was treated exemplifies the kind
of challenge parents might mount.[32]

Paulina's case points out ways in which factory children were
subjected to competing forms of authority and discipline. Even if
fathers (or widowed mothers) collected the wages of their children, they maintained this semblance of economic control at the
expense of the moral authority that had previously gone with it.
For those who lived in factory housing, further elements of family autonomy were relinquished as owners dictated standards of
behavior.

31. Among the works dealing with the relationship between the decline in
available land and the decline in patriarchal authority during this period are:
Robert A. Gross, *The Minutemen and Their World* (New York, 1976); Hal S. Barron,
Those Who Stayed Behind: Rural Society in Nineteenth-Century New England (New
York, 1984); Prude, *Coming of the Industrial Order;* and Ryan, *Cradle of the Middle
Class.*
32. Tucker, *Samuel Slater,* pp. 139–141; Prude, *Coming of the Industrial Order,*
p. 119. For an example of a factory avoiding local help in western Massachusetts,
see Christopher Clark, *Roots of Rural Capitalism: Western Massachusetts, 1780–
1860* (Ithaca, N.Y., 1990), p. 111.

In Slater's factories, at least during the 1830s, most workers fit this pattern. Barbara Tucker estimates, for example, that in 1832 74 percent of the work force at one of Slater's mills was drawn from kinship groups; the remaining workers, who were paid as individuals, were either skilled men or a few of the female weavers. The same proportions did not hold true at other mills employing family labor; in some cases, individuals outnumbered family contract workers. At the Annawan factory in Fall River, for example, more than two-thirds of the employees were paid as individuals. As in Slater's mills, family workers tended to be children working without parental supervision. Among the households headed by males which contributed children, only 17 percent also contributed fathers.[33]

The way workers were paid in the Annawan factory over-lapped to a great extent with the kind of work they did. The weavers, who were young, single, and female, were paid individually (even if they were living with their families). In most cases so too were the machinists and mule spinners, the skilled male workers in the factory. Few of these men officially contributed to a family wage, and few of them collected the wages of their children. Machinists, mule spinners, and weavers further distanced themselves from factory intrusions into their personal lives by living outside company housing in many cases.

Both in their housing choices and in their method of wage payments, these workers represented a strong contrast to those employed in the carding and spinning rooms. In those parts of the factory were concentrated the family wage workers and those who lived in company housing. Parents who were not employed by the factory collected the wages of their children, but like Walter Brown they surrendered other aspects of their authority.

This surrender of authority may be the reason skilled male

33. Tucker, *Samuel Slater,* p. 146; Annawan payroll records, FRHS. In the spring of 1832, 199 out of 286 employees (69.5 percent of the work force) were paid as individuals at the Annawan factory. The 87 individuals who were contributing to a family wage constituted 41 households, 12 of which were female-headed and 29 of which were male-headed. As was the case elsewhere, mothers simply did not work in the factory. Of the 29 fathers, 5 worked in the factory: Thomas Davis was a mulepiecer; Taber Cory and Benjamin Davis were unskilled laborers; Elisha Fuller was overseer of the carding room (where his daughters did *not* work); and Pelham Wood was a mule spinner.

factory workers did not put their children to work in the mill. The data here is skimpy but suggestive. Many of the skilled male workers at the Annawan factory were machinists, who tended to be young and mobile anyway. Thus the median age of machinists at the factory was twenty-three, and two-thirds were unmarried.[34] But even those who were married and who had children old enough to work in the mill did not put their children to work there.[35]

Perhaps skilled male workers did not want their children to work in the mill or to contribute to a family wage. If factories did indeed trample on parental authority, it would have been a reasonable motivation for keeping the children out of the mills. Skilled workingmen could thereby establish their independence from factory owners not only through the control of their skills but also through the control of their families. Similarly, while company housing might be an economic bargain, living elsewhere probably contributed to greater feelings of independence.

But challenges to the authority of male householders took place beyond the confines of the family contract system, particularly as "dependent" workers (women and children) became increasingly independent economically. The young women who worked in Lowell had always fit this pattern, as Thomas Dublin has so vividly demonstrated. Living independent of their families and paid cash wages as individuals, these young women were able to further their own individual aspirations in terms of education, marriage choices, and consumption. Family connections were an important avenue for finding work, but otherwise the young women maintained their economic independence.[36]

34. Some 32 machinists were employed at the Annawan factory in March 1832. I was able to determine the ages of twelve and the marital status of twelve using vital records and census data.

35. Caleb Cook's daughter Anganett was born in 1823 but never showed up in the mill records, though her father was employed there through 1835. Robert Cook's son Samuel worked in the mill for eight and a half days in March 1832, for which Robert's account was credited $2.84. But this was the only time Samuel worked, an indication that Samuel was not contributing to the family wage in any meaningful sense. A similar conclusion might be drawn about Elisha Carpenter, who collected a grand total of 32 cents for his daughter's weaving in 1832, and 39 cents for two days of his son's work in April 1833. (Annawan Ledger, FRHS.)

36. Dublin, *Women at Work*, pp. 23–57.

Growing ranks of young men in the factories also fit into this pattern. Machinists, in particular, often came from the countryside in search of work and relied on relatives to find them a place in a machine shop, a destination viewed as far more desirable than textile production. Charles Metcalf was exhausted by the pace of work he encountered in the spinning rooms of Lowell. Soon after his arrival there from his family's farm in Winthrop, Maine, he wrote to his parents that spinning was "rather hard work and I get very tired by night and feel thankful when Sat. night comes so that I can have a short respite." He went on to explain, "My fingers are so tired to night that I can scarcely hold on to my pen much less write a legible hand." To make matters worse, conditions in the spinning room were ruining his health: "My nose bleeds every day more or less not much however owing probably in part to the irritation arising from the cotton flying about and partly from the temperature of the room and fatigue."[37]

Charles had his sights fixed on the machine shop, and his cousin Shubael Adams was on the lookout for him, steering him away from dead-end prospects. Shubael wrote to Charles's mother:

> Within a few days he [Charles] has had a chance to go into the shop, but I did not advise him to accept—I think there will be a chance there soon however that will be an object for him to accept, unless he should conclude to remain in the mill—His work at present is hard and pay low, and the prospect of promotion not immediate, and I think I shall advise him when a good opportunity offers itself in the shop to accept and leave the mill.[38]

The practice of inside contracting made the choice of entry-level jobs in machine shops a critical one. Some master machinists were serious about their responsibility to train raw recruits, others were simply looking for unskilled labor. When

37. Shubael F. Adams to Chloe Metcalf, April 29, 1844 (Metcalf Collection, MATH).
38. Ibid.

George Richardson arrived in Lowell in the spring of 1846, his uncle took him to the machine shop to help him find a position. Unfortunately, Richardson's uncle did not appear to have the inside connections and information Shubael Adams did, and Richardson's initial experience was not promising. Before inviting him into the machine shop, the foreman put him to work as a manual laborer for six weeks. Richardson worked in the shop for eight weeks, but, feeling dissatisfied about his progress, he quit to find a job elsewhere. After wandering about the countryside for a couple of months, Richardson made up his mind to become a machinist and returned to Lowell. The Lowell Machine Shop was not his first choice, but he could not find work at more desirable establishments.[39] The autonomy that master machinists enjoyed at Lowell made family connections especially important.

Relatives provided connections for these young men and women, but they were entering a world of individual economic independence from their original households and approaching the peak of their earning years. A type of family relationship would be formed in many of the boardinghouses, both those run by companies and those maintained by individuals. Yet to a large extent these were voluntary relationships, easily altered as the individual moved from one situation to the next. Indeed, they existed to sustain the individual and were subordinate to the individual, rather than vice versa.

While these voluntary family relationships were the norm in Lowell, they were also becoming increasingly important in other arenas of industrialization, as individual family members began receiving their own wages. Mary Blewett describes how female shoebinders, working in their homes rather than in a factory or shop, were by the 1830s paid their own independent wages. The wage rates were lower than those paid in textile factories, so they did not confer the same degree of economic independence, but they were paid directly to the women who did the work. Thus, even if these women were contributing to a family wage they were doing so on a "voluntary" basis.

39. "George Richardson on the Witness Stand," Appendix 7 in Gibb, *The Saco-Lowell Shops*, pp. 642–647.

A similar situation may have existed for young women in Fall River. Most of the young women who married in that town during the middle of the 1840s described themselves as wage earners. While approximately one-third of the women were housekeepers, 20 percent listed themselves as factory workers, and 41 percent listed themselves as garment makers of one sort or another.[40] Most of these women were probably collecting their own wages.

Even within factories that had employed a family system of labor, the involuntary family wage shifted to a voluntary one. In part, the shift to individual wage payment was encouraged by a change in technology. As power looms were introduced, mills began to recruit independent female wage earners to operate them. Barbara Tucker notes that in the mid-1830s Slater tried to pay his female weavers independently, no doubt in recognition of the increasing number of single women, rather than children, who were tending power looms. Parental protests led him to abandon the attempt, however, and he did not succeed in making the change until the 1840s. The records of the Blackstone Factory suggest that by 1843 most workers were being paid individually, although in a few cases parents still collected for their children. In Fall River, the Annawan factory stopped keeping family accounts in the late 1830s.[41]

By the 1840s, as a result of these changes in the textile mills in southern New England, a voluntary instead of involuntary fam-

40. Information derived from the Fall River marriage records, 1844–1845, MSA. Occupations of women were recorded systematically for women only during this brief period, yielding the following results:

Occupation	Percentage	N
Housekeeper	31	15
Factory worker	20	10
Garment maker	41	20
Teacher	4	2
Other (farmer & laborer)	4	2
Total	100	49

41. Tucker, *Samuel Slater*, p. 225; Blackstone Records, MSS 9, Subgroup 1, Series D, vol. 579, RIHS.

ily wage economy had become the norm for a broad spectrum of working people. As single wage earners often living on their own, many of these young people would be able to support themselves. But once they married and began to have children, few men would be able to support their families on their own wages alone. Thus the family wage existed as a potent reality, either present or future, in the lives of this emerging working class. And as Bruce Laurie argues, declining wages of artisans in relationship to a rising cost of living meant that skilled as well as unskilled workingmen increasingly had to rely on additional sources of income, which were often controlled by other members of their families.[42] If the external mechanisms of family contract labor ceased to guarantee the contribution of wages to the family pot, internal mechanisms were needed.

While middle-class families were promoting moral restraint and emotional ties to protect their children in a new economic world, working-class parents may have been promoting similar ideals to protect themselves, particularly in their relationships with their teenage children, who were in such a liminal phase of their lives. One must also wonder what future these young people saw for themselves if they were to stay in the mills for any length of time. Family survival and moral restraint would go hand in hand, giving questions of moral authority important economic overtones.

42. On the changing relationship between wages and the cost of living, see Bruce Laurie, *Artisans into Workers: Labor in Nineteenth-Century America* (New York, 1989), pp. 59–60; and Faler, *Mechanics and Manufacturers*, pp. 97–99.

Chapter 2

Labor Reform in the 1830s:
Men's and Women's Struggles

When Walter Brown challenged the authority of Parris Richmond over Paulina in 1832, he did so in the wake of widespread unrest among factory workers and artisans in the region. The New England Association of Farmers, Mechanics, and Other Workingmen, which emerged in the early 1830s, was not the first organized protest to emerge in the region. It was, however, the first organization to attempt a broad coalition of skilled and semiskilled workers in factories as well as traditional trades, and the first to unite workers from most of the New England states. It combined several strains of labor activism which had previously been independent of one another, merging community protests with a burgeoning trades union movement.

The attack on paternalism which had been at the center of the Richmond-Brown case would be played out along several avenues in this broader labor movement. As labor reform surged forward in two distinct phases, first in 1832 and again in 1834, the struggle for a ten-hour day would be the major issue. This was essentially a struggle to control the world of leisure, to separate it from the workplace, and thus to attack the paternalistic presumptions of employers who controlled almost every waking hour of their employees. But this was also a struggle in which workingmen would confront their relationship with fellow wage earners who were women and children, such as Paulina Brown, and in this case they would fashion their own sort of paternalism.

A Community of Workingmen

The coalition of factory workers and artisans that emerged throughout New England in 1832 was an important innovation in labor-organizing. In 1824, factory workers had coalesced briefly in Pawtucket, in a strike that involved the community as well as workers in the factory. Female operatives had even organized their own independent procession, much to the amazement of local observers. Skilled workers in Boston had established trades unions by this time, and in 1825 journeymen housewrights struck (in vain) for a ten-hour day, claiming not only that their hours were too long but also that they had difficulty supporting their families on current wages.[1]

The labor-reform movement, on the other hand, began in Providence in September 1831, as factories prepared to light up for the winter. A rumor took hold among machinists in Providence that mills in Taunton would be discontinuing the practice. In a hastily convened meeting, Providence machinists resolved to follow suit, demanding a workday that would last only from sunup to sundown. They organized a committee to contact other machine shops in the state and scheduled a meeting for the end of October.[2]

Their second meeting drew representatives from factory towns all over Rhode Island and Massachusetts. Providence, Cumberland, Woonsocket, Warwick, Cranston, Pawtucket, Valley Falls,

1. For further discussion of these early New England labor movements, see Gary Kulik, "Pawtucket Village and the Strike of 1824: The Origins of Class Conflict in Rhode Island," *Radical History Review* 17 (Spring 1978): 5–38; John Commons et al., *History of Labor in the United States*, vol. 1 (1918; New York, 1966), pp. 159–162, 302–332; Gary Kornblith, "From Artisans to Businessmen: Master Mechanics in New England, 1789–1850" (Ph.D. diss., Princeton University, 1983), pp. 501–522. The Workingmen's Party, which emerged in Massachusetts in 1830 and 1831, touched on some issues that were important to workingmen, but Ronald Formisano demonstrates that it existed more as a shadowy faction within the National Republicans led by "ruffle shirt radicals" than as an independent movement of workingmen. Leaders tended to be merchants, businessmen, or prosperous farmers. See Ronald Formisano, *The Transformation of Political Culture: Massachusetts Parties, 1780s–1840s* (New York, 1983), pp. 225–226.

2. Kornblith, "From Artisans to Businessmen," p. 504; *Providence Patriot and Columbian Phoenix*, October 1, 1831; October 15, 1832.

Coventry, Burrillville, Lowell, Fall River, Taunton, and Seekonk were represented. The machinists altered their demands slightly, probably to make the movement attractive to members of the building trades as well. Instead of fighting against "lighting up," which was strictly a factory issue, they opted instead for a ten-hour day. This would have more appeal to carpenters and masons who did not work after dark in the cold of winter but faced grueling days in the summer. Delegates to the October meeting thus drew up a written constitution and signed a pledge: after March 20, 1832, they would not work more than ten hours a day without adequate compensation.

The mechanics continued to meet in their hometowns throughout the winter, organizing committees to convince their fellow workingmen to take the ten-hour pledge and sign the workingmen's constitution. A larger meeting to be held in Boston was planned for February, no doubt with the hope of steeling workingmen to confront their employers in what was clearly shaping up as a showdown.

The workingmen had couched their demands in extremely conciliatory, almost deferential language. "We disclaim all hostility to the interest of the employer," they proclaimed in the preamble to their constitution. "Our only object is, to promote the reciprocity of the community, without which, no such thing as equal rights can be said to exist."[3] Indeed, most of the workingmen organized by community rather than trade, and membership in their organizations was not restricted to wage earners, as it was among journeymen in the various trades of New York and Philadelphia. Instead, anyone of "good moral character" was invited to join. Masters and small employers were perceived as potential allies, not as enemies. The community the workingmen sought to construct would constitute an alternative, and hence a denial of the notions of community that provided the basis of factory paternalism.

Despite the mild-mannered language and open membership requirements, employers viewed this new organization as a

3. *New England Artisan and Laboring Man's Repository* (Pawtucket, Providence, and Boston), January 5, 1832 (hereafter, *The Artisan*).

direct challenge to their prerogatives and responded quickly with punitive action. One large establishment in Providence dismissed "almost an entire set of hands," an event that was repeated in Taunton. In Woonsocket Falls, the "lord paramount" of the village closed the schoolhouse to a meeting of workingmen. And in Lowell, Kirk Boott fired Willard Guild from the Lowell Machine Shop as punishment for attending one of the meetings in Providence. (Workingmen in Lowell retaliated by electing Guild to the state legislature in Boott's place.) Factory agents in Fall River were particularly alarmed, as some of them contemplated calling out the militia. "X.Y.Z." reported similar opposition among employers in New Bedford, whom he ridiculed for their " 'animous' vote not to employ any man, that will not conform to the old established custom. This will make fine openings for their journeymen, and is what some of them have long desired."[4]

Reports of these attacks were carried in *The Artisan*, which had commenced publication in January 1832 under the direction of the group's publishing committee and its new editor, Jacob Frieze. Frieze was a minister at the Universalist church in Pawtucket during the 1820s and had edited a reform newspaper, *The Liberalist and Wilmington Reporter* in Wilmington, North Carolina, before moving north. But the editorial committee justified their selection of Frieze by noting that he had "been brought up to, and labored in a mechanical profession."[5] The newspaper was published once a week, first in Pawtucket, then in Providence, and finally, the following year, in Boston. In its reports of organizing efforts throughout the region, it provided encouragement to the workingmen who were trying to organize.

When the Boston meeting was finally held in the Marlborough Hotel at the end of February, the list of delegates revealed the extent to which the movement was catching on among workingmen throughout New England. Boston was represented by eighteen delegates, Charlestown by eleven. The composition of the

4. *The Artisan*, January 5, 1832; February 2, 1832; February 16, 1832; March 22, 1832.
5. *The Christian Leader*, June 10, 1880, p. 8; *The Artisan*, January 5, 1832.

Providence delegation suggests how the movement was broadening occupationally: of eight representatives, only three were machinists. Three were carpenters, one was a master bookbinder, and another was a clerk from the Providence Furnace Company. Delegates from smaller factory towns were also present: North Providence, Pawtucket, Scituate, Warwick, Coventry, and Cranston in Rhode Island; New Bedford, Amesbury, Gloucester, Taunton, Springfield, East Cambridge, Fall River, Saugus, Medway, Dorchester, and Lowell in Massachusetts; New Market, Pembroke, Great Falls, and Dunstable in New Hampshire.[6] The delegates formally named their organization the New England Association of Farmers, Mechanics, and Other Workingmen and returned to their hometowns ready to push for what might best be called a general strike.

One *Artisan* editorial early in March, which enjoined readers to be prepared to switch to a ten-hour day on March 20, attempted to embolden them with assurances of community support. At the same time, however, it warned its readers: "The manufacturers boast that they will close their gates and stop their wheels." While acknowledging that temporary unemployment might indeed ensue, the newspaper reminded the workingmen that they, more than the manufacturers, had the power to determine whether the factories would run. Workingmen could *"compel"* manufacturers to shut down "until they become willing to listen to the demands of justice."[7] After a New Bedford employer dismissed ten or twelve hands from his shop for signing the constitution and threatened to close up his business if necessary, "F.P.S." made a similar assessment: "It is reasonable to expect from what has already been manifested, that there will be a struggle between the employers and the employed; and as we anticipate the conflict, let us be prepared."[8]

Hundreds of workingmen continued to attend meetings in each of these towns, leading one writer to estimate that by March 20 some 20,000 workingmen would rise up to assert their

6. *The Artisan*, February 22, 1832.
7. *The Artisan*, March 8, 1832.
8. *The Artisan*, March 15, 1832.

rights, a view echoed by the workingmen of Fall River, who resolved "that those who would resort to arms, to cheat mechanics of their just dues, have to contend with more than twenty thousand legitimate descendants of the heroes of our Revolutionary conflict, who will not brook insult, nor tamely submit to premeditated injury."[9]

Actual numbers were probably much more modest. New Bedford reported that 400 mechanics had attended one of its meetings and that 300 had signed the constitution. Providence also claimed 300 members.[10] The local groups organized extensive canvassing committees to gain more signatures and even adjusted their membership requirements in an attempt to accommodate a wider range of problems.

The Providence organization may have begun among machinists, but carpenters were providing most of the leadership by March. A committee of twenty-five appointed to get signatures to the constitution in early March included twelve carpenters, but only two machinists, along with a mason, a cabinetmaker, a jeweler, and a clerk. The decline of leadership from ranks of the machinists may have been due to pressure from mill owners, but the movement remained committed to including factory workers in the struggle. The Providence group even voted to let factory workers join their organization by paying 50 cents but without signing the constitution (and without taking the ten-hour pledge) right away. Instead, the Providence organization voted "that members under contract, be requested to render their names to the Secretary, and the time at which their contracts expire."[11]

This provision was probably aimed at the mule spinners, who were also becoming interested in the movement. Like most mill workers, they worked on yearly contracts, which were usually negotiated in the spring. Enforcement of contracts might be lax in normal times, but a strike was different. Thus Seth Luther cited an example of a machinist in Dover, New Hampshire, who

9. *The Artisan*, March 1, 1832; March 8, 1832.
10. *The Artisan*, March 8, 1832; March 15, 1832.
11. *The Artisan*, March 1, 1832; March 22, 1832.

had served in the state legislature as a representative of the Working Men, despite attempts by the foreman of the machine shop to intimidate him into not running. When the machinist had served his term and returned to his old place of employment, he was informed he could no longer work there because he had broken his contract to work for a year. According to the machinist, the only contract he had signed was to work for a particular wage for a year.[12]

The mule spinners met in Providence on February 18, 1832, to establish the New England Association of Mule Spinners for Mutual and Friendly Support and Co-operation—a combination of a friendly society and a trade union. Dues were comparatively steep ($5.50 to $6.00 to join, plus 12½ cents a week) and were to provide a fund to support workers who quit or were fired from their jobs for defense of the trade (such as preventing a reduction of wages). To ensure that employers understood the collective nature of the undertaking, mule spinners were required to quit in a body, not individually, when engaging in protest. They also set other rules for the workplace: no more than one set of mules was to be engaged, and only the sons of mule spinners were to be instructed in the trade.[13] Wages were another critical issue in their conflicts with employers that spring.

The mule spinners, as distinct from other workingmen in the New England movement, were organizing a specific trade organization rather than a community-based one, with regulations that were much more like those found among trades in Philadelphia and New York than among most working people in New England. Yet they cooperated with the broader New England movement as they moved to solidify their position, and they were viewed as supporters of labor reform.

The payroll records that still exist suggest that mule spinners

12. Seth Luther, *An Address to the Working Men of New England, on the State of Education, and on the Condition of the Producing Classes in Europe and America* (New York, 1833), pp. 24–25. *The Artisan*, March 1, 1832, noted "It is customary with manufacturing establishments not to settle with persons in their employ when the employed wish to withdraw their services before the expiration of their engagements."

13. *The Artisan*, March 15, 1832.

went out not on March 20 but on the days their yearly contracts expired. Thus, those at the Annawan factory in Fall River were among the first to strike, quitting on March 12 and taking the young mule piecers with them. Those at Slater's Steam Cotton Factory in Providence struck two-and-a-half weeks later, on March 30.[14]

While these different departure dates undermined the drama of a mass walkout, the early commitment of some may have given courage to others. The mule spinners in Fall River, for instance, were held up as an example for the entire labor movement in the region. *The Artisan* reported particularly strong solidarity among spinners in Fall River, who in one way or another bedeviled the efforts of agents to find replacements. One agent had apparently traveled the countryside for days in an attempt to find new mule spinners and had managed to come up with two, who "on hearing the state of things, after their arrival there, took *'French leave.'* " According to *The Artisan*, "The wages set by the mule spinners have been offered, and, in some establishments, are paid; but the reason the Fall River manufacturers cannot obtain help at these rates, is because the spinners are pledged not to run mules from which others have been discharged."[15]

Payroll records from both the Annawan factory and the Steam Cotton factory suggest that the mule spinners were more vulnerable than the newspaper indicated. Of the seven mule spinners at the Annawan who went out on strike in mid-March of 1832, five would never return. James Johnson stayed out only a few weeks, returning in April; Benjamin Nickerson returned to the factory a year and a half later in August 1833; but the rest disappeared. Meanwhile, the company quickly found replacements to take over some of the mules: Pardon White, Benjamin Greene, and Elijah Harris began working a couple of days after the strike

14. Annawan Factory Records, Account Books, 1830–1840, FRHS; Slater Mss., Steam Cotton Factory, vol. 17, March 1832, HBS. Participation of mule spinners in Fall River was deduced from debit and credit ledgers of the Annawan factory. All mule spinners collected wages on March 12. Day books were not available, as they were for the Slater Mill.

15. *The Artisan*, March 22, 1832.

began. Benajah Whitemore was hired in mid-April, Benjamin Bryant in the beginning of May, and Pelham Wood in the beginning of June. Before the strike, mule spinners were receiving 11 cents per 100 skeins and they would continue at those wages after the strike—indeed, until 1834, when prices were knocked down to 10 cents per 100.[16]

At the Steam Cotton factory all ten mule spinners (including the overseer) stayed out for only a week after they walked out en masse on March 30. By the second week of April, almost all were back at work, producing greater amounts of yarn than they had the previous month. One reason for their capitulation may have been Slater's ability to line up scabs. During the last two weeks of March the factory had located sixteen mule spinners engaged "to commence the second Monday in April next." Although four "backed out" and one was "not certain," there were still enough men listed to keep the machines running. Slater also managed to find excuses to shut down most of the rest of the factory. Payroll records indicate that machinery was being repaired, but it may have been a thinly veiled threat of a lockout as well.[17]

Records from the Annawan factory suggest that, regardless of intentions, not everyone was free to act in the same way with regard to the strike. The workers who were paid as individuals were the ones who walked out. For example, the mule spinners at the Annawan were paid this way—if they had children who worked, the children did not work in the same factory. Neither were most of them dependent on the mill for a roof over their head. Indeed, the only mule spinner who returned to work at the Annawan, James Johnson, was also the only one who lived in company housing. The overseer of the mule piecers, James Elsbree, who refused to strike, also lived in company housing.[18]

The mule piecers may have faced even stronger constraints. Although all the young piecers went out on strike, one of the four who quickly returned, John Kennedy, was living in company housing, as were three of the replacements. John Kennedy's re-

16. Annawan Ledgers C and D, FRHS.
17. Slater Mss., Steam Cotton Factory, vol. 17, March 1832; vol. 11, March 1832, HBS.
18. Annawan Ledgers, 1830–1840, FRHS.

turn may have also been dictated by another form of need. Most mule piecers (both strikers and scabs) were children contributing to a family wage collected by parents, but Kennedy's family situation was particularly tough. His father, Patrick Kennedy, had been killed a few months earlier while attempting to chip ice off the picker house waterwheel. John and his two brothers had become a major source of support for their family. Another striking mule piecer who quickly returned was John Ricketson, who had similar pressing family obligations. His father, Gilbert, had been a successful mule spinner in earlier years, but the elder Ricketson had not worked since May 1831, and John's other siblings had ceased working at that time also. John's wages of 33 cents a day were not much, but they were all that was going into the Ricketson account at that time.[19]

Other young men willing to scab in the strike were almost all contributing to a family wage and found the opportunity to move into the mule room an opportunity for slightly higher wages, usually on the order of about 2 cents to 8 cents a day. It was a pathetically small amount, but actually a 10 percent increase for most of them.

The mule spinners were not alone in resisting manufacturers and employers throughout the region. When March 20 came, many workingmen throughout New England either began working ten hours a day or refused to work at all. In Boston, shipwrights and carpenters moved to a ten-hour day. Housewrights in Fall River did likewise. In Lowell, where 350 men had signed the workingmen's constitution, the building trades moved to ten hours, "and about fifty others quit work from the machine shop and have nothing else to do, but to *electioneer* in a good cause." In Valley Falls, Central Falls, and Pawtucket, Rhode Island, about 100 men joined them, most of them machinists.[20]

About 500 mechanics in Providence left their jobs, including carpenters, machinists, and mule spinners. A few of the men in the building trades in Providence did not have to strike, because their employers acquiesced to a ten-hour day—at least for the

19. Ibid.
20. *The Artisan*, March 22, 1832; March 29, 1832.

time being. Tolman & Bucklin, for example, the large architectural and land development firm, put their work crews on ten-hour shifts. On the other hand, the Steam Factory Machine Shop closed down, while the Providence Calandering and Bleaching Company immediately began to hire scabs and was able to re-open quickly with a shoestring crew. One writer in *The Artisan* described the early fervor the strike created in Providence when he noted: "Our meeting on Saturday evening was attended by more than 1,000 persons. The hall was completely filled."[21]

An examination of existing payroll records confirms much of this reporting. We do not have the actual time books for the machine shop at Slater's Steam Cotton Factory, but the cash book for that period shows that the wages paid at the machine shop in March and April of 1832 were, respectively, 62 percent and 66 percent of the wages paid in February.[22] If the machinists did go out on March 20, this drop can be explained only by the walkout of virtually all the men in the machine shop.

At the Annawan factory, for which we do have records, this is precisely what happened. On March 20 the machine shop was almost deserted. Of twenty-eight men who were employed there, only eight remained, including the superintendent, his assistant, and three of the four apprentices. The men stayed out through the first week of April, but by April 9 many of those who were going to return were back in the shop. Half of the twenty strikers returned.[23]

For Lowell it is difficult to tell exactly which machine shop was struck. Machine shop activity was spread through different divisions of the Locks and Canals Company, which was responsible for the construction and maintenance of buildings and equipment, but none of those men seem to have walked off their jobs. A list of leaders in the movement suggests that most of the momentum in Lowell may have shifted to the building trades, as it had in Providence.[24]

21. *The Artisan*, March 22, 1832; April 5, 1832; April 19, 1832; and March 29, 1832, respectively.

22. Slater Mss., Steam Cotton Factory, vol. 3, 1827–1839, HBS.

23. Annawan Factory Day Book, 1832, FRHS.

24. The names of fifteen leaders in Lowell showed up in the pages of *The Artisan*. Nine could be traced through the city directory of that year: two were

Regardless of these efforts, the strike ended in defeat by the middle of April. In May, construction companies such as Tolman & Bucklin rescinded their ten-hour days, precipitating a walkout by their workmen. But by then the carpenters were acting on their own in Providence.[25] The only place the ten-hour struggle would continue was in the shipyards of Boston. The shipwrights and caulkers had adopted the ten-hour day on March 20 (probably six o'clock in the morning to six o'clock in the evening, with a two-hour lunch), but two months later merchants held a meeting and agreed not to give work to employers who hired men on the ten-hour system. Journeymen refused to work on those terms, and a struggle that would last all summer ensued. The journeymen were concerned about other inequities as well. They were not paid for their time when they had to travel to get a ship (at least in some instances), nor were they paid for their time when they worked a few hours but then stopped because of inclement weather.[26]

The journeymen won a partial victory in July when the merchants of Boston, claiming fear of the cholera epidemic sweeping the country, authorized master carpenters and caulkers to allow their journeymen a two-hour lunch break during August, though they added with great emphasis that the men "SHALL commence the days work at sunrise, and terminate it at Sunset." Ronald Formisano points out: "The epitaph of the strike . . . was written in September when a demoralized Workingmen's association met and repealed the provision that allowed it to fellowship only with those workers adhering to the ten-hour standard."[27]

A coalition of mill owners and merchants had demonstrated a strength far beyond anything wage earners could muster. While the masters who were leading the industrial transformation in cities of the Middle Atlantic states would acquiesce to the demand for a ten-hour day, New England capitalists would not. But

---

machinists, three were masons, three were housewrights, and one was a surveyor of work.

25. *The Artisan*, May 24, 1832.
26. *The Artisan*, June 7 and 21, 1832.
27. *The Artisan*, July 26, 1832; Formisano, *Transformation*, p. 230.

the strength and resistance of these capitalists is perhaps less impressive than the way male factory workers and traditional artisans had united in this struggle, with a clear recognition of the extent to which their economic destinies were intertwined. Mule spinners and machinists, carpenters and masons, had joined together in an alliance that would resurface in coming years.

When the Boston Trades Union was formed in 1834, it would continue in the distinctive tradition of New England organizing, though it may have been a bit more conservative than its predecessor. The new organization was defined by trade, and masters seemed to have taken a more active role in leadership. On March 6, 1834, Charles Douglass, who had taken over from Jacob Frieze as editor of *The Artisan*, called a meeting of the delegates of fourteen trades from the city of Boston, as well as representatives from Charlestown and the Lynn Female Society, to order. Curriers, cabinet and pianoforte makers, tailors, masons, coopers, shipwrights, rope makers, painters, iron founders, printers, house carpenters, sail makers, machinists, blacksmiths, and whitesmiths all sent representatives. Inspired by the New York Trades' Union, they read the constitution of that organization and then wrote their own. They also passed a series of resolutions supporting *The Artisan*.[28]

Although it took its cues from the New York organization, the Boston group retained the distinctive structure of New England labor organizations: masters as well as journeymen were invited to join. Thus, soon after the formation of the Boston Trades Union, "A Boston Mechanic" wrote to his peers in New York:

> Since the interest of all who obtain their living by honest labor is essentially the same, since the bos [*sic*] is often brought back to journeywork by hard luck, and the journeyman may expect in his turn to become an employer, while both of them are invariably imposed upon and treated as if belonging to an inferior grade of society by those who live without labor, it surely seems quite desirable that in a union of trades for the common benefit, both journeyman and employer should come together.

28. *The Man* (New York), March 12, 1834.

The author of this letter, drawing a clear line between producers and nonproducers rather than employers and employed, praised the Boston Trades Union for uniting the latter: "In the delegation from the same trade, you find the journeyman and his employer colleagues in the Convention, both feeling that in the great interest of redeeming the character and condition of labor, it is their duty to unite and co-operate." The writer urged New York workers to follow that example "so as the inclinations of the employers will permit."[29]

The unity of masters and journeymen within the Boston Trades Union represented a point of continuity with the ideology of the New England Association of Farmers, Mechanics, and Other Workingmen, but there were ways in which the two groups differed. First, employers seem to have taken a more active role in this organization, and for this reason the United Benevolent Society of Journeyman Tailors refused to join, complaining, "We are informed that a great number of the Employers represent their Journeymen, which we are of the opinion that they could not do fairly." The tailors suggested that, instead, "the Journeymen and Employers form separate bodies, and that each body send their own representatives to the general Convention of the Trades' Union."[30] This division did not take place, and the tailors were conspicuously absent from the grand Fourth of July parade staged by the Boston Trades Union in 1834.[31]

Also absent from this trades organization were factory workers. Machinists joined, for in Boston there were workshops in which they were employed, but there was no sign of the mule

29. *The Man*, May 30, 1834.
30. *The Artisan*, July 26, 1834.
31. The *Boston Daily Advocate* described the procession in detail. Led by the Mechanics' Rifle Company, 130 cabinet and pianoforte builders followed, then 56 printers with a printing press, 160 housewrights, 64 shoemakers, 88 masons, and 88 rope and sail makers. Most spectacular was the frigate *Mechanic*, 27½ feet long, drawn by 24 white horses and followed by 66 shipwrights, then 42 machinists, 64 painters, 58 stonecutters, 51 coopers, 70 "black and white smiths," and 27 members of the Mechanics' Apprentice Library Association. *The Advocate* counted just over 1,000 marchers, while *The Artisan* estimated between 2,000 and 2,500. Of the trades that originally sent delegates to the first meeting of the Boston Trades Union, not only the tailors but also the curriers and iron founders appear to have been absent. (Both articles in *The Artisan*, July 12, 1834.)

spinners, who had been so active a couple of years earlier. Their absence may have been a result of the local character of the trades union, it may have been an indication of growing exclusivity among artisans in Boston, or it may have reflected very different conditions in the countryside, where many factory workers, including mule spinners, faced wage cuts in the textile industry and were perhaps less inclined to consider unity with employers a desirable goal. While artisans in Boston were expressing their unity, industrial workers in the countryside were organizing strikes.[32] This time, however, women rather than men were the heart and soul of these protests.

"Dependent" Workers

Although one distinguishing feature of the New England Association of Farmers, Mechanics, and Other Workingmen was its attempt to unite traditional artisans and factory workers, the women who constituted such a large part of the work force in textile production were largely ignored in organizing efforts, though they may have been interested. Thus, in 1832, at the same time that the mule spinners were beginning their strike at the Annawan factory in Fall River, a large number of female workers either went on strike or were laid off. In a highly unusual move, the factory paid up wages to about half the weavers, all of whom were women, on March 12 and 13. Whatever the disruption, it was brief. Many of the women were back on the payroll by the end of March. But the reason we know nothing about this disruption is that the activities of these women were never mentioned in *The Artisan*, though the activities of male workers in Fall River were covered extensively.

The fact that these women went unnoticed underscores an-

32. The cuts were apparently widespread. According to *The Artisan* of June 7, 1834, "about three months ago, a heavy reduction of wages took place in all the principal manufacturing establishments throughout New England. It commenced at Lowell, the headquarters of manufacturing monopolies, and like the Asiatic cholera, soon extended into all the other villages, carrying desolation 'distress,' and misery into the bosom of many poor but industrious families."

other important characteristic of this movement: gender, rather than skill, unified participants. Operating in the world of male citizenship (and republicanism), members of the New England Association viewed their relationship with women and children in similar terms: as dependents to be protected, rather than as independent wage earners of equal status. This orientation would provide a bridge between artisans struggling for a ten-hour day, and mule spinners who were more concerned about wages than they were about time. The mule spinners' demand that their sons be educated in the trade (which seldom happened, if payroll records are any indication) suggests that they were concerned about their place within their households as well as within their trade.[33]

The relationship between "independent" and "dependent" workers was partially articulated in the demands for education. In the preamble to their constitution, workers in the New England Association demanded the right to be consulted on the hours and prices of their labor, not only to obtain a comfortable livelihood but also so that their children might "be afforded the necessary means and opportunity to acquire that education and intelligence absolutely necessary to American freemen." Another article warned that without education the most factory children could hope for in the future was to obtain the position of overseer.[34]

As Seth Luther, a former carpenter, stumped the New England countryside in the early 1830s, he stressed again and again the problems of illiteracy among children in the factories. Describing "the *pale, sickly, haggard,* countenance of the ragged child, haggard from the *worse* than *slavish* confinement in the cotton mill," Luther went on to point out: "If 13 hours actual labor is

33. For a discussion of the importance to mule spinners of being household heads, see Marianna Valverde, " 'Giving the Female a Domestic Turn': The Social, Legal, and Moral Regulation of Women's Work in British Cotton Mills, 1820–1850," *Journal of Social History* 21 (Summer 1988): 619–634. Jonathan Prude also found few kin relationships between spinners and piecers in *The Coming of the Industrial Order: Town and Factory Life in Rural Massachusetts, 1810–1860* (New York, 1983), p. 119.

34. *The Artisan,* January 5, 1832; March 23, 1832.

required each day, it is *impossible* to attend to education among children, or to improvement among adults." Luther went on to cite a report by workingmen in Providence that found that "in Pawtucket there are at least *five hundred children* who scarcely know what a school is . . . and to add to the darkness of the picture . . . in all the mills which the enquiries of the committees have been able to reach, books, pamphlets, and newspapers are *absolutely prohibited."*[35]

The protection of children was an effective issue from a variety of perspectives. First, it would arouse middle-class sympathy as well as working-class concern. Child labor had become the symbol of the worst excesses of British industrialism, and it was the horror of British factory abuse that Luther was trying to evoke in his "Address to the Working Men of New England." Child labor was the most important indicator that "we are, in these United States, following with fearful rapidity the '*Splendid Example of England.'* "[36] Moreover, by asserting their role as advocates and protectors of these children, workingmen could also reassert their traditional role as male heads of household against incursions of authority by paternalistic factory owners, even though many of the men participating in the ten-hour struggle had not yet begun to head their own households, and even though some skilled workingmen made it a point to keep their children out of the factories. A metaphorical relationship between father and child was thus created between two groups of industrial workers.[37]

Yet because they asserted themselves as protectors, members of the New England Association of Farmers, Mechanics, and Other Workingmen also saw limits to their relationship with these workers from a strategic point of view. They felt that young

35. Luther, *Address*, pp. 20–21.
36. Ibid., p. 10.
37. Sally Alexander makes a similar point about labor unrest in England during this period: "In the minds of these different groups of male workers, their status as fathers and heads of families was indelibly associated with their independence through 'honourable' labor and property in skill, which identification with a trade can give them." See Sally Alexander, "Women, Class, and Sexual Differences in the 1830s and 1840s: Some Reflections on the Writing of a Feminist History," *History Workshop Journal* 17 (Spring 1984): 137.

or female factory workers, particularly family wage workers, would not be able to negotiate successfully with their employers but would require the intervention of the state. In making this assessment, they collapsed beliefs about gender into those about childhood. One writer, for example, noted that women who quit at a factory in Exeter, New Hampshire, were required to give two weeks notice or lose whatever wages were forthcoming, but that men were not. The writer surmised that this disparity was due to one reason only: "Men are not so easily frightened into submission as girls."[38]

This perception inspired the workingmen to petition the state for the protection of dependent workers. In August an article addressed to the workingmen of New England appeared in *The Artisan*. "A large proportion of the operatives in our factories, are and must continue to be, a helpless population," the writer claimed. *"It is indispensible that they should be put under the unremitted supervision and protection of the law of the land."* The New England Association had begun a petition drive to reduce working hours legislatively, a petition that seemed aimed primarily at factory operatives, though its wording was vague. The Memorial to the House of Representatives and Senate noted that "numerous bodies of monopolists in New England, by the facilities granted them for the accumulation of wealth, and their consequent power and influence in society, controlled by avarice and cupidity, triumph over the salutary prescriptions of the constitution, [and] have erected themselves into a self-created aristocracy." Arguing that these developments threatened to demolish the freedom of others, the memorialists concluded by appealing "to your honorable body" and "respectfully ask[ed], if within the limits of your legislative powers, that a law may be passed limiting the hours of labor at ten per day." Petitions from Rhode Island apparently made it to Congress, for *The Artisan* reported that they were denounced there. Workingmen in Rhode Island also submitted petitions to their state legislatures as *The Artisan* cheered them on. "Employers may *growl* a little; but be not disturbed; they won't *bite*," the article reassured its readers.

38. *The Artisan*, April 5, 1832.

"They cover up facts to promote their interest; let operatives unveil those facts to promote the cause of humanity. Public opinion will protect them against abuse."[39] Such legislation would benefit not only women and children, but adult men as well—advancing to protect the interests of "dependent" workers, these workingmen would also be protecting themselves.

An assumption that guided the petitioning efforts of male workingmen in 1832 was that women and children were the same category of workers: dependents, who were unable to organize themselves to combat their employers. This perception would continue, even as the activities of female industrial workers in 1834 challenged these assumptions. When the Boston Trades Union organized in the spring of 1834, they did so in the wake of widespread unrest among women workers, which demonstrated the ability of women to organize and introduced a new set of issues into the male-dominated labor movement.

The Trades Union acknowledged female organizing by allowing women's groups to send delegates to the meeting as long as the representatives were male, suggesting both a concern workingmen had about the propriety of women speaking in public, and a belief that the leadership, if not the rank and file of their organization, should be male. The Lynn Female Society was the only group to respond, however, sending Israel Buffum and William Phillips to represent them at the original meeting in March. They did not participate in the great Fourth of July parade, however. Female textile workers who were staging a strike in Lowell during the March meeting in Boston sent no one to represent them. Because male factory workers, such as mule spinners, were also absent, women may have avoided the movement because they were factory workers; but the women in Lowell may have been unwilling to appoint male spokesmen as well. Their female leaders in Lowell were particularly noted for speaking in

39. *The Artisan*, August 16, 1832; April 5, 1832; June 28, 1832; April 19, 1832. For a recent reassessment of the literature on protective legislation, see Kathryn Kish Sklar, " 'The Greater Part of the Petitioners Are Female': The Reduction of Women's Working Hours in the Paid Labor Force, 1840–1917," in *Worktime and Industrialization: An International History*, ed. Gary Cross (Philadelphia, 1988), pp. 103–133.

public. Despite their absence from the Boston meetings, their turnout over a wage cut forced the workingmen to take notice of them and to view them, like the female shoebinders, as potential allies.[40]

The presence of women in the larger regional movement presented several problems for the men. Women in New England were organizing over the issue of wages, while men were focusing, by and large, on time. This was not surprising, since the wage cuts in factory work, at least, had a gender bias: piece rates rather than day rates had been cut, and most men in factories were paid by the day.[41] The only male textile workers to feel these wage cuts were mule spinners in southern New England (who do not appear to have organized a protest over these cuts). But how should women organize? Should women organize themselves as men did? If so, how would issues of propriety be balanced against independence? Was the relationship between male and female workers economic or familial? Were women to present themselves as fellow wage earners or as sisters and daughters?

It was a tricky issue, because in many cases women were hired at lower wages than men as various trades were industrialized. But in the pages of *The Artisan*, at least, women received some support. "A.Z.," for example, was concerned that even skilled female workers, such as mantua makers and tailoresses, were still barely able to provide for themselves. Moreover, the writer claimed, women who did work formerly done by men were often found by their employers to be better workers "because their habits are more regular"—but they were never paid as much as men, though they suffered "more from acute disease than any

---

40. *The Man*, March 12, 1834; Frederick Robinson, *Oration Delivered before the Trades Union of Boston and Vicinity, on Fort Hill, Boston, on the Fifty-eighth Anniversary of American Independence* (Boston, 1834), p. 32; Mary Blewett, *Men, Women, and Work: Class, Gender and Protest in the Early New England Shoe Industry, 1780–1910* (Urbana, Ill., 1988), pp. 35–41. For a description of the women's strike in Lowell, see Thomas Dublin, *Women at Work: The Transformation of Work and Community in Lowell, Massachusetts, 1826–1860* (New York, 1979), pp. 90–95.

41. Dublin, *Women at Work*, p. 102.

others of the working class." Shoebinders and seamstresses were even worse off.[42]

Charles Douglass, as editor of *The Artisan*, echoed this view in presenting his support for the workingwomen of Baltimore who demanded higher wages in the fall of 1833: "If we have a pair of pantaloons well made, it is of no consequence to us whether the labor was bestowed upon them by male or female hands." The article also stressed, however, that women must take responsibility for organizing themselves and not depend on others. "Women are entitled to the same amount of wages as men, for the same quantum of services, and ought to receive it. But nothing will be done to improve their condition so long as they are careless and indifferent about it themselves."[43]

However, Douglass was not as sympathetic to the issue of female wages as these comments suggest. When the women in Lowell began to show a similar move toward collective organization a few months later, Douglass was quick to acknowledge them. In the middle of March 1834, soon after their strike had begun, he made an appearance at Jefferson Hall in Lowell, both to encourage the women in their organizing activities and to critique their goals. He urged them to make a shorter workday their first concern, arguing that their lengthy workdays were currently constructed "merely to satisfy the unjust and unreasonable demands of avaricious employers."[44] By ignoring the issue of wages, Douglass did not show much sensitivity to the plight of workingwomen or their demand for a wage level that, Thomas Dublin has pointed out, carried with it economic independence. Indeed, Douglass encompassed the female discourse of labor protest within that of the men, subordinating the issue of wages, which women had put forth, to the issue of time.

Despite his reservations about their goals, Douglass applauded their organization. Indeed, he saw a potential audience for a new female labor newspaper (since *The Artisan* was not interested in appealing to them) he planned to call *The Female Advocate and*

42. *The Artisan*, November 9, 1833.
43. *The Artisan*, September 26, 1833.
44. *The Artisan*, March 22, 1834.

Factory Girl's Friend. Describing his potential readers as sisters, daughters, and future mothers, Douglass condemned the "attempts that have been made in different quarters to overawe and impose upon female industry, by a reduction of wages at the pleasure of the employer, and a disposition to treat them as hirelings and dependants." It was particularly offensive that they had received "no respect on account of their sex, of their usefulness, or of their general character," a deficiency that justified "a firm union among females to resist oppression, and make a common cause in defence of their natural rights."[45]

Douglass's talk stressed not only the "natural rights" of these women but also the respect due them "on account of their sex." They might be workers, but they were female workers, and this introduced a different set of problems when it came to their taking his earlier advice to "unitedly resolve to better their present circumstances." Their activities would be limited and shaped by public expectations of proper female behavior. For example, respectable women were not supposed to speak out and act publicly, but that created an important problem: how could they organize to defend themselves when that very act might undermine public sympathy?[46]

New England workingwomen, keenly aware of these limitations, moved carefully, as they had done in the past. The female weavers who had turned out in the Pawtucket strike of 1824 had organized themselves with hardly a word spoken. The female shoebinders who were organizing in the mid-1830s met in churches, particularly in a Quaker meetinghouse, where women were allowed to speak freely. In Dover the factory women who were protesting the same wage cuts that had occurred at Lowell turned out at the city hall, but they refused to march publicly and kept to their rooms for much of their protest. Their resolutions condemned their employers for "attempting to abase and insult them," and the women went on to argue that they viewed

45. *The Artisan*, July 26, 1834.
46. For an important discussion about how the propriety of female activism was related to whether the cause being espoused was radical, see Lori Ginzberg, *Women and the Work of Benevolence: Morality, Politics, and Class in the Nineteenth-Century United States* (New Haven, Conn., 1990), pp. 25–35.

"both the ungenerous accusation of our effecting '*riotous com-binations*' and the poor compliment of our being '*otherwise respectable*' with like feelings of contempt: and consider them both as in the last degree insulting to the daughters of freemen."[47] Being daughters of freemen did not merely harken up images of liberty and equality; it was an important badge of respectability. Indeed, the concept of respectability merged with and depended on a notion of independence for these women.

The women who were on strike had to contend not only with the opposition of their employers but also with the comments of their male supporters, who were clearly uncomfortable with the behavior of female operatives. The *Bunker Hill Aurora*, in an article reprinted in the *New Bedford Weekly Courier and Workingmen's Press*, defended the turnout of women in Lowell by arguing: "It is a method of displaying their independence which very naturally occurred to them, as they gathered together from their various apartments, in addition to the influence of precedents elsewhere, '*in the other sex.*'" Arguing that one or two of the women might deserve censure for their activities, the article continued: "The alleged weakness of the sex is sufficient to excuse for the rest, and ought to be so regarded by gentlemen of thought and feeling. It were against the character of women, if not beyond the power, to restrain herself under these circumstances." The newspaper concluded that the "weakness and humble sphere of life" of female operatives demanded that male newspaper editors show "charitable consideration."[48] The *Gazette* in Dover, New Hampshire, provided a similar defense of the female operatives in that town: it was reassuring that principles of liberty were so deeply ingrained that "even helpless females will rise *en masse* to resist the oppressions of '*haughty insolence,*'" the newspaper argued. Echoing the views of the *Bunker Hill Aurora*, the newspaper added: "They need now the encouragement and assistance of the stronger sex, and they will assuredly receive it."[49]

The newspaper editors who "defended" these women were

47. *Gazette* (Dover), reprinted in *The Man*, March 8, 1834.
48. *New Bedford Weekly Courier and Workingmen's Press*, March 5, 1834.
49. *Gazette*, reprinted in *The Man*, March 8, 1834.

probably middle-class labor reformers who had more in common with such men as Horace Greeley and George Lippard than with leaders of the labor movement; their newspapers were certainly intended for broad circulation in their communities. Thus the somewhat questionable line of defense that rooted these protests in the "weakness of the sex" and the inability of women to restrain themselves must be viewed in the context of middle-class labor reform literature that focused voyeuristically on the degradation of working-class life and the helplessness of its victims. At the same time, however, these portrayals underscore the very real community constraints women faced in organizing, constraints that converged with the restrictions the Boston Trades Union placed on women's participation in the larger labor movement.

As organized workingmen took up the cause of female workers, they ignored the issue of wages and turned instead to the issue of time. Charles Douglass, who had argued that mill owners demonstrated a lack of respect for factory girls on account of their sex, usefulness, and character, would also express reservations about the character of factory operatives. Attending the Trades Union National Convention in Philadelphia in 1835, he would urge another petitioning campaign for legislation to force factories "to shut their mills at a regular hour." He described the young men and young women who worked there as dupes who had traded their characters for wages. The young men "for a few pence more than they could get at home . . . are taught to become the willing servants, the servile instruments of their employer's oppression and extortion!" The young woman who followed a similar route "earns a little more money for a short time; but as surely loses health, if not her good character, her happiness!" The wages that factory operatives earned were construed not so much as a source of independence as a sign of avarice. Thus managers of mills, "knowing these adventurers have come for gain, . . . commence a direct appeal to their feelings of avarice—to persuade them to work overhours."[50]

The larger, national body voted the proposal down, fearing any

50. *The Man*, September 18, 1835.

involvement with politics, but Douglass's argument fit well into the discourse about women that was emerging within the National Trades Union. As Christine Stansell argues, the organization adopted a protectionist stance toward workingwomen which was predicated on the belief that the true place of women was in the home, where they would be protected by workingmen, rather than in the workplace, where they lowered wages and put their morals in jeopardy. Women were of weak character, a failing that encompassed both sexual immorality and the inability to organize; thus workingmen felt it their duty to speak for the women.[51] In New York, workingmen focused more on the issue of female competition and the lowering of wages; in New England, concern was expressed more in the conflict over time.

Male labor leaders and labor reformers regarded female labor protests primarily as an indicator of larger problems in the economic order. Thus they applauded the activities of the women, but they also worried about their propriety. Women were not accepted as full or equal partners in the labor movement, and their issues were not accorded equal status. By 1835 the New England Association of Farmers, Mechanics, and Other Workingmen had returned to its earlier position of pressing petitioning as the only viable way to protect "dependent" workers.

51. Christine Stansell, *City of Women: Sex and Class in New York, 1789–1860* (Urbana, Ill., 1987), pp. 137–141.

Chapter 3

Control of Culture:
Education, Morality, and Religion

Women were excluded from the struggle for a ten-hour day because of concerns about character and propriety, but they were excluded also because the cultural terrain being contested was defined as male rather than female. The workingmen who were struggling for a ten-hour day were attempting both to create and to control a world of leisure. Leisure, as they conceived it, was primarily a world of male respectability, defined as such because of its public and secular character and because of the questions of citizenship and economic exchange it raised. Both these issues became especially pertinent in the context of expanding white male suffrage and the growing dominance of a market society.

In one of the earliest articles printed in *The Artisan,* a contributor argued that shorter hours were needed to improve the mind for intelligent citizenship. This education was particularly important given the brute economic force used to buy votes. "Thousands of American freemen have been obliged to succomb [*sic*] to their employers and cast votes to sustain their party views, or in default thereof, to relinquish their business and submit to privation and distress." A later article would complain of a man who was fired for being an anti-mason.[1] And Seth Luther would claim that a factory agent in Mendon who represented owners living in

1. *The Artisan,* February 2, 1832; August 2, 1832.

another state had "shut down the gates, and marched ninety workmen up to the polls, who established a road, and sent a representative to General Court, in defiance of the inhabitants."[2] This attack on the way aristocrats—which included capitalists, merchants, lawyers, and in many cases, employers—manipulated the political system would feed into the movement of workingmen to elect their own candidates to political office.[3] But also crucial to this attack was the need to critique and control measures for education.

Knowledge and Power

The demand of the New England Association of Farmers, Mechanics, and other Workingmen for shorter hours had been tied to concerns for the schooling of children, but their interest in education extended further. They also wanted a meaningful education for adult workingmen in society. Seth Luther focused on the lack of schooling for children, but he pointed out that adult workingmen also had problems in continuing their education. "E.R.A." in New Bedford would describe education as the key to virtue and happiness, a key that workingmen needed to acquire. "K.L.M." would write to *The Artisan* on the importance of schools for workingmen, arguing that if workers would "only acquire a thirst for education" they would seek to recover those inalienable rights "which by artifice have been alienated."[4] Limited educational opportunity affected far more than intellectual achievements or upward mobility; it structured power relationships as well, creating a hierarchy that was unfair and unnatural. As one

2. Seth Luther, *An Address to the Working Men of New England, on the State of Education, and on the Condition of the Producing Classes in Europe and America* (New York, 1833), p. 35.

3. *The Artisan*, December 28, 1833. On the problems of putting this political plan into practice, see the report on problems in Fall River in *The Artisan*, November 22, 1833. For further discussion of the interaction between the Workingmen's movement and the Workingmen's party, see Ronald Formisano, *The Transformation of Political Culture: Massachusetts Parties, 1790s–1840s* (New York, 1983), pp. 222–244.

4. Luther, *Address*, p. 30; *The Artisan*, May 31, 1832; October 25, 1832.

of the first articles in *The Artisan* stressed, understanding was not natural, but learned, and more often than not owed "its birth to fortuitous circumstances." The article went on to enjoin its readers not to regard those who have had access to education as "demi-gods," as if fate had decreed that they should rule and the rest should obey. "It is in this way that knowledge gives power— It is for this reason, more than any other, that the labors of the many are made subservient to the interest and pleasure of the few." As a result of this subservience, "little reciprocity and social feeling exist between the two or more classes in society."[5]

Writers for *The Artisan* were careful to point out that the acquisition of knowledge did not simply require more time and more schools. How the knowledge was acquired mattered even more. New England workingmen, more than workingmen elsewhere in the country, were extremely sensitive to the way the dissemination of knowledge, and not simply its absence, was used as an instrument of domination. This became especially clear in their discussion of lyceums.

Lyceums and lecture series were becoming an important part of the cultural and intellectual landscape of antebellum New England. On any given night in cities and towns throughout the region, speakers expounded on issues of science, self-improvement, politics, literature, and moral reform. Some lectures took place in exclusive clubs and libraries, and others were costly enough to keep the masses away. But more often than not, they were priced and advertised with a popular audience in mind.

Indeed, one of the defining characteristics of the lyceum movement was that the lectures were disinterested, nonpartisan efforts on behalf of the public good. Despite this ideology of inclusiveness, Donald Scott has pointed out that lyceum lectures were in fact created by and for the white, Anglo-Saxon, urban middle class. Artisans and mechanics might attend, and young professionals invariably were present, but factory workers seldom darkened the door of a lecture hall. More exclusive in nature than its supporters acknowledged, while claiming to embody the interests of all, "the public lecture system was in fact an institu-

5. *The Artisan*, January 5, 1832.

tion for the consolidation of the collective cultural consciousness by which this group [the middle class] came to assert a claim that it was the real American public."[6]

The Boston Associates had made lyceums and lectures in Lowell a centerpiece of their strategy to draw workers from the countryside and had attracted some of the most famous speakers in the nation to the city. The mill owners subscribed to the belief that lyceums were instruments of uplift, bringing education to large masses of people, and many of their factory operatives agreed. Members of the New England Association of Farmers, Mechanics, and Other Workingmen, however, were less sanguine. They viewed most lyceums as elitist organizations that undermined the confidence of working people. Regardless of a lecture's content, the nature of the performance made a difference—lecturers were empowered at the expense of their audience.

With this perception in mind, the Boston Mechanics' Lyceum added declamation to its curriculum in June 1832. According to the projectors of the Lyceum, who included English-born instrument maker Timothy Claxton as the organization's president, this was a far more useful course to pursue than simply attending popular lectures, for mechanics needed to improve their speaking abilities and confidence. In this way "the members acquire a habit of doing their own studying and speaking, and consequently of calling into exercise the faculties of their own minds, and using the means for improving their own manner of delivery." These newfound abilities would be a vast improvement over the tendency of those attending a lecture to "retain little of the instruction they receive, and . . . to go away with the impression, that because the lecturer's duty is performed, their own task is as certainly completed."[7] In promoting this participatory approach

6. Donald M. Scott, "The Popular Lecture and the Creation of a Public in Mid-Nineteenth-Century America," *Journal of American History* 66 (1980): 801, 809. See also Mary Kupiec Cayton, "The Making of an American Prophet: Emerson, His Audiences, and the Rise of the Culture Industry in Nineteenth-Century America," *American Historical Review* 92 (June 1987): 597–620.

7. In light of the emphasis which was placed on public speaking, it is worth noting that women were allowed to attend meetings as guests of male members. The rules for female participation, however, were different. According to Claxton,

to lyceum activities, Claxton was also drawing on experience. In 1826, he had helped to set up the Boston Mechanics' Institution, which failed after a few years, in part because of "its unsocial character: . . . no library, reading room nor classes" had been established. Claxton continued his educational campaign when he became president of the Boston branch of the New England Association of Farmers, Mechanics, and Other Workingmen. He supported both a ten-hour day and education when he spoke to the organization, arguing that "for want of mental cultivation, men do become dupes of those better informed."[8]

This attack on the power relations implicit in the educational process was even more explicit in the critiques that came from New Bedford: popular lyceums were not only hierarchical, they provided a forum for the rich to dominate the poor through ridicule. Thus, the *New Bedford Workingmen's Press* asked: "Why cannot both the old and the young, the plebian and the patrician meet together for mutual improvement, and impart to each other their honest views regardless of age or condition?" It went on to answer the question by pointing out: "It is a matter of policy with 'the few' to divert the attention of the plebian community from such objects, that they may better effect their diabolical purposes—and further, such is the state of society, we are considered underlings." Citing the unfair association of wealth, education, and domination, the article continued: "The wealthiest man among us is the best. And he who has no other recommendation than unsullied character and an hard pair of hands must, agreeable to popular doctrine, move on among the 'unblest.'" As a result of this division between nonproducers and producers, education became not only a source of greater knowl-

---

women "were permitted to hand in pieces of composition, which were read at the meetings." One of the earliest topics debated at the lyceum, on March 26, was "Are Females endowed by nature with intellectual abilities equal to those of the other sex?" *The Artisan*, November 8, 1832; Timothy Claxton, *Memoir of a Mechanic: Being a Sketch of the Life of Timothy Claxton, Written by Himself* (New York, 1839), p. 90.

8. Timothy Claxton, *Memoir of a Mechanic*, p. 83; *The Artisan*, April 5, 1832. For further discussion of Claxton and the Mechanics' Institution see Gary Kornblith, "From Artisans to Businessmen: Master Mechanics in New England, 1789–1850" (Ph.D. diss., Princeton University, 1983), pp. 457–461.

edge but also a basis for verbal abuse. "The former, having more time for study, become the most intelligent, and when associated with the latter professedly for improvement, are too apt to take advantage of honest error, and by means of *satire* to destroy their confidence and kill their ambition; thereby subverting the very purposes for which they associated." The article would conclude by arguing that "there can be no such thing as the cooperation of all classes," and by recommending that "the Mechanics, Farmers, and other Workingmen, those who are satisfied with the simple appellation of 'common people' . . . form themselves into associations for mutual improvement, independent of the self-styled 'gentry.' "[9]

Another essay lauding the New Bedford Lyceum followed the lead of this first article, noting that at most lyceums workingmen were frowned on or treated sarcastically if they tried to speak on an issue. Lyceums, the author noted, "instead of demolishing the partition walls which divide class from class, lay them broader and more formidable than before." For this reason the New Bedford Lyceum, with its 120 members, was an important step forward for workingmen. As the article went on:

> Lyceums in order to be useful to the producing classes should be managed altogether by themselves. They should be places of public resort for the less favored by fortune, where they could meet together and discuss questions important to their own welfare, and not as they now are, establishments controlled by the aristocracy, where the people are required to meet at set times to hear a flippant lawyer or some other candidate for popular favor display his college learning in the use of hard words and unmeaning phrases, which are of no sort of consequence to those who get their bread by the sweat of their brow.[10]

While most criticisms of lyceums focused on context and style, some pointed out that the content also reinforced existing power relations. "An old Friend" wrote that popular lectures on the

9. *The Artisan*, November 15, 1832.
10. *The Artisan*, April 4, 1833.

sciences were meant to divert working people from questions of political economy. Workers would not challenge the unfair distribution of goods as long as this was the case. "So long as the industrious classes leave the control of our schools to those who have an interest in keeping them in the dark," the writer warned, "so long as our honest mechanics will run after *chosen* Lecturers, who will teach them the movement of celestial bodies; and the structure of the interior of our terrestrial globe, and keep cautiously to themselves the important knowledge of securing the better half of the good things of this world, *without labor,* so long will it be vain to undeceive them."[11]

Workingmen did not view their lyceums simply as self-help solutions to improve their economic circumstances. They were also attacks on the way knowledge was disseminated and appropriated to maintain existing power relations. Knowledge was political in the broadest sense of the term. Culture had to be understood in the context of power relations, according to the New England Association. Workingmen might share a culture with their employers, but they did not share its control equally.[12]

Morality functioned in a similar way, as part of a social and economic exchange that operated on several different levels. Employers particularly had charged this issue by rooting so much of their paternalistic position in their claims to be guardians of morality who instilled virtue in their workers by requiring long workdays.

Employers in New England had long argued for the moral benefits of the all-day system. When Boston housewrights challenged their wages and long hours as unfair in 1825, they confronted masters who defended long days as the basis for Boston's reputation as the city "of early rising and industry." Moral problems would proliferate if apprentices and journeymen were left

11. *The Artisan,* November 9, 1833.
12. Formisano, writing on the relationship of the New England Workingmen to the political parties of the state, argues: "The apparently moderate and conservative exhortations to workingmen to cultivate learning and to produce their own leaders were thus challenges to them to overcome the continuing and inhibiting influence of deference in political life" (Formisano, *The Transformation of Political Culture,* p. 243).

to their own devices, seduced from industry, and exposed to temptation. "That we consider idleness as the most deadly bane to usefulness and honorable living," they argued, "and knowing (such is human nature,) that where there is no necessity, there is no exertion, we fear and dread the consequences of such a measure upon the morals and well being of society." Their sentiments were echoed by the capitalists funding the building trades, who felt that shorter days would open "a wide door for idleness and vice."[13]

This point of view was still being argued by employers in the 1830s (and would continue to resurface in the 1840s), as a letter to the *New Bedford Weekly Register* in 1832 made clear. "There are some who object to the measures lately taken by the working class of people," "A Working-Man" wrote, "because they are designed to give journeymen and apprentices more time than they have under the present custom. They say this time will be spent improperly, in visiting 'grog shops,' &c; and that vicious habits will be the consequence." The writer of this letter suspected that working people were more respectable in the uses of their leisure time than employers might argue, but even if they were not, he pointed out, "then so much the greater is the necessity allowing them time and opportunities for intellectual and moral improvement." *The Artisan* endorsed this point of view, arguing that if journeymen and apprentices did patronize grog shops it was only because they were kept in ignorance and oppressed by their employers. Another writer removed the issue of drinking from this class perspective by arguing that workingmen were about as likely as their bosses to patronize bars.[14]

This paternalistic system was to be replaced by the moral self-reliance and independence of workingmen. Morality was to be an issue of their individual control, rather than an employer's responsibility, achieved in the world of leisure instead of in the

13. "Resolution of Master Carpenters, from the *Columbia Centinel*, April 20, 1825," John Rogers Commons et al., eds., *A Documentary History of American Industrial Society* (Cleveland, 1910), 6:70–71. Resolutions of "gentlemen engaged in building the present season," *Columbia Centinel*, April 23, 1825, in Commons, *Documentary History*, 6:79.

14. *The Artisan*, January 26, 1832; March 8, 1832.

world of work. Thus the workingmen pushed for a radical disjunction between the worlds of work and leisure, worlds of discretely banded lengths of time. To the extent that we can glimpse this world of leisure envisioned by workingmen in the 1830s, it was the public life of lyceums and reading rooms, not the private world of domesticity. They were interested in redefining the moral dimension of community relations, rather than family life.

In many respects, the demands the members of the New England Association were making for moral self-reliance converged with emerging middle-class values, but it would be a mistake to assume that this convergence represented a broader consensus. Middle-class morality was more firmly rooted in home life, and particularly in a mother's shaping hand.[15] The New England Association emphasized the way in which a much broader environment, particularly an unrelenting workplace, atrophied the development of self-reliance. The workingmen's critique played on the paternalistic presumptions of employers to suggest that they were not living up to their claims of being good "parents" to their employees. Both employer and employee were entering into the discourse on self-reliance, but taking very different positions.

Further differences emerged in the conflict over morality as members of the New England Association argued that there were two standards of morality: one for the rich and one for the poor. Samuel Whitcomb, for example, in his address to the workingmen of Dedham, argued that there were "two distinct codes of morality" in American society. "That by which we judge the poor, industrious common people, bears the marks of a *christian* origin," he pointed out, while "that intended for the opulent and elevated, shows a strong resemblance to Mahometanism." The wealthy were allowed to defraud creditors and still hold high political office, whereas "the smallest defect in the character, manners, or education of the plain common citizen is known to everyone and animadverted on with severity."[16]

15. Mary Ryan, *Cradle of the Middle Class: The Family in Oneida County, New York, 1790–1865* (New York, 1981), p. 147.
16. Reprinted in *The Artisan*, February 2, 1832. See also the editorial in the November 8, 1832, *Artisan*, which argued that "so many instances occur of

Another article argued that respectability was a term for external appearance not inner moral worth, so that the poor man had no chance of being known as anything more than "decent" no matter how honest he was, and the rich man could be respectable no matter how he had accumulated his wealth—that is, "shaving notes, lending money at exorbitant rates, over reaching in trade, palming off bad articles on neighbors, or profiting from bankruptcy." The author then went on to describe how a poor man might gradually move up the ladder to respectability. "At his first start in life he is unnoticed. But when he is found to be a 'money getting' character, no matter *how* he gets it, unless is he *known* to steal it, he is a *likely* man." After a few years of financial success, the next stage was to become "a *knowing* fellow," though this paragon of virtue might actually demonstrate few qualities other than the ability to make money. "At length as he advances in the world, and quits labor himself, he becomes 'respectable.' And finally, when sufficiently rich to quit business, and live on his income, he becomes '*highly* respectable.' "[17] Following a similar line of reasoning, another article argued that wealth in itself was not bad but that it was often achieved dishonestly. Moreover, the rich received more respect than the poor, and this was not fair because both deserved respect equally.[18]

The arguments about the respectability of wealth would resonate with members of the New England Association on two levels. For many of these people the emerging distinctions between manual and white-collar work were becoming more potent; the promise inherent in artisanal occupations began to fade, and white-collar occupations began to carry more prestige

---

extreme poverty and hopeless wretchedness among families who are industrious, whilst the idle and the profligate remain in the secure enjoyment of ill-gotten riches, there must exist rottenness somewhere."

17. *The Artisan*, February 2, 1832. As another contributor would point out in condemning imprisonment for debt, "The spendthrift, the speculator and the bankrupt, honest or dishonest, unless fraud can be proved upon him, who has contracted debts up to the amount of even $100,000, is in little or no danger of the operation of the law" (ibid., April 6, 1832).

18. *The Artisan*, June 14, 1832. A similar point was made by "B," who argued that "individuals are respected, cherished, promoted and obeyed, for their wealth" (ibid., September 13, 1833).

and possibility for economic advancement. All this fractured the notion of a middling strata, which had existed before as a virtuous anchor in the community.[19] When members of the New England Association identified themselves as workingmen, they did so to emphasize the respectable nature of their manual labor. But they did so knowing full well that more powerful people in society were using the term "workingmen" to signify exactly the opposite or to suggest a moral hierarchy. Thus "A Boston Mechanic" would ask what Judge Story meant when referring to the "upper classes" and the "lower classes": "Does he mean, that riches, or talent, or patrician blood makes 'upper classes,' and poverty and labor, and plebian blood, together with living in a hut, makes 'lower classes[?]' "[20] Mechanics intent on undermining this hierarchy chose their issue well.

The distinction between inner moral worth and the outward display of respectability was both a defining feature and a central contradiction in emerging bourgeois ideology, for the notion of character suggested that inner moral worth could be displayed publicly, and as such was a valuable form of social currency for members of the middle class.[21] Workingmen who criticized the moral hypocrisy of the middle class were clearly attuned to an emerging bourgeois discourse on character formation, and they recast that discourse to show its inequities, oppressiveness, and contradictions.

This critique of morality makes the membership requirements of the New England Association all the more intriguing. Good moral character, rather than wage-earning status, was the major criterion for membership in the local organizations of the New England Association of Farmers, Mechanics, and Other Workingmen. For example, the Boston and Roxbury Mill Dam Association was open to all persons of good moral character who would sign the constitution (stating that they would not submit to any

19. Stuart Blumin, *The Emergence of the Middle Class: Social Experience in the American City, 1760–1900* (New York, 1989), esp. pp. 66–107; Ryan, *Cradle of the Middle Class*, pp. 171–185.

20. *The Artisan*, November 8, 1832.

21. Karen Halttunen, *Confidence Men and Painted Women: A Study of Middle-Class Culture in America, 1830–1870* (New Haven, Conn., 1982), pp. 33–55.

deduction by their employers). The New Bedford Association stipulated a similar requirement. Even the constitution of the larger regional organization stated that anyone of good moral character could join. Why was morality rather than wage-earning status the dividing line? In part, the wage-earning status, which was so central to the industrialization of cities in the Middle Atlantic states, was only part of the equation in New England.

The true enemy, according to the New England Association, was not simply the employer, but also the idle capitalist who might control from afar the activities of masters and overseers as well as journeymen and operatives. Even farmers were subject to preying capitalists who were taking increasing control of the real estate that by rights belonged to farmers. Thus an open letter to the farmers of New England warned them "that the amount of debt due from the farmers to the merchants, to individual capitalists, and to the banks, constitutes a charge upon their industry and the income of their Estates, which must ultimately expel them from their houses and farms."[22]

In one respect, this analysis was part of the producer ideology that distinguished between those who produced goods for society and those who did not, not between the employer and the employed. While this distinction was becoming increasingly outdated and counterproductive in many contexts, in New England it had taken on a new vitality.[23] Much of the industrialization in New England was indeed controlled by a powerful group of capitalists, who were often protected by a legal web of incorporation and limited liability and who set the economic pace for the

22. *The Artisan,* August 16, 1832. For a more extensive discussion of the rural dimensions of the workingmen's movement, see Christopher Clark, *The Roots of Rural Capitalism: Western Massachusetts, 1780–1860* (Ithaca, N.Y., 1990), pp. 204–209.

23. Bruce Laurie argues that in Philadelphia, for example, the producer ideology "left the worker vulnerable to the appeals of middle-class radicals, whose translation of the producer ideology deflected attention from employers to financiers, and lured him into fighting rear-guard battles against the money changers." See his *Working People of Philadelphia, 1800–1850* (Philadelphia, 1980), p. 202.

entire region. Journeymen carpenters and masons, as well as machinists and operatives, were as likely to be employed by a corporation or capitalists with far-flung networks as by a master. Both merchants and manufacturers had assumed leading roles in opposing the attempted strike during March. Masters, bosses, and small employers were as much at the beck and call of large capitalists as were wage earners, and members of the New England Association were trying to convince these small employers of this.

Equally important, the New England Association had invested the notion of morality with a critique of emerging class relations. Membership in a society that required good moral character would become an institutional embodiment of this critique as support for a ten-hour day was merged with good moral behavior. The criterion for membership in the New England societies, which was linked to morality rather than wage-earning status, baffled workers from other areas. But within the context of struggle in New England it made tremendous sense. Working people had defined their goal as a shorter work day, and any employer acquiescing to this demand would be welcome to join. By stating the criterion of membership as moral character, however, workingmen were claiming the moral mantle for themselves and leaving all those who equated virtue with long hours (as did most employers) out in the cold.

The struggle for cultural control did not end with education and morality; to a lesser extent, religion also represented contested terrain. Although the topic was not discussed extensively, it did receive some treatment in the workingmen's press as another way in which employers could dominate employees. Seth Luther argued that religious demands were one of the ways in which mill owners enslaved the "bodies and souls" of their men, controlling the way they "think, act, vote, preach, pray, and worship." Among the specific examples of abuse he listed was the rule at Waltham "that all who go to work there are obliged to pay for the support of the minister employed by the Corporation." He would cite similar examples at Leicester, Massachusetts, Saxonville, Framingham, and the York Mills in Saco, Maine, all of which infringed on one's liberty of conscience "in direct violation of the law of the land."[24]

"Othman" complained in one article that forced attendance at church by mill corporations got in the way of educational pursuits. "Sunday is a day to which mechanics look forward with pleasure," he explained, "in which they can communicate their tho'ts to their friends; a day in which they wish to employ themselves in reading, or viewing the works of nature, and if they are to attend public worship constantly, I ask, where is their time for information?" Othman insisted that he was not criticizing the idea of public worship, but rather its forced interference with educational and social development that provided workingmen with the means "to be respectable and good." Thus "Othman" concluded, "If God has required of us to serve him the first day of the week, man ought to allow us, by law, the third day, a Sabbath for ourselves."[25]

"Othman," like the radical workingmen of Philadelphia at this time, may have felt more of an affinity with the Enlightenment religious beliefs of the eighteenth century than with the evangelicalism of the nineteenth century—more of a commitment, that is, to a belief in God through knowledge rather than through prayer. "Othman's" critique of religion also fit well with the "republican religion" described by Sean Wilentz for New York City during this period. Workingmen there might subscribe to a wide variety of religious beliefs, but they shared a distaste for anything that smacked of social or spiritual inequality in religious practice. Forced public worship challenged the independence of workingmen.[26]

Workingmen in New Haven suggested a similar concern about religious sources of dependency when they met to select delegates to the workingmen's convention in the winter of 1833. In

24. Luther, *Address*, p. 29.
25. *The Artisan*, February 9, 1832.
26. Laurie, *Working People of Philadelphia*, pp. 67–83; Sean Wilentz, *Chants Democratic: New York City and the Rise of the American Working Class, 1788–1850* (New York, 1984), pp. 77–87. For further discussion of Enlightenment religion, see James Turner, *Without God, Without Creed: The Origins of Unbelief in America* (Baltimore, 1985), pp. 35–72.

discussing the problem of education, they complained: " 'Working men' will soon find (in many places they now find) the useful branches of knowledge giving place to Sunday School lessons and the preachings of theological school masters and school mistresses." Calling instead for a republican education, the workingmen of New Haven coupled their critique of religious appropriation of education with its domination by the wealthy, so that education was "basely perverted to favor the views of the accumulator." Such an education was designed to make workingmen "useful servants of the rich, to administer to luxury by their skill in arts and manufactures, and to suffer exaction, injustice and oppression without rebellion."[27]

The dependence created by the churchgoing policies of employers could be translated easily into a problem of gender. One commentator elaborated on the distinctions between religion and knowledge in heavily gender-laden terms. Religion without knowledge, "degenerates to superstition; a cruel fickle fiend, that at one time woos man to her arms, and caresses him with all the fondness of love; and at another time binds him on the wheel and applies her cruel tortures, or immolates him at the stake. Where religion most flourishes, most benefits man, most honors her divine original, she is found hand in hand with knowledge." The author, in this case, was arguing for the morality that the workingmen considered so important, but it was a morality produced by a union of the masculine world of knowledge and the feminine world of religion.[28]

The relationship of the workingmen's movement to religion in the 1830s was not only more muted by also more complex than its relationship to other areas of cultural terrain. Unwilling to reject it outright and suspicious of its intrinsic value, these workingmen saw formal religion as something to be controlled and contained, for it represented a point of opposition to the secular world of male respectability and independence. Just as their

27. *The Artisan*, November 9, 1833.
28. *The Artisan*, February 9, 1832. For a discussion of the way in which morality and virtue were becoming gendered in the late eighteenth and early nineteenth centuries, see Ruth Bloch, "The Gendered Meanings of Virtue in Revolutionary America," *Signs* 13 (Autumn 1987): 37–58.

concept of morality had more in common with republican ideals of virtue than with evangelical ideals of personal piety, the world of religious belief was distinct (and supposed to remain distinct) from the world of economic relations. Many of these workingmen may have participated in some form of religious activity, but this participation existed apart from their moral practice and political imagination.

Chapter 4

Popular Religion
and Working People

When the Boston Trades Union attempted to celebrate the Fourth of July in 1834, it was shut out of twenty-two of the city's churches. *The Artisan* demanded to know how respectable members of the union could have been dealt such an insulting blow when they numbered "among them a large proportion of church members and pew holders, by whose money and labor almost every church has been built."[1] The following week, Andrew C. Davison wrote that he was not surprised that the union was being attacked for being "enemies of the Christian religion." The arguments of heresy and infidelity had been used before "whenever knowledge was contending against Ignorance, and had reduced to shreds all other arguments." The charge against these men was as unfair in 1834 as it had been when leveled in earlier centuries. Davison would defend the Christian beliefs of members of the union, arguing that "the proportion of unbelievers in the christian religion to believers is not greater than one to a hundred." Their Christian beliefs had been called into question only because they had sought to obtain their rights.[2]

Davison's attack on the clergy of Boston for refusing to open their doors to the Trades Union is not so surprising. It is consistent with the conflict between workingmen and religion which

1. *The Artisan*, July 12, 1834.
2. *The Artisan*, July 19, 1834.

characterized the labor movement throughout the North during this period. What is surprising, however, is his contention that the vast majority of the members of the Trades Union in that town were Christians and church members. Was he right? What was the role of religion in the factory towns and industrializing cities of New England?

Newspapers, diaries, and letters, as well as some of the church records that have survived, make it clear that Protestant religion was an ongoing, viable part of emerging working-class life during the 1820s, 1830s, and 1840s, particularly in the factory towns of New England. It is virtually impossible to read the surviving correspondence and diaries of early industrial workers without finding a reference to religious activities that reflect serious spiritual involvement. Revivals, camp meetings, and lively preaching were arenas of entertainment, sociability, and struggle, as well as intense religious commitment.

Successful revivals might draw in an entire town, saved and unsaved alike. Much of the meeting would be filled with those who were saved, or those who were anxious about the state of their souls, or those who were backsliders. But there were also curiosity seekers, troublemakers, reluctant relatives, and travelers who were simply passing time until the next stage departed. These spectacles of salvation provided good town drama—for free.

The remaining descriptions of revivals in factory villages portray a tumultuous scene in which the saved and the damned fought border wars on the fringes of the meetinggrounds, making visible the realities of what was otherwise an invisible struggle. Hiram Munger, a former mill worker and an itinerant preacher who made his way through the villages and mill towns of New England, first as a Methodist and later as a Millerite, provided vivid memories of such experiences. He never preached at a revival without confronting members of "the Cain family," and apparently he never failed to overcome them.

When rowdies in Plainville, Massachusetts, attacked a Millerite camp meeting in the summer of 1842, tearing down the tent of black worshipers, singing obscene songs, and running their horses through the grounds, Munger fought back. He organized the forces of good for an ambush the following morning and succeeded in tying the interlopers up with a clothesline. A couple of years later, at a revival in the factories of Chester, Connecticut, Munger chose the more peaceful approach of simply praying at the rowdies who were disrupting the meeting by throwing eggs. The prayer and preaching turned out to be so powerful that the Cainites decamped and their instruments of attack were transformed into an excellent breakfast.[3]

Catherine Reed Williams, a severe critic of Methodist camp meetings, recorded her horror while visiting a tumultuous event in Smithfield, Rhode Island, the location of one of the Slaters' factories, during the early 1820s. Entry to the campground was possible only by traversing a road on which alcohol was being bought, sold, and consumed to great excess. "The brutal intoxication and profanity visible on the road home was truly shocking," she recalled. The "mob" (as Williams referred to the drunks) was so menacing, particularly to women, "that the Methodists had sent for two or three sheriffs to come and keep order."[4] Yet Williams found the scene within the campgrounds to be small improvement. The intermingling of men and women was a sign of promiscuity, and their fainting, shrieking, and preaching a scandal.

In such scenes the everyday order of things was challenged, and so too were most forms of traditional authority. It is not surprising that these spectacles bordered on the riotous. Indeed, a riot is exactly what the *Boston Daily Advertiser* called the crowd assembled to hear Jacob Knapp, the Baptist itinerant, preach in Boston in January 1842. He "collected so disorderly an assemblage, in and about the church in Bowdoin square, on Wednesday evening, that the interference of the Mayor, with the aid of the

3. Hiram Munger, *The Life and Religious Experience of Hiram Munger, Including Many Singular Circumstances Connected with Camp-Meetings and Revivals* (Boston, 1881), pp. 42–44, 82.
4. Catherine Reed Williams, *Fall River: An Authentic Narrative* (Providence, R.I., 1834), pp. 177, 179.

police, was necessary to disperse the crowd and restore order." Apparently the scene was repeated the following night:

> The crowd assembled anew, with additional numbers, doubtless drawn there from curiosity, to see how the affair would end. At the request of the Mayor the corps of Lancers were ordered out in aid of the police, and although a great crowd was assembled, they were dispersed, we believe, without any act of violence.[5]

Itinerant preachers who fueled these events fostered the attack on established order by turning their lack of education and status into an asset. They captivated their audiences with a visual and verbal style that their critics regarded as little more than cheap theatrics at best, and disgusting blasphemy at worst. Edward Carpenter, an apprentice cabinetmaker in Greenfield, Massachusetts, whose diary did not reveal him to be a young man overly concerned with religion, still attended both the Unitarian and the Methodist meetings in town, for entertainment as well as spiritual uplift. On April 27, 1844, for example, he noted in his diary that he had gone with his cousins Jane and Cynthia Slate to the Methodist church, where they "heard a very comical preacher, he used a great many odd expression he was from Ohio. A backwoodsman I presume."[6]

John Ingersoll, a young store-clerk and Whig who heard Knapp preach in Baldwin Place on January 3, 1842, was somewhat repelled by the performance. "I did not like his style of delivery," he complained in his diary, describing Knapp's expression as coarse and harsh. "His comparisons were many of the(m?) low and vulgar; for instance comparing woman to a turtle as carring [*sic*] every thing on their backs and the like.—a large number of enquirers filled the anxious seats."[7] Knapp was clearly a show-

5. *Boston Daily Advertiser*, quoted in the *Fall River Gazette*, January 27, 1842.

6. Edward Carpenter, Diary, April 29, 1844 (Manuscript Collection, AAS). For an annotated edition, see Edward J. Carpenter, "The Diary of an Apprentice Cabinetmaker: Edward Jenner Carpenter's 'Journal,' 1844–1845," ed. Christopher Clark, in *Proceedings of the Antiquarian Society* 98 (1988): 303–394.

7. John G. Ingersoll Diary (1839–1843), January 3, 1843 (John G. Ingersoll Papers, Essex Institute, Salem, Mass.).

man who drew large audiences wherever he went. At times, though, his theatricality got him into trouble. At one point in his career he was charged with wearing old clothes to obtain a more sympathetic response in offerings. Although deeply hurt by the charges, Knapp pressed on and was eventually cleared.[8]

Catherine Williams found the preachers at the camp meeting in Smithfield to be little improvement over the drunken mob that milled around outside. She was clearly horrified by the black preacher who stood on a stump claiming " 'Some say poor niger hab no shoule. Vel dat I dont know, but dis I know, I got something in my body make me feel tumfortable' (clapping his hands vehemently upon his huge chest)." Said Williams, "A peal of laughter, long and loud from the profane rabble, was the response."[9]

Williams claimed to be sympathetic to female preachers, but she found those at the camp meeting coarse: "A young female whose appearance bespoke her to be under twenty, was exhorting. The first words we distinguished were these, that she 'did not want a copper of their money—No I dont want your money,' she repeated, 'not a copper of your money only the salvation of your souls.' " Another female preacher whom Williams found in more decorous circumstances to be a very good speaker was in this case unappealing, "the great effort of retaining such a masculine attitude entirely destroying the effect." A third preacher was "bold and uncouth" as she "called upon people loudly to repent 'to-day and save their souls.' "[10]

Almond Davis, writing a far more sympathetic portrayal of Salome Lincoln, who left her work as a weaver in Taunton to become an itinerant preacher connected with the Methodists and Freewill Baptists, would speak more favorably of Salome's powerful preaching style. "In private . . . she was naturally reserved and retiring in her manners. But in the pulpit, she was bold and attracting; and as she began to warm up in the spirit of her discourse, this reserve was entirely gone." In part this trans-

---

8. Jacob Knapp, *Autobiography of Elder Jacob Knapp, with an Introductory Essay by R. Jeffrey* (New York, 1868), pp. 131–132.

9. Williams, *Fall River*, p. 183.

10. Ibid., pp. 181–182.

formation was tied to the prophetic nature of female speaking; Salome believed she was transmitting the word of God. She therefore described how she summoned her courage to deliver her first sermon while she sat in a neighbor's kitchen waiting for a prayer meeting to commence: "While in prayer, the power of God was manifested—and the fear of man taken away," she recalled. "I then arose and began to speak. The promise of the Lord was verified—'Open thy mouth wide, and I will fill it.'"[11]

These preachers and their religion were part of a popular religious tradition recently described by Nathan Hatch as emanating from the American frontier during the years after the Revolution. Their preaching style was rooted in their own reading of the Bible rather than in formal theological training. Their personal experiences and stories they had heard were the basis for their sermonizing, a testimony to their faith in God. As they attacked the coldness of an established and professional ministry they adopted a stance that was both anticlerical and antiauthoritarian. Their language, which was often anything but respectable, fueled the fires of the Second Great Awakening and eventually became so powerful that middle-class ministers and more established congregations attempted to appropriate the tradition.[12] No doubt much of this frontier religious culture was brought by rural immigrants to the mill towns where they sought work or was already planted in rural communities where factories sprang up, for revival meetings swept through factories as well as rural areas.

When Nancy Towle left her home in New Hampshire to begin her life as an itinerant preacher in the second decade of the nineteenth century, she traveled to many of these new factory towns, such as Burrillville and Pawtucket, Rhode Island, and Blackstone, Massachusetts. In 1822, she visited a Methodist camp meeting in Smithfield in Rhode Island (which may well

11. Almond H. Davis, *The Female Preacher; or, Memoir of Salome Lincoln* (New York, 1972) [c. 1843], p. 44.

12. Nathan O. Hatch, *The Democratization of American Christianity* (New Haven, Conn., 1989), pp. 57–58. On the use of this style by middle-class preachers, see David S. Reynolds, "From Doctrine to Narrative: The Rise of Pulpit Storytelling in America," *American Quarterly* 32 (1980): 479–498.

have been the same one Catherine Williams visited), where she met two powerful female preachers, Mrs. Thompson and Susan Humes. Towle would speak of the female preaching at this camp meeting in far more favorable terms than Williams had, saying of Humes, "Her melting addresses to both saints and sinners, exceeded what I had ever witnessed before, in either male or female." Humes's preaching had a powerful impact on Towle, penetrating her heart: "I felt myself, at this time, especially called away from the vain formularies and the customary devotions to which many of the different communities extant adhered: and as a being, accountable for my doings alone to the LORD JESUS CHRIST;—to try to listen to the voice of His Spirit, in my own soul."13 The power of this kind of preaching was felt in other factory towns as well.

Jacob Knapp's 1842 campaign moved from Boston into the surrounding area, stopping in Lowell for a five-week visit and one of Knapp's sweetest victories. The Lord descended on the work force with such power that the superintendent in Lowell was forced to shut the factory down. "The operatives were nearly all on their knees, in prayer for themselves, or for their unconverted associates. In fact, the entire factory was an anxious room." Knapp estimated that at the end of his five-week visit fifteen hundred people had been converted, pouring into the Methodist, Congregational, Episcopal, and Baptist churches.14

This was certainly not the only time a factory would be disrupted by religion. For example, Barbara Tucker notes correspondence from the Slater factory agent Alexander Hodges in 1839, reporting that attendance of factory operatives at the Methodist camp meeting was widespread enough to curtail operations at the factory.15 Rebecca Ford, at work in a textile factory in Middlebury, Vermont, in the winter of 1843, described a re-

13. Nancy Towle, *Vicissitudes Illustrated in the Experience of Nancy Towle in Europe and America* (Portsmouth, N.H., 1833), pp. 37–38. Towle was the daughter of a militia captain and had been a schoolteacher before embarking on her career as an itinerant preacher.
14. Knapp, *Autobiography*, pp. 138–139.
15. Barbara Tucker, *Samuel Slater and the Origins of the American Textile Industry, 1790–1860* (Ithaca, N.Y., 1984), p. 165.

vival that lasted twelve weeks in which "we went to meeting evening and work days so we had not any time to write[.] the Lord has graciously revived his work about two hundred and fifty have been made happy in a saviour."[16]

Given the disruption created by these outbreaks of religious enthusiasm, it is difficult to believe that factory owners and agents would tolerate Protestant workers, let alone encourage them. Yet in varying degrees, in their attempts to create a more disciplined work force as well as fulfill part of their self-ordained role as paternalistic factory owners, most employers did support religious endeavors. In many factory towns, employers funded at least one church for their employees, though in each town the pattern differed. The Lowell corporations originally deducted money from the wages of female operatives to support the Episcopal church and eventually required regular church attendance by employees. By 1845, twenty-three churches were listed in the Lowell city directory, including four Congregational churches, three churches each for Baptists and Universalists, two each for Freewill Baptists, Wesleyan Methodists, Unitarians, and Catholics as well as two Methodist-Episcopal churches, and one for the Adventists.[17]

Samuel Slater was equally assiduous in promoting religion. When Congregationalist minister Ephraim Abbott started his mission to Rhode Island in 1812, he was welcomed by Slater and began by preaching at the schoolhouse of Slater's factory in Smithfield, Rhode Island. According to Abbott, sixty-four families were connected with the factory, though among them he found only ten Baptists and five Congregationalists. Considerably more turned out to hear him preach: 100 in the morning and 150 in the afternoon.[18]

16. David A. Zonderman, "From Mill Village to Industrial City: Letters from Vermont Factory Operatives," *Labor History* 27 (1986): 277.

17. Hannah Josephson, *The Golden Threads: New England's Mill Girls and Magnates* (New York, 1949), p. 47; Lowell City Directory, 1845; Thomas Dublin, *Women at Work: The Transformation of Work and Community in Lowell, Massachusetts, 1826–1860* (New York, 1979), p. 78.

18. Ephraim Abbott, "Journal of a Mission of Two Months in the State of Rhode Island, September 27–28, 1812" (Manuscript Collection, RIHS).

Slater supported the Baptists and the Methodists as well as the Congregationalists. In Webster, he helped finance the building of the Methodist church and parsonage and provided continuing economic support when necessary. Like the Lowell corporations, the Slater family expected its employees to attend church services.[19]

In Woonsocket, Rhode Island, where churches sprang up in the wake of factory development, mills provided empty factory rooms for fledgling congregations. The Quakers were the long-established and languishing denomination until the early 1830s. In April 1832, St. James Episcopal Parish was formed in Bernon Village, where a large percentage of British immigrants lived. Leading the names on the petition for incorporation was Samuel Greene, agent for the Bernon mills, where the congregation met until a meetinghouse had been built. The Universalists, formed in 1834, met at the Dexter Ballou schoolhouse and the Social schoolhouse, both of which were no doubt attached to the Ballou Mills and Social Mills owned by Dexter Ballou & Company. The Congregationalists, also organized in 1834, met at the Dexter Ballou schoolhouse as well, until they moved to Globe Village (where comparatively few foreign immigrants resided).[20]

The Mendon (Massachusetts) Freewill Baptist Church was the independent creation of village residents, many of whom worked in the Blackstone mill. But in the middle of the 1830s, as they attempted to build a church and establish a settled minister, they sought assistance from the Blackstone Manufacturing Company, which agreed to contribute $200 to the minister's salary in 1837 and "the refusal of their meeting house." This was probably a reference to the Congregational church built by the Blackstone Company in 1836. In any event, it is clear from company ledgers that, between 1837 and 1841, Maxey Burlingame, who was minister for the Freewill Baptists, was on the company payroll. In

19. Tucker, *Samuel Slater*, p. 164. Tucker also cites support from mill owners in nearby Wilkinsonville, Manchaug, and South Sutton.

20. Erastus Richardson, *History of Woonsocket* (Woonsocket, R.I., 1876), pp. 75–86; S. C. Newman, *A Numbering of the Inhabitants: Together with Statistical and Other Information Relative to Woonsocket, R.I.* (Woonsocket, R.I., 1846).

1837, he was paid $220 per year (partly in cash, partly in goods) for his preaching. By 1841, his salary had risen to $300 per year.[21]

Even where outright grants were not made from factories, owners might actively fund and lead congregations, which they encouraged (or pressured) employees to join. Peter Smith, co-owner of one of the major machine shops in Andover, Massachusetts, was delighted when the men in his machine shop began to attend revival meetings at Old South Church in 1831, even though they did so at first "out of a spirit of opposition more than from a desire to be spiritually benefitted." He brought them home for religious instruction, encouraged them to attend prayer meetings, and gave thanks for their conversions.[22]

Religion was, in short, a strongly contested terrain in which working people and employers had very different interpretations and goals. Employers had much to gain from religion. For example, Paul Johnson argues convincingly that the theology of nineteenth-century Protestantism was a crucial component in legitimizing the social relations of wage labor. A belief in free moral agency rather than predestination stressed that each individual was responsible for achieving his or her own salvation. In what was essentially a blow against the old patriarchal artisanal order in which masters assumed moral as well as economic responsibility for their journeymen, evangelical employers could feel justified in expecting moral behavior from their employees, without taking responsibility for them. Because evangelical religion offered such obvious rewards for employers, Johnson assumes that any workingmen who joined churches in later revivals were pressured to do so by their employers.[23]

Paul Faler studied the shoemakers of Lynn and noted the way Protestant morality promoted internalized values of self-

---

21. This was probably the last year payments were made, because the rest of the page was not filled in, but lack of later ledgers makes this difficult to prove. See "A History Record of the Rise, Progress number and Transitions from [unclear] to Time of the Mendon Freewill Baptist Church," Typescript copy of church records, May 20, 1837, private collection. Blackstone Manufacturing Records, MSS 9, Subgroup 1, Series B, vol. 182, Book O, RIHS.

22. Peter Smith, *Memorials of Peter Smith* (Cambridge, Mass., 1881), pp. 36–37.

23. Paul Johnson, *Shopkeeper's Millennium: Society and Revivals in Rochester, New York, 1815–1837* (New York, 1978), pp. 137–141.

restraint and hard work, values that were compatible with the demands of industrialization. These shared values between master and journeyman, as well as shared religious affiliation in the Methodist church, undermined conflict between wage earners and employers in the shoe trade.[24]

Barbara Tucker goes even further in emphasizing the role Protestant religion had in establishing the hegemony of manufacturers in Samuel Slater's empire. According to Tucker, Methodism in particular helped to create not only a disciplined work force but a docile one as well. Methodism impressed on workers the importance of obedience and respect for authority and thereby strengthened the paternalistic ethos in Slater's factory villages, as workers deferred to the authority of overseers and agents.[25]

Certainly these churches, even without the direct support of factory owners, were upholding values that would be important to mill development. Barbara White, a young woman working in the cloth room at the Blackstone Company, was brought before disciplinary committees from both the Burrillville and Mendon Freewill Baptists when she stole some cloth from the factory. Her co-worshippers made sure that she returned the cloth and that she "made an open, frank and voluntary Acknowledgement; and gave us good satisfaction as to her sincere penitency respecting that unhappy Affair."[26]

But religious commitment was far from a one-dimensional experience. It met a broad spectrum of needs—social, economic and spiritual. To begin with, religious activities could compete with the demands of factory life as often as they supported factory discipline. The revivals that shut down textile factories were hardly consistent with the demands of producing on a regular basis for a national market. And Jonathan Prude notes that, while manufacturers may have wanted to promote stability

24. Paul Faler, *Mechanics and Manufacturers in the Early Industrial Revolution, Lynn, Massachusetts, 1780–1860* (Albany, N.Y., 1981), pp. 102–106, 137.
25. Tucker, *Samuel Slater*, pp. 163–185. Anthony Wallace (*Rockdale*, pp. 288–294), also argues that Protestant religion encouraged a more docile attitude among factory workers.
26. Records of the Modern Freewill Baptist Church, May 28, 1825 (Private collection).

among their workers by encouraging religious involvement, voluntary departures from local mills actually increased after revivals took place. Salome Lincoln, as she began her itinerant ministry, funded her forays into the countryside with brief stints at local factories. And she used her developing speaking abilities to great effect in 1829, when she and the other female weavers at the factory in Hopewell turned out to protest a wage cut. After parading down the main street dressed in black silk dresses, red shawls, and green calashes, the young women proceeded to a hall near the town common, where Salome "eloquently addressed them at considerable length, on the subject of their wrongs; after which they quietly returned to their homes."[27] Thus not all mill owners and factory agents were anxious to encourage evangelical fervor. Betsey Pierce, for example, was fired from Lowell's Hamilton Company in 1836 because she "pretended sickness to go to meeting."[28]

Hiram Munger recalled his conflicts not only with rowdies but also with a factory agent by the name of Hanshaw in Ludlow, Massachusetts, who was concerned about the foothold the Methodists were establishing in his village. Hanshaw banned praying in company tenements and threatened to fire anyone who would not abide by his rules. His edict, however, only fanned the flames of revival. The relationship between Methodism and industrious work habits apparently made little impression on the agent, for when one factory worker emerged from an all-day meeting victorious over the devil and claiming she was able to do more work than before, the agent was only strengthened in his resolve to quench the spreading flames of revival. Fortunately, he became so overwrought that he dropped "like a dead man" in his tracks and remained incapacitated for the next three months while the revival flourished. While the providential nature of Munger's stories might leave us with some suspicion about their complete

27. Jonathan Prude, *The Coming of the Industrial Order: Town and Factory Life in Rural Massachusetts, 1810–1860* (New York, 1983), pp. 125–126, 153–154; Davis, *The Female Preacher*, p. 51.

28. Carl Gersuny, " 'A Devil in Petticoats' and Just Cause: Patterns of Punishment in Two New England Textile Factories," *Business History Review* 50 (1976): 141.

accuracy, they clearly portray the tension he believed existed between the demands of his religious faith and those of the mundane world of work.[29]

More prosaic, but potentially more threatening, were the day-to-day requirements of Protestantism that competed with the rigors of factory life. The maintenance of Christian faith required constant watchfulness. Attendance at church services was time-consuming, as was reading the Bible, a fundamental responsibility of Protestant faith. Charles Metcalf, who worked in one of the spinning rooms at Lowell until he could begin training as a machinist, complained to his parents that he was too tired after work to attend religious services. "There is a young peopls meeting Sab. nights at 5 and prayer meeting at 6½ oclock also on Tuesday and Friday evenings, but I get so tired week nights that I cannot keep awake," he wrote. Even Sunday services were proving to be too much because the congregation sat through most of the service at John Street Congregational Church. "It is almost impossible for me to keep awake on the Sab. at church as the congregation do not rise in prayer time as they do in W[inthrop, Maine], they rise the first and last times singing," Charles explained. "And the consequence is that as I am on my feet all the time in the week and sitting nearly all the Sab. that I get asleep and it makes it very unpleasant for me as I try hard to keep awake, for I do not like to be seen sleeping in church."[30]

Christian fellowship was a powerful draw for young mill workers and artisans, not only for the religious inspiration they found but also for their social lives. It was an important avenue for structuring new relationships within laboring communities, though precisely for that reason it could be a source of tension. One of the first things Sarah Hodgdon did on arriving in Lowell during the summer of 1830 was attend the Freewill Baptist Church in Lowell, on the invitation of another young woman she had met. Sarah herself belonged to the Freewill Baptists, so it would have been the logical congregation for her to join. However, she also attended Methodist services with her cousin

29. Munger, *Life and Religious Experience*, pp. 32–34.
30. Charles Metcalf to parents, April 27, 1844 (Metcalf Collection, MATH).

Wealthy Page, and when her Freewill Baptist friend discovered this, Sarah reported that "she grew cold and indifferent towards me." Sarah was also disturbed that she was expected to pay pew rent. As Wealthy reported in one of her letters, "It has grieved me very much to see the coldness which she has been treatd with since we have been here by [them] that call themselves free will Baptist. I think they are as they might be calld self will and rightly namd." Wealthy offered to find a place at the Methodist church for Sarah and her friend Elizabeth, but the young women were torn about what to do. "They thought they should like to go to their own meeting but since they have been talkd so hard to for not hiring a seat and [not] going too ther meeting all their time they have almost concluded to go with me."[31]

When Charles Metcalf arrived in Lowell in 1844, he promptly joined the John Street Congregational Church. Although he originally boarded with his cousin Shubael Adams, Charles found the living situation to be spiritually unrewarding. He eventually moved and found a roommate at Mrs. Hurd's boardinghouse who was a member of the same congregation. The two men took turns each night reading to one another from the Bible. "It seems like home," he reported to his parents, "for till I came here I heard not a blessing asked at table or a prayer except on the Sab or at meeting. I was homesick for the domestic altar."[32]

For mill workers who constantly moved from one factory town to the next, a religion such as Methodism justified the constant mobility even as it provided them with a community that was not rooted in one place. According to Catharine Read Williams, Sarah Maria Cornell converted to Methodism in 1827, while she was working at a mill in Pawtucket. As Sarah subsequently moved to jobs in Lowell, Dorchester, and finally Fall River, she reassured her worried family about her constant mobility with a justification of religious principle. Writing to her sister that she was not "a moving planet," she instructed her to tell their mother that she was "connected with a people that do not believe in

    31. Weathy Page to "Friends," June 1830, reprinted in Thomas Dublin, *Farm to Factory: Women's Letters, 1830–1860* (New York, 1981), p. 45.
    32. Charles Metcalf to parents, April 27, 1844 (Metcalf Collection, MATH).

tarrying in any one place for more than one year or two years at most at any one time." She went on to explain the religious precedent by saying, "I am with them [the Methodists] in sentiment in believing with the Apostles that we should be as strangers and pilgrims having here no continuing city or abiding place, but seek one to come."[33]

It is difficult to confirm the authenticity of these letters because they were published in a book that may have blurred fiction with fact. However, the sentiments Sarah expressed to justify her mobility echo those of young women in England at this time.[34] Moreover, the importance of the newfound community of Methodism was borne out in trial documents about Sarah's death. Sarah was excluded by the Methodists in Lowell after her minister, Ephraim Avery, discovered that she had been treated for gonorrhea and had had sexual intercourse with several different men. After facing this disgrace, Sarah moved on to mills in New Hampshire and Fall River, where she desperately attempted to gain admission to the Methodist churches in those towns, a task that was virtually impossible without a letter of character.[35]

While religious commitments clearly opened up important avenues of sociability, it would be a mistake to view religion only as a force for unification among working people. Inhabiting a contrasting world were the rough and godless workers who often

33. Williams, *Fall River*, pp. 135–137.

34. Catharine Williams claimed to be writing a history of Fall River, Massachusetts, which began with a chapter on the town's glorious participation in the American Revolution, but all the following chapters were devoted to examining Sarah's life and death. This approach is quite similar to the fiction of such men as Charles Brockden Brown, who used domestic tragedies as allegories of political problems. For further discussion of this style, see Jane Tompkins, *Sensational Designs: The Cultural Work of American Fiction, 1790–1860* (New York, 1985), pp. 40–61; and Jay Fliegelman, *Prodigals and Pilgrims: The American Revolution against Patriarchal Authority, 1750–1800* (New York, 1982), pp. 237–240. For a discussion of religion and mobility among young women in England at this time, see Deborah M. Valenze, *Prophetic Sons and Daughters: Female Preaching and Popular Religion in Industrial England* (Princeton, 1985), p. 65.

35. *The Correct, Full and Impartial Report on the Trial of Rev. Ephraim K. Avery, before the Supreme Judicial Court of the State of Rhode Island at Newport, May 6, 1833, for the Murder of Sarah M. Cornell* (Providence, R.I., n.d.), pp. 76–88.

disrupted church services and camp meetings or in other ways made life miserable for believers. Matthias Haines, a pious youth from New Hampshire, lasted only a week at a Dorchester furniture factory, where his roommates kept him up until the wee hours of the morning playing cards. "No sleep for poor me," he confided in his diary. "I had to lay and endure the noise but this I could have borne very well but to hear the language they uttered was enough to sicken any one." Charles Metcalf wrote of a similar concern in Lowell. "I come in contact with and necessarily hear persons use profane language every day," he complained, "and I feel that there is danger of the moral sensibilities becoming blunted by contact with vice of any kind."[36]

Religious activities provided contradictory results in the laboring communities of New England. They might support factory discipline even as they undermined it, or encourage ties among some workers while undermining their relationships with others. The colloquial unlettered style of evangelical ministers provided an important challenge to the traditional authority of elites, both within the churches and beyond. The same impetus that Nathan Hatch describes as providing an important basis for an emerging democratic culture would also undermine the deference that mill owners and industrial elites craved, particularly as part of their paternalistic labor policies. Working people drew on their own feelings and experiences as a competing basis of spiritual authority. This attack on the religious authority of the respectable could not help but have broader ramifications within the workplace and family organizations. But it is worth remembering that the challenge of popular religion was primarily a spiritual one whose struggle was to some extent predicated on an acceptance of already-existing social and economic relationships, rather than an explicit attempt to change them. Moreover, the radicalizing potential of popular religion was further compromised by its impact on individual family relations, an arena more susceptible to spiritual challenge.[37]

36. Mathias Haines, Diary, January 9, 1841 (Manuscript collection, New Hampshire Historical Society); Charles Metcalf to his mother, June 2, 1844 (Metcalf collection, MATH).

37. For an excellent discussion of the way religion can challenge a broad range of social relationships without attempting to do so, see Rhys Isaac's discussion of

Family, Gender, and the Attack on Authority

Religious commitment in the nineteenth century demanded autonomy on the part of converted individuals. Indeed, the formation of conscience and the creation of individual autonomy were inextricably bound together. Because so many of the converts were young, in their teens and early twenties, and because so many were women, this phenomenon had to affect family relations, since both groups were expected to assume subordinate positions within their families. It is therefore not surprising that almost all the surviving correspondence between mill workers and their families touches on religious activities.[38]

In some cases, young workers sought to allay family fears by suggesting continuities with family life in the country. When Rebecca Ford described her sister's conversion during a Methodist revival in Middlebury, Vermont, to her brother back home, she commented: "It would do you good to see them meet in class for they are wide awake I tell you."[39] Martha Russell, working at a mill in Andover, Massachusetts, reassured her mother in Newbury, Maine, about her religious condition away from home: "It is a dull time with religion here yet I do believe there is a remnant of praying souls & I do have there prayers[.] Truly I think we have one of the best Methodist ministers here that ever was his name is A. D. Merrill." Martha had also found religious renewal at a summer camp meeting on Cape Cod which she attended for a week in August 1840. "I believed god was there," she said. "In very deed it seemed to me that it might be allmost compared to heaven with many for it seemed there happiness was completed many did I meet with & converse with there that I shall proveably never meet again until we meet at the bar of god."[40]

More often, however, issues of individual autonomy and family rejection had to be negotiated. James Metcalf joined a Congrega-

the Baptists in *The Transformation of Virginia, 1740–1790* (Chapel Hill, N.C., 1982), pp. 161–177.

38. Joseph Kett, *Rites of Passage: Adolescence in America, 1790 to the Present* (New York, 1977), pp. 62–85.

39. Zonderman, "From Mill Village to Industrial City," p. 277.

40. Martha Abbot Russell to Benj. & Mehitable Russell, 1840 (Russell Letters, AHS).

tional church upon arriving in Lowell, but contemplated switching congregations to give himself greater autonomy. He was tired of singing in the church choir as a way of gaining a seat at services. "[H]ad rather pay a fair price for a seat and be my own master," he wrote to his mother, hard on the heels of announcing that he had received his first pay raise from 60 to 70 cents a day.[41]

His sister Mary Metcalf encountered even more difficult problems. Mary had not undergone a conversion experience before arriving in Lowell, and would not for several years. It was only in 1846, when Mary was working in the household of a Methodist preacher that she was finally converted. Through the clergyman's influence and the counseling of her friend Lizzy Brown, Mary pushed through the tortuous paths of self-doubt to surrender in faith in God. But the conflict between her Congregational upbringing and her new Methodist associations was clear in her letters home. The battle for her soul took place in the Congregational church as well as at Methodist class meetings, leaving her somewhat confused about her allegiances. "I shall go in the future to the Methodist S.S. and meeting in the forenoon and the Cong. in the afternoon. do not like the Cong minister Mr. Perry at all for a minister, know he is a good man but still he is not interesting," she wrote to her mother. "I do not feel like meddling with doctrines much[.] I dont feel as if it would alter my moral obligations in the least whether I believed the doctrine of Saints Persevereance or Election. Wish you would write and tell me what doctrines it is that you love and I will try to love them too although I do not think it will be asked at the gate of heaven whether any one is a methodist or a Congregationalist." Salome Lincoln would have probably sympathized with Mary's dilemma. Her father was a Christian Baptist and her mother a Calvinist Baptist who would later join the Freewill Baptists; Salome herself would alternate affiliations with the Reformed Methodists and the Freewill Baptists, depending on where she lived, though she was married later by a Congregational minister.[42]

41. James Metcalf to his mother, November 9, 1845 (MATH).
42. Mary Metcalf to her mother, May 28, 1846 (MATH); Davis, *The Female Preacher*, pp. 21, 32, 34, 143.

Other young mill workers also broke with family religious traditions. Benjamin Wilbur's mother saw to it that he was brought up in the First Baptist Church of Fall River and that he attended Sunday school regularly, but at the end of the 1830s, as the Universalists gained a foothold in Fall River, Wilbur committed himself to the new church. It is probably more than coincidence that this commitment coincided with his new career in block printing, for the Universalists in Fall River attracted a large following among the block printers. Although still living at home, Benjamin would construct new religious ties that reinforced his new occupational relationships.[43]

Catharine Read Williams's depiction of Sarah Maria Cornell is also in accord with Wilbur's experience. Before her expulsion by the Methodists, the young woman explained to her family how her new religious ties had satisfactorily replaced familial and community bonds. Although deprived of "every earthly connexion," she explained, "I am walking hand in hand with a large circle of dear friends to Mount Zion the city of the living God."[44]

Sabrina Bennett's embrace of Universalism in Haverhill, Massachusetts, provoked criticism from members of her family. Her correspondence reveals that it opened up a wide range of new friends for her, but her cousin Olive Sawyer was clearly concerned. Writing of her brother Samuel, who had toyed with Universalism the previous winter, Olive suggested that Samuel's recurring bouts of bilious fever were due to his unkept promises to the Lord to seek true religion. "O Sabrina universalism wont stand by in a dieing hour," Olive warned. Two days later, she appended a note to her letter saying that Samuel had finally found religion: "He says he never knew what it was to be happy before he found religion. O he cant believe universalism now although he tried to last winter."[45]

Sally Rice alternated between domestic wage labor and factory work in New England and used religion as an excuse for not returning home. She was partly motivated by the material benefits of wage labor, for as she pointed out to her parents, "I am now

43. Benjamin Wilbur, "Reminiscences" (Typescript, FRHS).
44. Williams, *Fall River*, p. 137.
45. Dublin, *Farm to Factory*, pp. 62–64.

most 19 years old[.] I must of course have something of my own before many more years have passed over my head." But religion provided her with justification for leaving home. "I should be with a profane Sabbath breaking set," she wrote of returning home. "I have lived amongst desent people so long that I dont want to go home. . . . I have but one life to live and I want to enjoy myself as well as I can while I live. If I go home I can not have the privelage of going to meting nor eny thing else." The following year, trying to explain her "feelings as a daughter and a sister," Sally informed her family that she had joined the Congregational church, "and now its members and my Pastor is very dear to me how can I bare the thought of leving it." Still refusing to come home, Sally urged her parents and brother to sell their farm and move closer to her so she could take care of them.

In Sally's mind, economic responsibility was inextricably bound up with religious responsibility, as she spoke of settling her parents on "some pleasent farm where they will not have to work so hard." She spoke at length of her concern for her family's spiritual condition, urging them at one point to "rest not untill you find peace in the savior build a family Alter and Let not a day pass with out reading a portion of scripture and ofering up a prayer to the giver of every good and perfect gift."[46] Sally's newfound economic independence and religious independence were mutually reinforcing.

The same was true for Martha Russell, who devoted much space in her letters to religious activities and reflections on her own mortality. But neither necessarily led to a spirit of denial or dependence. Although she began a letter to her mother by noting, "I have sought for happiness in the things of this world but I can truly say I have never found any & am resolved in the strength of god to seek for that happiness the world cant give nor take away," her concluding remarks set a different tone. Having bought a piece of calico for her mother to make a dress, and velvet to make her father a vest, she admonished them, "I want you to put them

46. Sally Rice (Union Village), 1839 and March 4, 1840 (Hazelton Rice Papers, Dover Free Library, East Dover, Vt.). Some of this correspondence is in *The New England Mill Village, 1790–1860*, ed. Gary Kulik, Roger Parks, and Theodore Z. Penn (Cambridge, Mass., 1982), pp. 387–392.

on & were them I do not send them for you to lay away in the drawer for remember those garments must soon bee laid aside by us forever." Faced with her own mortality in conjunction with her economic independence, she advised her parents: "Let us strive to make our selves comfortable & those around us as far as is our priviledge[.] I believe that is my determination & ever has been since I provided for my self."[47]

The spiritual independence and new social ties that came with religious activism might be acceptable in some families but threatening to others. Ephraim Abbott, for example, often spoke directly to women and children in factory villages about their religious feelings. On November 22, 1812, he "preached to the children and young people about 100 of whom came together." He also spoke on several occasions to Miss Mary Bushe. Mary was about thirty years old but had been sick for fourteen years with an illness that appeared "to have been occasioned by working beyond her strength." She was also limited in her religious relationship with her parents, for they were Quakers. Thus, Abbott noted, "She has not been able to hold christian communion with them; for her sentiments are Calvinistic." This complicated the networks of mutual support which grow from religious involvement, so Abbott interceded for her with the Quakers and later noted that William Buffum "promised me that he would do something by way of Charity for Mary Bushe, who has been very burdensome to her family, which is not forehanded."[48]

Some of the women Abbott encountered were interested in religion but found their husbands opposed. When Abbott was doing his rounds at Slater's factory (presumably in Smithfield), he spoke to one head of household, Mr. Syria Smith, who was unwell. Abbott suggested that his illness might provide time for reflection, but he received a sharp retort from the invalid, who "complained that ministers called upon the sick & frightened them when their judgement were weak . . . & that he had his own salvation to work out." That same day, Abbott spoke to Mrs.

---

47. Martha Abbot Russell to Benj. & Mehitable Russell, 1840 (Russell Letters, AHS).
48. Abbott Journal, October 15, 1812, and December 21, 1812 (RIHS).

Joslin, who had "lately obtained a hope concerning herself."
Unfortunately, her husband, who was a Quaker, was "unwilling
that she should receive the ordinances of the Gospel." A week
later, Abbott spoke to a man "who said he thought a person might
be just as good without making a profession as with. His wife has
lately entertained a hope concerning herself & he is unwilling
that she should join any church."[49]

Abbott ran into his strongest criticism from a man named
Obediah Winsor whose wife and parents were professors of religion. Abbott took supper with the family one evening and was
foolish enough to ask the man "if he had taken any thought for
the supper, that GOD has prepared for his children." Winsor
subjected the minister to a barrage of verbal abuse, maintaining,
among other things, that "ministers were a pack of good for
nothing fellows going about to get their living out of other people, that the Bible was a pack of lies & I [Abbott] knew it." Winsor
went on to suggest that Abbott "was a liar, a thief, & a villain
going into all the poor houses after black women & squaw and all
filthy women." After Abbott left Winsor's house, he discovered
his horse's mane had been cut.[50]

Abbott was not the only evangelical minister to be regarded
with suspicion. Jacob Frieze, a few years before he assumed a position of leadership in the labor movement, was the Universalist
minister in Pawtucket. In this capacity, he waged a bitter attack
on the revivalist activities at Daniel Greene's Baptist church,
where Calvin Philleo, visiting from Suffield, Connecticut, had
staged a revival in 1829. According to Frieze, Philleo "succeeded in converting to his faith, some twenty or thirty persons,
women and children, exclusively; with perhaps one solitary exception."[51] Philleo's following as well as his teaching were mutu-

49. Abbott Journal, December 8, 1812, and December 19, 1812, (RIHS). For
similar concerns of husbands about their wives' participation in evangelical
religion, see Johnson, *Shopkeeper's Millennium*, p. 108; Mary Ryan, *Cradle of the
Middle Class: The Family in Oneida County, New York, 1790–1860* (New York,
1981), pp. 75–77.
50. Abbott Journal, December 24, 1812 (RIHS).
51. Jacob Frieze, *Letter to Rev. Mr. Philleo Dedicated to the People of Pawtucket*
(August 27, 1829); Jacob Frieze, *A Sermon, Delivered at the Universalist Chapel, in
Pawtucket, R.I. on Monday, September 27, 1829* (Pawtucket, R.I., 1829), p. 25.

ally reinforcing sources of concern. Frieze complained that Philleo painted a brutal portrait of God (who should be regarded as a kinder parent). Most horrifying was the portrait of God "as having 'a cord around the consciences of sinners, and winding that cord with a crank, until He drawed them to himself'; then severing it in twain and dropping them into your endless hell!" Frieze would reprimand Philleo by saying "you should learn to treat the Divine Being with more respect, than to present him to our view in such a low, vulgar, and contemptable [*sic*] figure, fit only to excite the scoffs and laughter of fools."[52]

Frieze was outraged not only by the content of the revival meetings but also by their frequency and timing. "Prayer Meetings, Conference Meetings, Church Meetings, Meetings for Preaching, and other Meetings without names" had been held "for weeks past, to at least sixteen in the week." The meetings disrupted normal family relations, for they were "attended at all hours, by mostly the same persons, from sunrise to midnight; to the great annoyance of husbands, disturbance of the community, and the neglect of children, business and family cares—to say nothing of the exposure of health."[53]

To maintain family stability, Frieze warned: "Fathers and mothers, bar your doors against the foul monster, that under the garb of sanctity, would invade your peaceful abode, and spread terror and dismay among the children of your love: that would alienate their affections from you, and teach them to utter curses on your head."[54] While Frieze employed the image of parents protecting their children, it was women, in particular, whom he considered vulnerable:

52. Frieze, *Letter to Rev. Mr. Philleo*, p. 3.

53. Jacob Frieze, *Two Discourses Delivered in the Universalist Church in Pawtucket on Sunday, August 30, 1829, on the Subject of Religious Excitements* (Pawtucket, R.I., 1829), p. 32. Midnight meetings were not unheard of. Elder Lorenzo Johnson described how on the final day of a protracted meeting in Sandwich, Massachusetts, a midnight sermon was proposed and Salome Lincoln was asked to give it: "At the appointed time, Sister Salome accompanied by one or two female friends, took the stand and announced her text—'And at Midnight there was a cry made; *Behold* the Bridegroom cometh; go ye out to meet him!—Matt. xxv6'" (Davis, *The Female Preacher*, p. 47).

54. Frieze, *Two Discourses*, p. 18.

Refuse to listen to his harangues, but in the presence of father, husband or protector; and which the common principles of female delicacy demand of you. Absent yourself from his midnight haunts, except in their company; and which, a proper respect for your own reputation should induce you to do; and my word for it, you will soon cease to see such a person prowling around your houses day and night, to gain admission in the absence of father and husband.

Fearing that women would not be able to resist the dangerous revivalist, men in the village prepared to defend their womenfolk. Frieze challenged Philleo: "I understand you have promised to call on every family in the place. Some of the MEN, I among the number, would like to be home at the time. Or can you more readily convert the FEMALES solus?—You Understand me."[55]

Frieze believed that women were inherently more susceptible to evangelical appeals than men were. It was not because they were "of a constitutional weakness of mind," he reasoned. Rather, it resulted "from a peculiar delicacy of feeling and sensibility, the ornament of the female breast, denied to the other sex; and, of which, superstition makes use as one of the fittest instruments for its purpose."[56] Frieze's attack on female participation in revivals as superstition was a powerful way of masking the female assertiveness that came with submission to God rather than man.

It was also in many of these popular evangelical denominations, particularly among Freewill Baptists, that female preaching was allowed. Nancy Towle preached among the Freewill Baptists, Christians, and Methodists in her travels, though she declined membership in any of them. Stressing the importance of the independence that came from refusing to join a church, Towle noted, "I am . . . accountable to no mortal, for my procedure—nor hath any human being any control over me." Free of institutional fetters, Towle was able to campaign against a growing evil within Christianity: "that of excluding female gifts from

55. Frieze, *Letter to Rev. Mr. Philleo*, p. 8.
56. Frieze, *Two Discourses*, p. 21.

the Church of God." Taught to be subordinate and passive, denied the role of teachers, it was no wonder than women did not fulfill their spiritual potential, she argued. Towle challenged the religious constraints placed on women and sealed her testimony "in vindication of the rights of woman!" Female preachers like Towle brought an additional level of assertiveness to evangelical religion.[57]

Frieze's attack on evangelical religion suggests not only the threat it posed to family relations of working people, but also a gendered dimension in the distinction between "rational" and evangelical religion. In a discussion of male and female responses to revivalism, Barbara Epstein notes that Unitarianism and Universalism were good compromises for men who did not want to deny their worldly interests when they embraced religion. And a survey of fourteen Universalist and Unitarian churches in New England by Paul Goodman demonstrates that these churches were less heavily female than evangelical churches. Although we have no records for Frieze's Universalist church in Pawtucket, similar gender ratios might well have existed there.[58]

Jacob Frieze's attack on Calvin Philleo blatantly revealed the way evangelical religion undermined male authority in the family. The women who joined evangelical churches entered into new relationships in which their ministers—instead of their fathers or husbands—assumed positions of moral and spiritual authority. The vivid and even crude revivalistic preaching, which challenged the authority of elites and elevated the speech of the common farmer or workingman, also served to undermine that workingman's authority within his own family.

The fears that relationships between evangelical clergymen

57. Towle, *Vicissitudes Illustrated*, pp. 11–12, 28, 244–253. For an important discussion of preaching by Quaker women during this time, see Joan Jensen, *Loosening the Bonds: Mid-Atlantic Farm Women, 1750–1850* (New Haven, Conn., 1986), pp. 145–166.

58. Barbara Leslie Epstein, *The Politics of Domesticity: Women, Evangelism, and Temperance in Nineteenth-Century America* (Middletown, Conn., 1981), pp. 49–50; Paul Goodman, *Towards a Christian Republic: Antimasonry and the Great Transition in New England, 1826–1836* (New York, 1988), p. 93. Goodman cites here the Rev. Bernard Whitman, a Waltham Unitarian who "argued that women leaned towards evangelical Christianity because they were more 'impressionable,' less rational, and more readily swayed by the Calvinist clergy."

and their female followers engendered would be played out in the scandals about illicit relationships that erupted periodically.[59] For example, Pawtucket was rocked in the mid-1830s by revelations that Elder Ray Potter had impregnated a young woman in his congregation. Potter was a colorful and popular preacher who had helped form the Freewill Baptist Church in Pawtucket during a revival in 1820. A couple of years later he split from the church in a conflict with Daniel Greene, which may have been induced by social as well as theological differences. In any event, Potter formed his own church, which was not affiliated with any other—Freewill Baptist or Calvinist. Potter's congregation was noted for its female following. In January 1837, for example, the local newspaper slyly noted that a lecturer on moral reform spoke at Potter's church "without having any offensive bearing on the persons present—a large majority of whom, of course, were females."[60]

Two weeks later, Potter published a public confession that he had "committed a great sin."[61] Potter claimed that "one unfortunate incident" had resulted in a young follower's pregnancy, but most in town believed the affair had gone on for ten years and that Potter had had affairs with more than one young woman. Particularly suggestive of his lecherous ways was the revelation of a covenant between Potter and two young women that "we will ever be unto each other constant, faithful and confidential friends." One of the women was the mother of his unborn child; the other was thought to have been similarly involved.[62]

Community outrage was vented in a "turn-out." The demonstration was menacing enough that Potter fled town upon hearing that it was planned. But his supporters described to him what he had missed. "After marching through the place and

59. For a discussion of similar concerns about sexual impropriety in the First Great Awakening, see Susan Mary Juster, "Sinners and Saints: The Evangelical Construction of Gender and Authority in New England, 1740–1830" (Ph.D. diss., University of Michigan, 1990), pp. 55–61.

60. *Pawtucket Chronicle*, January 13, 1837.

61. "Confession of Ray Potter," n.d. (broadside); *Pawtucket Chronicle*, February 3, 1837.

62. *Pawtucket Chronicle*, April 7, 1837.

making sundry exhibitions to disgrace me, I was burnt in effigy in front of the meeting house where I had formerly preached," Potter complained. His sin was not so much fornication as the betrayal of the trust his position as a clergyman gave him. Thus Potter noted: "Some of the leaders of this 'sin avenging' company were most notorious for their licentious lives."[63]

The "turn-out" against Potter was not the first of its kind in the town, for the *Pawtucket Chronicle* also reported: "This is the second offense perpetrated by a clergyman in our village in a few months—and when the story is told in other places, for the honor of Pawtucket be it remembered that both offenders had to flee before the indignation of her justly excited citizens."[64]

Of course, the preeminent case of this era and region to crystallize the tensions created in factory towns over the relationships between ministers and female converts was the trial of the Methodist minister Ephraim Avery for the murder of Sarah Maria Cornell in 1833. Sarah had followed Avery to Fall River in a desperate attempt to reclaim a letter of admission to the Methodist church. She was working at a mill in town and was pregnant when she was found hanged in the Durfee haystack, leaving behind several letters implicating Avery in both her downfall and her demise. Avery was eventually acquitted, after a long string of witnesses was paraded through the courtroom to testify to Sarah's wayward activities and vindictive nature. Despite this testimony, however, there was a massive outcry against both Avery and the Methodists for their attack on female virtue. Jacob Frieze once again took up his pen, this time under the name of "Aristides." "The whole machinery of the Methodist Institution has been brought into operation, and its artillery made to bear on the battlements of the hall of justice," he claimed. Frieze was particularly outraged that, after Avery was acquitted, the Methodists agreed to restore him to his pulpit. Frieze considered Avery guilty "not of wilfully murdering Sarah M. Cornell, but

63. Ray Potter, *Admonitions from "The Depths of the Earth"; or, The Fall of Ray Potter in Twenty-Four Letters* (Pawtucket, R.I., 1838), p. 37.

64. *Pawtucket Chronicle*, February 3, 1837. See Kett, *Rites of Passage*, pp. 47–48, for comparable discussion of "turn-outs" against schoolmasters who were thought to have abused their authority.

guilty of the means by which she came to her death."[65] Methodism, in other words, had destroyed the family bonds that might have protected Sarah. Although Frieze was no longer editor of *The Artisan* when he penned his attack, he was urged on by the labor newspaper.[66]

While Frieze confined his attack on the Methodists to family issues, Catherine Williams transformed it into a question of social status. Many revival preachers, she argued, were "ignorant persons; people, who, if they knew their proper places in society, would be hewers of wood and drawers of water, rather than teachers." It was outrageous for the poor to support their own ministers. Those of comfortable economic circumstances could provide their neighborhood "with ever so many good, respectable, competent teachers," according to Williams, who concluded: "that a preacher, who cannot be supported without drawing upon the charity of poor factory girls, ought to go in and go to work himself."[67]

Implicit in Williams's attack was an acknowledgment of the way the evangelical religion of working people posed a challenge to their "betters." They might not propose a change in social and economic structure, but their avoidance of more elite leadership undermined patterns of community deference. As Frieze's comments made clear, however, the potency of this challenge was limited by the fears about family authority which evangelical religion created for workingmen. Workingmen would have to renegotiate their relationship with religion if they were going to use it more effectively. The Washingtonian temperance movement would help them do it.

65. Aristides, *Strictures on the Case of Ephraim K. Avery* (Providence, R.I., 1833), pp. 5, 92. Frieze is noted as the real author of this piece in the Rider Collection (John Hay Library, Brown University). For a full discussion of this case, see David Richard Kasserman, *Fall River Outrage: Life, Murder, and Justice in Early New England* (Philadelphia, 1986).

66. *The Artisan*, September 19, 1833.

67. Williams, *Fall River*, p. vii.

Chapter 5

Exemplary Lives:
The Washingtonians
and Social Authority

For workingmen who were concerned about the way evangelicalism was disrupting their families, displacing them morally and spiritually, Washingtonianism provided an important counterpoint. Washingtonianism was the arena in which displaced fathers reasserted their moral authority within the family as they attempted to create new bonds of domesticity. The Washingtonian movement began with a few reformed drunkards in Baltimore in 1840, but it became so successful that within a few years it had become many other things as well. Youth groups, women's groups, and mainstream temperance societies all adopted the name of Washingtonianism. By the mid-1840s there might be several Washingtonian societies operating in any given town, sometimes in harmony with one another and sometimes at each other's throats. But despite this diversification in membership, "reformed drunkards" would remain the heart of the movement's identity: they were its leaders, they were its speakers, and they quickly became the targets for criticizing the movement.

Washingtonianism hit New England with full force in the spring of 1841 as John Hawkins, in particular, inspired audiences in Boston with the story of his descent into alcoholism and regeneration through the Washingtonian movement. Reformed inebriates from Boston began speaking in other towns throughout the region, so that, in June 1841, societies were organized in Newburyport, Lynn, and Fall River, and in July an organization

was formed in Providence. By the end of 1841, supporters estimated that 5,000 people had signed the pledge in Boston and that
73,000 had signed the pledge in all other states.[1]

This may have been an overly optimistic assessment, but local
reports suggest the popularity of the movement. In October 1841,
some 488 women and 802 men had signed the Pledge in Providence, Rhode Island. By the summer of 1842, the Providence
Washington Total Abstinence Society claimed 1,320 members,
and a newer organization in town called the Sixth Ward Washington Total Abstinence Society claimed an additional 300 members. The society in Fall River was considerably smaller, with
332 members listed a year after its organization. In Watertown,
Massachusetts, 390 members had joined the society by October
1841—some 190 men and 200 women; Worcester had 550 members. In Lynn, the Washingtonians appear to have been far more
successful; in their first year they enrolled 1,030 women and 840
men, and another 1,077 names were added to the Washingtonian
pledge the following year, and 300 in 1843, bringing the total to
about 3,200.[2]

The "reformed drunkards" who formed the core of the movement probably accounted for about 10 percent of the membership. Ian Tyrell, for example, found that 50 out of the 550 members of the Washingtonian society in Worcester were reformed
drunks.[3] Of the 2,000 men and women who signed the Wash-

1. "A Teetotaler," *The New Impulse; or, Hawkins and Reform: A Brief History of
the Origin, Progress, and Effects of the Present Astonishing Temperance Movement,
and of the Life and Reformation of John H. W. Hawkins, the Distinguished Leader*
(Boston, 1841), pp. 15–18; *A Concise Statement of the Origin, Progress, and Present
Condition of the Washington Total Abstinence Society of Newburyport and Vicinity*
(1845), p. 2; *First Annual Report of the Washington Total Abstinence Society, Lynn,
1842*, p. 4; Record of Fall River Washington Total Abstinence Society, 1841–1842
(Manuscript collection, First Baptist Church bank vault, Fall River); Records,
Providence Washington Total Abstinence Society, 1841 (RIHS).

2. Records, Providence Washington Total Abstinence Society, October 18,
1841 (RIHS); *First Quarterly Report of the Watertown Washington Total Abstinence
Society,* October 18, 1841 (Boston, 1841); *First Annual Report . . . Lynn, 1842*, p. 6;
Essex County Washingtonian (Lynn), January 26, 1843 and February 1, 1844. The
wide disparity in numbers from one town to the next may mean that some towns
were reporting everyone who had signed the pledge, while others were reporting
those who actually belonged to the organization; there could be a difference.

3. Ian Tyrell, *Sobering Up: From Temperance to Prohibition in Antebellum
America, 1800–1860* (Westport, Conn., 1979), p. 162.

ingtonian pledge in Lynn during the first year of the movement's existence, 225 were drunkards. Of the more than 1,200 pledge-signers in the Providence, 175 were reformed inebriates. The rest of the organization was a support group.[4]

Workingmen's Domesticity and Manly Morality

In addition to focusing on drunks, Washingtonianism also fo-cused on men. The rhetoric of the reformed drunks was distinctly masculine, and it was these reformed drunks who were the lead-ers and speakers of the Washingtonians. In telling their stories, Washingtonians were in effect recreating the culture of the tav-ern without alcohol; if their stories were not about family de-struction, they were masculine tales of adventure and conquest.

The Lynn society gave further statistics that bear on this point. Of the reformed drunkards claimed, 150 were heads of families and 75 were young men. There were apparently no women in the movement who were considered to be "reformed drunks." Yet the very same report that contained these statistics also presented excerpts from the diary of their leader, Captain Carroll, describ-ing his visits to drunkards and attempts to reclaim them. On December 1 he visited a "Mr. X." "His wife was also very intem-perate, so much as to make herself, husband and family com-pletely miserable," Carroll noted. "They were a pitiable sight, being destitute of food, fuel, and indeed everything necessary for the comfort of a family. After conversing with them upon the folly of their course, and the propriety of living a different life, they both signed the pledge, and I furnished them with wood and other things necessary to make them comfortable."[5] Here was a female who was clearly a reformed drunk, but she had no place in the statistics of the Lynn Washingtonians. At its heart, Wash-ingtonianism was a male movement.

In the numerous temperance publications issuing from New

4. *First Annual Report . . . Lynn, 1842*, p. 6; Records, Providence Washington Total Abstinence Society, October 9, 1841.
5. *First Annual Report . . . Lynn, 1842*, p. 9.

England, virtually nothing was said about female drunkenness.[6] Women did participate in the movement actively, but as subordinates or in separate auxiliaries. In Lynn, the women formed a companion organization to the male Washingtonians, but after a year the two organizations merged and women assumed five of ten places on the committee. Most of these women were wives of men who were leaders in the movement and were identified as such, using their husbands' names (i.e., Mrs. John Norwood). The women would also form a Washingtonian Sewing Circle, headed by many of the same people, and when the Young Men's Charitable Temperance Society was formed the following year, so too was a Young Ladies Charitable Temperance Society.[7]

In Lynn, as in most places for which we have any record of female activity, women collected, made, sold, and sometimes distributed articles of clothing to families of reformed drunks. This was also one of the main activities of the Factory Village Temperance Society in Andover.[8] In addition, women also supplied food for parties and parades. In Marblehead, women may have been even bolder. Soon after a Martha Washingtonian Society was formed in that town, it was reported that they "purpose visiting every house in town to obtain signatures to the pledge."[9]

The orientation toward reforming male household heads also showed up in the movement's literature. While young and single

6. In this respect, the situation in New England appears to be different from that described by Ruth Alexander in "'We Are Engaged as a Band of Sisters': Class and Domesticity in the Washingtonian Temperance Movement, 1840–1850," *Journal of American History* 75 (December 1988): 763–785. Lori Ginzberg notes, however, that public discourse did not admit that women engaged in immoral behavior, regardless of what the actual case might be. See Lori Ginzberg, *Women and the Work of Benevolence, Morality, Politics, and Class in the Nineteenth-Century United States* (New Haven, Conn., 1990), pp. 13–14.

7. *Essex County Washingtonian*, January 19, 1843; February 23, 1843; February 1, 1844; May 9, 1844.

8. Factory Village Temperance Society Minutes, 1842–1857 (Manuscript Collection, AHS). Other examples of this kind of activity may be found in the report at the third annual meeting of the Washingtonians in Lynn, which stated that women collected and distributed most of the garments for the society (*Essex County Washingtonian*, February 1, 1844). The Martha Washingtonians in Providence numbered about 300 and were also engaged in ministering to the needy (*The Samaritan* [Providence], April 1843).

9. *Essex County Washingtonian*, May 12, 1842.

men received some attention from the Washingtonians, it was family men who were of primary concern. As the *First Annual Report* of the Lynn Washingtonians suggested, "The husband has been given back to his despairing wife—the father to the foresaken child; and the house which was before the place of wretchedness, poverty and cruelty, has been turned in to the home of gladness, abundance and love."[10] In the second annual report, the Lynn Society again highlighted the heads of households who had been reclaimed. Of those who had signed the temperance pledge, "we can reckon something like 500 men who are heads of families, who have foresaken the intoxicating bowl; and instead of being, as formerly, a source of grief to their families, have become their support and comfort." Excerpts from Captain Carroll's diary deal almost exclusively with male heads of households who were drunk and whose families had fallen on hard times.[11]

The society in Newburyport echoed this emphasis, bragging that within a few months of the society's founding "over two hundred were reformed from drunkenness, many families were delivered from poverty and wretchedness, and the children of these families by the kindness of friends, were able to attend school, and meetings of religious worship."[12] The Fall River Washingtonians, an all-male organization, stated in their preamble an "earnest desire to repair as much as in us lies, the injury we have done to society, to our families and to ourselves."[13] In other words, the fathers repented.

The narratives of reformed drunkards likewise centered on their failures as fathers. John Hawkins had become a drunk while an apprentice in the hatters trade and had been a persistent source of anxiety to his own family.[14] Charles Newton, a reformed drunkard in the Worcester Washingtonians, described "the virtues, and the wretchedness of an affectionate wife, whom

10. *First Annual Report . . . Lynn, 1842*, p. 5.
11. *Essex County Washingtonian*, January 26, 1843.
12. *Concise Statement . . . Newburyport* (1845), p. 2.
13. Record of the Fall River Washington Total Abstinence Society, Preamble (n.d.) (Manuscripts collection, First Baptist Church, Fall River, Massachusetts).
14. "Teetotaler," *The New Impulse*, pp. 10–12.

he had reduced from happiness to misery, and driven in despair from his house, and from himself." A mariner in Newmarket, New Hampshire, spoke first of his travels in such places as India and London, then spoke of the way he had destroyed his family through drink: "My eldest son tore himself from his degraded father, and has never returned. My young heart's idol, my beloved and suffering wife, has gone broken hearted to the grave. And my lovely daughter . . . now sleeps by her mother's side." Deprived of his own family, he became a public father, restoring his "wandering brethren again to the bosom of society" and warning young people to take heed from his example.[15]

This focus on the fathers as drunkards (and reformed drunkards) is particularly interesting in light of the emphasis that mainstream temperance literature often placed on the sons. As William Breitenbach has pointed out, "The archetypical temperance tale featured a young man of fair prospects, prepossessing appearance, and fine intelligence, who fell to drunken poverty and a miserable death—all because his father taught him to drink."[16] As Breitenbach goes on to argue, these stories usually absolved sons of moral responsibility for their failings because vicious habits had been instilled in them when they were too young to be accountable—it was the fathers who had to accept the blame.

Breitenbach notes that there are a variety of reasons reformers directed their hostility at fathers, though he is most interested in the troubled relationship of reformers to the preceding revolutionary generation. The fact that these former drunkards called themselves Washingtonians suggests that they too were establishing ties to their revolutionary heritage. Washingtonians, however, wanted to rehabilitate themselves as fathers rather than sons. Jay Fliegelman has described the way the exemplary nature of Washington's life, rather than the greatness of his office, had become important in early nineteenth-century literature,

15. *Worcester County Cataract and Massachusetts Washingtonian,* March 22, 1843; *Portsmouth Washingtonian,* October 19, 1843.

16. William Breitenbach, "Sons of the Fathers: Temperance Reformers and the Legacy of the American Revolution," *Journal of the Early Republic* 3 (Spring 1983): 70.

replacing "the authority of position with the authority of character." As former drunkards took the pledge and recounted their life stories as examples for others, they too reoriented their basis of authority away from their position, toward their character. This reorientation toward character was particularly important as these men tried to find a place for themselves in families where their economic authority had been compromised in some instances or demolished by financial failure in others.[17]

The narratives of the Washingtonians, unlike those in mainstream temperance literature, were more often about the fathers who had been unable to provide for their families than about sons who had been profligate. Washingtonianism provided a way for these fathers to reestablish their moral authority (and possibly financial responsibility) within their families. If mainstream temperance literature absolved sons of their moral accountability in becoming drunks, placing blame on the fathers, Washingtonianism removed the responsibility even further, absolving fathers of blame as well. As W. H. Y. Hackett argued, "When a man in middle age opens his eyes to the truth, sees his real situation, and reforms himself, he is entitled to our respect and sympathy."[18]

Many Washingtonians did not place the blame for drunkenness on the individual, or at least were ambivalent about doing so. The use of the passive voice in reports of becoming a drunkard was one indication of this tendency. Charles Newton, for example, told of "the process by which he had been gradually led to the formation of intemperate habits, until he was plunged headlong into the vortex of dissipation and ruin."[19] One does not get the impression that Mr. Newton forged ahead willingly on the road of drunkenness, but that he was brought there by some force beyond his control. Mr. Beck of Philadelphia, when he told his

17. Ibid., pp. 74–75; Jay Fliegelman, *Prodigals and Pilgrims: The American Revolution against Patriarchal Authority, 1750–1850* (New York, 1982). For another discussion of the way Washington was mythologized, see Catherine Albanese, *Sons of the Fathers: The Civil Religion of the American Revolution* (Philadelphia, 1976), pp. 143–181.

18. *Washingtonian and Banner* (Portsmouth and Saco), March 9, 1843.

19. *Worcester County Cataract and Massachusetts Washingtonian*, April 5, 1843.

tale of woe to the Washingtonians of Portsmouth, New Hampshire, "told how he had by the rumsellers been robbed of his last cent, and afterwards kicked into the street to make the pavement his bed and the curb stone his pillow."[20]

James Gale created a similar impression when he detailed his life of misfortune in *A Long Voyage in a Leaky Ship; or, A Forty Years' Cruise on the Sea of Intemperance*. Gale had been born in Worcester County, Massachusetts, in 1795 and had faced a succession of financial betrayals. He worked at a twine factory for two months without receiving any wages. As a meat carrier a few years later, he was held responsible for collecting for the meat he delivered and ended up in debt to his employer eight months later because so many customers defaulted on their payments. Although swindled out of money by virtually everyone for whom he worked or with whom he did business, Gale stopped short of blaming them for all his misfortunes. "However wrong or improper may have been the course which individuals pursued, there was another and a more certain cause of all my ill. The fated cup was at bottom, and this it was that was working all my mischief."[21] Gale did not blame society or exploitative labor conditions for his failures, as he might have if he were a radical workingman. Neither did he blame himself, as the middle-class ethic of responsibility dictated. Nor did he blame his parents. The problem lay elsewhere: in the bottle. Wicked individuals were at least partially culpable for ruining Gale financially, but even here he qualified the blame, laying the "more certain cause" to alcohol, as if it could be personified into having a volition all its own.

The victims of alcohol were not free moral agents, and they could not be held responsible for their actions. In Lynn, some Washingtonians circulated a petition for the pardon of Isaac Leavitt, who had been condemned to death for murdering someone while drunk. William Barlow would argue in the pages of the

20. *Portsmouth Washingtonian*, August 3, 1843.
21. James Gale, *A Long Voyage in a Leaky Ship; or, Forty Years' Cruise on the Sea of Intemperance* (Cambridgeport, 1842), p. 36. Gale's comments on his various jobs in the meat business are particularly interesting because they show how unskilled laborers were forced to assume the financial risks of the operation.

Essex County Washingtonian that Leavitt was "no more account-able for deeds committed under its influence, than any man for the acts performed in a state of insanity produced by any other cause."[22]

Indeed, W. H. Y. Hackett of the *Washingtonian and Banner*, of Portsmouth, New Hampshire, and Saco, Maine, went so far as to reverse the lines of responsibility and blame society for the drunkard's problems, arguing, "The reformed drunkard has a great deal to forgive." He would suggest that any man who had lived a sober life should contemplate how horrible he would feel to be talked about as the drunkard had. "The drunkard is the victim of a wrong and perverted public sentiment. Drunkenness resulted from former usages of society as certainly as any effect flows from a cause."[23]

As the emphasis on reformed character replaced that of position for the morally rehabilitated father, brotherhood and equality rather than patriarchy and hierarchy were stressed. Love and moral suasion, staples of the emerging feminized families, were also stressed by the Washingtonians in opposition to external coercion. D. H. Barlow would claim in an editorial for the *Essex County Washingtonian* that the movement "visits with love and extends kindly aid to the inebriate, *while* he is an inebriate, and *because* he is an inebriate. And by this love and kindness it supplies both a *motive* to reform and the help which makes effectual the *endeavor* to reform."[24]

The Fall River society stressed the importance of remonstrating with backsliders "in a kind and affectionate manner." Gilbert Ricketson, a former mule spinner whose children worked at the Annawan factory, was one of the most prominent and colorful members of the Fall River Washingtonians, and he frequently underscored the superiority of moral suasion over legal coercion. Having served time in the New Bedford House of Correction, he was no doubt in a position to know. Recalling the degraded work he had been given, Ricketson observed that "he was considered a

22. *Essex County Washingtonian*, August 31, 1843.
23. *Washingtonian and Banner*, March 9, 1843.
24. *Essex County Washingtonian*, July 21, 1842.

first rate workman at the picking oackum business . . . if he had been allowed to have staid his time out he should have come out Master of Arts." Contrasting the effects of legal coercion and moral suasion in reclaiming drunkards, Ricketson elaborated on "the difference of being carried by force and confined in the house of Correction and that of going over on the 9th of September perfectly Sober with a Coach and four to the splendid Temperance Celebration composed as was supposed of Six thousand friends of Temperance."[25]

In Portland, Maine, "a True Washingtonian" recollected that early Washingtonians "went into the work of reformation as if they felt that all men were brethren; and as the manifestation of that kind spirit had reclaimed them, they believed it sufficient to reclaim others. The spirit of the Lord appeared to have taken possession of the hearts of Washingtonians, and wonderful conversions were made through their instrumentality." Hackett argued of Washingtonianism, "Love is the power which is, if rightly directed, to reform and rule the world."[26]

"C," writing for the *Washingtonian and Banner*, would use flogging to make a point: "The lash can never make men better. It may restrain for the time, but it never changes the bad disposition into a good disposition." The author would go on to argue that Washingtonians should learn from this example that "outward force, bodily restraint, corporeal punishment however administered cannot restrain the intemperate man or make better the keeper of the rumshop." Having discarded external coercion as both brutal and ineffective, the writer argued: "Men act according to the dictates of their character; and if we would change the *conduct* we must operate on the *character*."

In criticizing flogging, "C" also argued that a "ship is a world in miniature," and he went on to describe a plan for reformation that focused on a similarly male-oriented family: "The fathers must be made temperate, the family circle must be purified of alcohol. . . . We must reform the fathers and then will the children

25. Record of the Fall River Washington Total Abstinence Society, By-Laws, September 19, 1841.
26. *The True Washingtonian and Martha Washingtonian Advocate* (Portland), August 9, 1843; *Washingtonian and Banner*, February 3, 1843.

come forward in the world with characters which shall make them useful and happy men."[27] Regardless of their failures—indeed, because of them—the moral authority of fathers could be rooted in their characters rather than in their position. It was a process that inverted the normal basis for the creation of moral authority, a life of purity, but perhaps that was the point. The failures of the fathers were exceptions to the rule: both the exceptions and the rule were accepted.

The Social Authority of the Reformed Drunkard

The reformed drunkards who told these stories were establishing an inverted basis for moral authority not only in their households but also in society at large. This became particularly clear in the verbal performances of the Washingtonians. Charity work, newspapers, and the formation of local organizations and institutional networks were all a part of the emerging Washingtonian strategy. But the focus of Washingtonian reform was the reformed drunkard's confession. In stories repeated frequently at informal meetings or on public stages, verbal performance brought a challenge to society at large because it was the ability to tell these stories which gave drunkards the power of leadership.

Most of the early societies do not record specific rules about office-holding, though retrospective analyses suggests that only drunks were supposed to be leaders, as do indirect allusions at the time of the movement's founding. Thus, a description of the Washingtonian Total Abstinence Society in Boston described its officers, agents, and lecturers as men whose compensation was "the delightful reflection, that they have been raised from degradation and moral desolation."[28] The preamble to the Fall River Washington Total Abstinence Society noted: "We have personally experienced the degrading and disasterous effects intellectually, morally & socially, of the use as a drink of intoxicating liquors."

27. *Washingtonian and Banner*, January 19, 1843.
28. "Teetotaler," *The New Impulse*, p. 16.

Although it was not specifically spelled out in the bylaws of the Fall River organization, it had clearly been customary for former drunks to hold office. Attempts by the prosperous shoe manufacturer and main-line temperance reformer Richard French to assume a position of leadership in the organization later on provoked a crisis. According to Joseph Ward, one of his critics, French and a few of his friends proposed resolutions to change the bylaws and the pledge, "putting the gag to all those that adhear strickly to the . . . principles of the old . . . for no person to hold offices of any distinction but the Reformed Drunkards themselves."[29]

In Maine, a writer recalled that the early Washingtonians considered the influence of traditional temperance reformers so dangerous "that almost every Washingtonian Society had incorporated in its regulations, that no member should be admitted who had not drank intoxicating liquor within three or six months previous to his application to join."[30]

At least in the early days of the movement, however, there may have been little need to put these rules in writing, for the movement was so clearly associated with drunkards. The focus was on reclaiming them. They were the ones who inspired reverence as temperance orators, catapulting them into positions of leadership in the temperance movement. In Lynn, it was reported that "unless a lecturer has once been a drunkard, he cannot get a respectable hearing!" This did not particularly disturb the commentator, but he did point out that this meant the previous relationship between reformer and drunkard had been completely reversed: "The learned, the old fashioned reformer, the modern pharisee who exalts himself and despises others . . . do homage to their [the drunkard's] commanding, subduing and effective powers of eloquence."[31]

Many of the Washingtonian narratives focused on the previous drunken escapades of members in a playful manner sure to enter-

29. Record of the Fall River Washington Total Abstinence Society, Preamble; *The All Sorts* (Fall River), January 31, 1846.

30. *The True Washingtonian and Martha Washingtonian Advocate* (Portland, Maine), December 20, 1843.

31. *Essex County Washingtonian*, July 27, 1843.

tain listeners. Gilbert Ricketson was fond of providing such discourses for his Fall River compatriots. On one particularly slow night, he "gave a very animated history of part of his past life of his hair breadth escapes &c. one time in particular in Baltimore while with Capt. Cobb. . . ." Captain Carroll of Lynn had a similar style, for when he spoke to the Washingtonians of Danvers, A. R. Porter noted that the audience "expected something *funny*, no doubt from the well known character and genius of the speaker." Carroll did not disappoint them, as he "related several thrilling incidents which have passed before his own observation of the effects of Alcohol [and] detailed briefly some events in the history of his own life."[32]

The form of their narratives automatically encouraged people from the lower ranks of society to join in, because "true Washingtonian" narratives were colloquial and unlettered. These reformed drunkards were referred to as "gutter graduates," who had powers of speaking and understanding far superior to those of mere college graduates.[33] The Rev. Abbot, a former sailor and reformed drunkard, delivered a lecture in Springfield, Massachusetts, which the local Washingtonian newspaper described as "the most unlearned learned production which ever met our observation." Abbot was able to appeal to a broad and diverse audience precisely because he was uneducated. His training came from his experience as a sailor, traveling from one port to the next, not from schooling. Thus, the newspaper went on to report that Abbot had "an almost perfect disregard of the construction of the king's English, he had a touch of the idiom and the provincialisms of all the tongues of the earth—the quaint phrases . . . of every nation." Moreover, Abbot's lecture "appealed to the feelings of the audience." He used his speaking style to establish a rapport with the crowd.[34]

Unfortunately, it is virtually impossible to find any traces of these narratives in the written records of the period, for two of

32. Record of the Fall River Washington Total Abstinence Society, September 20, 1841; *Essex County Washingtonian*, December 15, 1843.

33. See, e.g., "Gutter Ahead of University," *White Mountain Torrent* (Concord), September 27, 1844.

34. *Hampden Washingtonian* (Springfield), December 22, 1842.

their primary characteristics were that they were spontaneous and oral in nature. It would never do to write out one's confession ahead of time. Thus, George Weeks of Milbury spoke to the Worcester society in May 1843 "in an off hand, unstudied speech, which was truly Washingtonian in its language, and sentiment." Elisha Burchard, when in Worcester, also "complied with that original rule, and practice of Washingtonianism." When he presented his "own experience in the career of alcoholic dissipation," he did so "spontaneously, off hand, as the heart, and the occasion may prompt, without the aid, or the incumbrance of any manuscript."[35] Spontaneity was juxtaposed against the reading of a prepared text. A speaker did not have to be literate to deliver an effective speech. Indeed, in order for a Washingtonian narrative to be authentic, it had to be composed and performed at the same time, at the moment the speaker and audience came into contact.

Even without the actual texts for these speeches, the rules governing their delivery suggest their subversive nature. An uneducated audience required an uneducated speaker. No wonder that another Washingtonian would argue in the pages of the *Worcester Cataract* that the most successful temperance reform had "not come from the educated or professional classes . . . [but] through the labors of men . . . whose worldly advantages had ever been limited and, therefore, whose arguments and illustrations were drawn mainly from the rich volume of their own experience."[36]

Assessments such as these contradicted the assumptions of moral reformers who felt that the educated and the elite should provide leadership to those of the lower ranks. The Washingtonians made it clear that the masses were neither instructed nor led effectively by their superiors, but rather by their peers. Moreover, because the subject matter was the speaker's past dissipation, those who considered themselves morally superior to the masses were locked out of positions of leadership in the move-

35. *Worcester County Cataract and Massachusetts Washingtonian,* May 10, 1843; May 31, 1843.

36. *Worcester County Cataract and Massachusetts Washingtonian,* May 31, 1843.

ment. Even if a middle-class reformer had groveled on a barroom floor, he would be loath to recall such an experience and trumpet it about.

Traditional temperance reformers, who had originally supported the Washingtonians, soon adopted a more critical posture, as they saw their own authority receding. In part, the uneasiness of middle-class reformers surfaced as they expressed a growing interest in legal suasion (prohibition) over moral suasion. The invocation of the law would be a sure way to undermine the emphasis that was being placed on Washingtonian narratives as an instrument of conversion. But equally important was their attack on the crudeness of Washingtonian narratives that seemed to focus more on an immoral past than on a moral present.[37]

In Lynn, the issue came up several times, beginning in the fall of 1842 when a writer who called himself "Plain Dealer" debated another called "A True Washingtonian" in the pages of the *Essex County Washingtonian*. When N. Crosby, Esquire, of Boston, spoke to the Washingtonians in South Danvers, advocating legal suasion for the rum seller, "Plain Dealer" expressed relief that Crosby's was not the standard Washingtonian narrative:

> It is refreshing in these times of *crude* and *coarse remarks* on this subject, to have sound views presented, in a chaste and gentlemanly manner. There is great danger that the public taste will be vitiated, by the style of address that is becoming too common among lecturers on temperance. . . . It is the duty of those who have spent their lives in the gutter, when they ask the attention of those who have not condescended to grovel with them, to clean themselves and to appear in their best array, both in *speech* and *person;* and not to endeavor to bring their hearers down to the condition in which they have been so depraved.[38]

These comments were answered the following week by "A True

37. For a discussion of the impact of these tales on literature, see David Reynolds, *Beneath the American Renaissance: The Subversive Imagination in the Age of Emerson and Melville* (Cambridge, 1989), pp. 67–74.

38. *Essex County Washingtonian*, October 27, 1842.

Washingtonian," who pointed out, first, that the attack was not simply on coarse language but on the reformed drunkards, who were the heart and soul of Washingtonianism, "a once degraded, though now respectable class." It was unfair, the writer went on, to criticize the reformed drunks, because "some of this class are not quite so polished in their language and because they do not and cannot appear in public with such '*an array [both in?] speech and person*' as do some of our lily-fingered declaimers." Plain Dealer did not consider the "gutter-graduate so important as a college-graduate . . . because, he cant discourse quite so learn-edly and elegantly as the latter."[39]

Referring to "Plain Dealer's" article as a "burlesque upon Washingtonianism" which did not "show Christian spirit," the author reminded his opponent of the godliness of the reformed inebriate, saying, "If he has been a little lower in the gutter than your correspondent, he bears no less the image of God." More to the point, however, "A True Washingtonian" launched a critique on the moral pretensions of bourgeois culture. "Have we not been bored again and again, in times past, by flowery language, by high wrought figures, &c? And what has been accomplished by all such performances?" he asked in exasperation. Arguing that such performances were worthless, he expressed relief that "God in his mercy raised up a Hawkins from the gutter and sent him forth to utter '*crude and coarse remarks*' to his brother drunkard."[40]

In focusing on the language of Washingtonians, several impor-tant issues were being raised. First, by inverting the style of middle-class reform, Washingtonians called attention to the con-structed nature of moral authority which fostered middle-class discourse.[41] Second, the enactments of these inversions in the first person raised some troubling questions. Drunkards had been talked *about* by respectable temperance reformers, and their degradation explored in great detail, so the stories them-

39. *Essex County Washingtonian*, November 3, 1842.
40. Ibid.
41. For a discussion of how inversions both define and question the absolute-ness of social boundaries, see *The Reversible World*, ed. Barbara Babcock (Ithaca, N.Y., 1978).

selves were not so much the issue. But rather than being the objects of temperance oratory, these Washingtonian narrators had made themselves the subjects by speaking their own stories and establishing a potent model of agency. This creation of agency, and the efficacy of the storytelling, as much as any inherent immorality, made their narratives a threat.[42] Thus, "A True Washingtonian" would argue:

> It is the unlettered *"gutter graduate"* standing up in his rude style presenting a history of his sufferings, which has touched the sympathies of the people, and brought conviction to the inebriate, and induced him to sign the pledge and quit forever the intoxicating bowl. If his coarse expressions have excited a smile, his doleful story has started the tear and enlisted the feelings of the philanthropic. True Washingtonianism does not despise the drunkard, or scout the reformed man for uttering some *"crude and coarse remarks."* And none, I think but a stony hearted man or a bigot could manufacture such a communication as the one under consideration.[43]

When "Plain Dealer" responded to this defense, he would continue to hammer away at the dangers of these drunkards speaking and the immorality of their performances: "I rejoice in their reformation, and all I ask of them is, to continue reformed in all respects, and not to glory in boasting of their degradation." Attempting to somehow recast the authority structure of the Washingtonians in midstream, "Plain Dealer" distinguished between the founding of the movement and its continued existence: "It may have been well for a *Hawkins* to have done this, but it will not do for every drunkard to attempt to follow in the track of *Hawkins* for he cannot do it. That *peculiar power* so success-

---

42. The distinction between the act of storytelling and the content of the stories is an important one and separates the activities of the Washingtonians from such middle-class sensationalists as George Lippard. This distinction is not clear to David Reynolds, who lumps both groups under the heading "immoral reformers" (*Beneath the American Renaissance*, pp. 54–91).

43. *Essex County Washingtonian*, November 3, 1842.

fully exerted by Hawkins, can never be attained by mercenary imitators."[44]

Another contributor to the *Essex County Washingtonian* also showed signs of concern about the narratives that were becoming popular among members of the organization, and he criticized the "expedients," both oral and written, which were being used simply "to attract attention." He went on to explain in more detail: "Some mis-spell their words in the Jack Downing, or Sam Slick style. . . . Others make all sorts of caricatures, and sad pictures to attract notice." These attempts, the author believed, were more appropriate for "the comic almanack" than for the Washingtonian movement.[45]

"G.H.C." demanded to know why working men insisted that "they must have facts plainly set off, without any attempts at beauty of style—theory must be broached in terms more common than concise and plain." Arguing that plain-speaking was not always the most accurate way to convey an idea, he criticized those who complained of "scholarship on the part of a lecturer, or a minister, for using language which in reality is much more easy to be understood by all, than what are styled the 'common terms.'—If an expression is *common* it does not always follow that it is *clear.*"[46]

When the Essex County Washingtonians convened in South Andover the following year, they met a rather "cold" reception for similar reasons, and John B. Souther, their president, blamed this coldness in part on the hostility of the faculty and students of nearby Andover Theological Seminary to their efforts. A writer from the seminary responded with an attack on "brawling characters" and "those men who go about telling their old drunken frolics *for a living.*" The temperance cause, he felt, had been degraded by the Washingtonian style. "Temperance Conventions should be better employed than in listening to silly, dogrel rhymes, sung by a poor, worthless fellow, who, for want of better employment, goes from town to town telling over his own misdeeds and degradation," the seminary student complained. This

44. *Essex County Washingtonian*, November 10, 1842.
45. *Essex County Washingtonian*, December 15, 1842.
46. *Essex County Washingtonian*, December 22, 1842.

approach to temperance reform, he believed, only undermined the entire temperance movement, making it ridiculous to the entire community. Challenging the type of leadership the former inebriates were creating with their stories, the writer continued: "We rejoice to have drunkards reform, but we cannot fall down and worship a reformed drunkard, neither can we consider him as entitled to our obsequious regard solely because he has once been a most miserable sot." The Washingtonians had gone too far if they thought they were somehow superior to traditional temperance reformers, and the writer suggested that they "abstain entirely from abusing other and better men than themselves."[47]

Washingtonians, of course, fought back against these charges and maintained that their style of colorful speaking was the only effective way to reform drunkards. "The Torrent Myself," writing for the New Hampshire paper, the *White Mountain Torrent*, argued: "Legislators, lawyers, doctors, and ministers cannot make us drunkards, neither can they make us sober." Lyman Beecher, he said, was a prime example of the ineffectiveness of middle-class reformers: "His sermons on intemperance were read and admired. But his influence was like that of the moon. He was *too far off*." Washingtonian Jonathan Kittridge, however, rose "up from the gutter, working with Herculean power, at the very foundations of King Alcohol's temple." It was when Kittridge and other Washingtonians began to rely on the legislature and the churches for leadership that the cause began to falter. The writer then went on to praise the coarse language of the Washingtonians and the simple people from whom it sprang, noting, "This world was never yet reformed by gentle milk-and-water addresses. If you would remove a great evil, you must go at it with a great soul, that scorns to spend its time in culling soft words from the dictionary." Casting the Washingtonians in the tradition of the Apostles, he reiterated the importance of their common origins in effecting significant reform:

> Jesus Christ was the greatest reformer this world ever saw, and he was the reputed son of a carpenter, born in a stable. . . . He knew if the gospel ever prevailed, it must be received by the

47. *Essex County Washingtonian*, January 25, 1844.

people, and he chose from among the people, his immediate disciples and Apostles. The twelve, so far as we know their origin, were men of low degree. Your high born, and rich, and educated, and well bred, *with rare exceptions*, are not worth a cent for reformers. . . . Give me the hatters, the blacksmiths, the farmers, the laboring people, for reformers. Such men as Hawkins, Mitchell, Robinson, Houston, and a host of others, right from the ditch. . . . I am a farmer. I call upon my brother farmers to look about them, and see what the temperance cause has done, and is doing for the laborer.[48]

Each time the Washingtonians recounted their narratives of metamorphosis from drunkenness to sobriety, they transformed themselves from objects of pity to agents of their own destiny. Their critique of middle-class claims to moral superiority was evident in their reversals of the conventions of reform discourse. But reversals, as many scholars have pointed out, do not necessarily indicate a desire for change. Indeed, the very success of reversible behavior depends on maintenance of the status quo.[49]

Religious Dimensions of Profane Experience

As these comments suggest, the conflict in New England between Washingtonians and main-line temperance reformers centered on the issue of religion as well as on the issue of legal coercion versus moral suasion. While both Washingtonians and main-line temperance leaders might agree that the massive reformation of drunkards was proof of divine intervention, they were not likely to agree on the role of the former inebriates in this great drama. John Marsh, an important temperance advocate who was a great supporter of the Washingtonians (at least in their early days), still challenged their independence and tried to subsume their movement under the broader plan of temperance reform, which had been developing for decades. He argued that

48. *White Mountain Torrent,* February 16, 1844.
49. *Reversible World* (ed. Babcock).

these earlier activities were "God's preparatory work. . . . The reformation of the drunkards of the nation could not have been accomplished without it; and if accomplished, public sentiment would not have sustained it." This argument had important implications: Marsh was claiming authorship of the Washingtonian reforms for the more traditional temperance group he represented. Indeed, he went on in his article to suggest that God's great plan of redemption might be beyond the understanding of the Washingtonians, saying, "They in their heart may have no reference to this great end. But God uses them as instruments of his own purposes."[50] By denying that the Washingtonians had any idea of the larger goals and meaning of the temperance movement, Marsh was also denying them the possibility of leadership. How could they lead a movement they did not even understand?

A similar issue inhered in the debate over the influence of popular revivalist Elder Jacob Knapp on the founding of the Washingtonians. It was Knapp's lecture in Baltimore which the founders of the movement had attended the night they were inspired to found the Washingtonians. Traditional temperance reformers, in an attempt to claim credit for the Washingtonian movement, eventually seized on this connection as an indication of their influence. William Mitchell, in particular, was outraged over this attempt to subsume Washingtonianism under the traditional temperance banner. The *New England Cataract, Berkshire, Franklin, and Hampshire Washingtonian* (which had just been started that summer of 1844 as a "Washingtonian" newspaper that supported prohibition) backed the traditional temperance reformers on this point, in an attempt to undermine the importance of the founders of the movement, which the newspaper claimed

was originated in God thro' his ministering servant Mr. Knapp, and started in the mysterious way with which we are all familiar. Now why should we wish to snatch the wreath from the

50. John Marsh, "The Hand of God in the Reformation of Drunkards," *American National Preacher* 17 (September 1842): 201, 197.

great ruler of events and place it on the brow of W. K. Mitchell or any other man? It is to the artist that belongs the credit of erecting a beautiful structure and not the tools used in constructing;—it is to the artist that belongs the credit of a beautiful painting and not to his brushes.

Again, the leaders of the Washingtonian movement, the reformed drunkards, were to be seen as little more than tools. If Mitchell was to receive any credit at all, "it must be for carrying out the principles revealed by God through his servant the Rev. Mr. Knapp."[51]

It is at this point—with the question of whether or not the Washingtonians were merely passive instruments of God's will who had no real understanding of his ends—that we can see the difference between the perspective of Marsh and prohibitionist Washingtonians versus a Washingtonian such as "A Teetotaler." From "A Teetotaler's" point of view, the reformed drunkards were not only leaders but also prophets. They had been saved by God, but at that point their passive role ended. Through their stories about their experiences of being drunkards, they were the only ones invested with the power to save other inebriates. Indeed, as a result of their past degradations, they possessed the emotions that were necessary to redeem other drunkards. Thus, "A Teetotaler" explained, "The grand success in the new system, is *the treatment exhibited by the reformer* to his poor fallen brother; his *humility in calling himself a drunkard,* in putting himself on a level with this loathsome offender." To call oneself a drunkard was the truly Christlike behavior. It was something other temperance reformers could never do, for as the author went on to point out, "*It is he who, having known and felt the same miseries,* and having the heart to feel for others' woes, has the self-denial, the magnanimity, the Christian virtue, to put his feelings in operation, and his Christian principle in practice, regardless of a haughty and sneering world."[52] As experience became the basis

---

51. *New England Cataract, Berkshire, Franklin, and Hampshire Washingtonian,* August 15, 1844.
52. "Teetotaler," *The New Impulse,* pp. 9–10, 19, 20.

of authority, the victim was transformed into the savior. Washingtonians cast themselves in the image of Christ and thus used the mantle of Christianity to legitimize their positions of leadership in the temperance movement.

This use of the Christian tradition is particularly interesting, for it points out the way in which the Washingtonians used Protestant beliefs to challenge mainstream evangelical temperance leadership. Most historians of the movement see the secular orientation of the Washingtonians as the main source of contention between that group and traditional temperance reformers. For example, Robert Hampel has noted that "evangelicals and non-evangelicals alike bridled at the secularity of many Washingtonian meetings, and found the open anti-clerical prejudice of others disturbing."[53] With William Mitchell, in particular, that was a problem, as religious dissent was transformed into blasphemy and Mitchell was toasted by some Washingtonian groups as "the saviour of the world."[53] Historians have attributed the piety in the movement, which is too blatant to ignore, to the employers and entrepreneurs in the organization rather than to the working people. Thus, Sean Wilentz argues that in New York City, where "pious masters" assumed many positions of leadership in the movement, "the pan-Protestant moralism characteristic of entrepreneurs always found a place in the new movement's public ceremonies."[54]

Certainly both Hampel and Wilentz are correct in pointing out how the secular aspects of the Washingtonian movement were a social threat, but we must remember that an equally important threat grew out of the Washingtonian's expression of religious commitment, and that it was by no means the religion of middle-class employers. The Washingtonian style of speaking was rooted

53. Robert Hampel, *Temperance and Prohibition in Massachusetts, 1813–1852* (Ann Arbor, Mich., 1982), p. 18; *New England Cataract, Berkshire, Franklin, Hampshire Washingtonian*, August 15, 1844.

54. Sean Wilentz, *Chants Democratic: New York City and the Rise of the American Working Class, 1788–1850* (New York, 1984), p. 311. Jed Dannenbaum makes a similar point about the anticlericalism of Washingtonians in Cincinnati (*Drink and Disorder: Temperance Reform in Cincinnati from the Washingtonian Revival to the WCTU* [Chicago, 1984], pp. 39–40). This moralism was particularly characteristic of the Washingtonians who supported prohibition.

in the tradition of rowdy revivalists rather than staid, middle-class preachers. As one critic pointed out, Washingtonian speakers "like the preachers at Camp-meetings, aim at coarse and vulgar expressions to excite a temporary smile."[55] In their telling of their life stories, they were drawing on pulpit storytelling traditions that had become important in revivalism. In evoking the tradition of the Christ's Apostles, they were drawing on ideals of primitive Christianity which were also a part of popular evangelicalism.

The religious elements of Washingtonianism, however, became subversive as the movement—particularly the movement committed to moral suasion and the efficacy of the reformed drunkards' narratives—became not a branch of the evangelical empire but a challenge to it as a surrogate religious movement. The radicalization of the religious impulse may have happened without Washingtonians being fully aware of it. Here was a problem that left more traditional reformers and religious leaders caught between a rock and a hard place. Many of these reformed drunkards welcomed contact with religious organizations and other moral reform groups. They patterned their own meetings on religious services and often opened with a prayer, followed by testimonies of members and punctuated by the singing of temperance hymns, all of which had the earmarks of a religious meeting. In Augusta, Maine, the Washingtonians even appointed one of their own members to be chaplain: "an aged brother whom we all respect and esteem."[56]

Ministers also often addressed the Washingtonians, or at least led the opening prayer. While this format no doubt grew out of respect for evangelical religious services, the result was that Washingtonians were, in effect, competing with traditional Protestant denominations. And as the Washingtonians continued to grow, ministerial support began to flag.

This issue proved to be a particular problem in Providence, Rhode Island. Ministers from a variety of churches addressed the Washingtonians of that town during the early days of their exis-

55. *Essex County Washingtonian,* October 27, 1842.
56. *The Washingtonian* (Augusta), July 14, 1841.

tence. But after about eight months, the organization had difficulty lining up religious speakers. The frustration of the group was clear when they resolved that "as we have applied to various Clergymen of this City for their aid in Preaching on the Temperance Cause . . . that we have not received. Therefore, Resolved that for the future we will do our own Preaching, and if they chuse to help us we will thank them."[57]

The local Washingtonian newspaper also noted the "spirit of indifference which has taken possession of, and the heavy torpor and lethargy which has fallen upon, the Clergy in reference to this holy cause." The paper went on to charge that once the Washingtonians had entered the temperance arena, the clergy had withdrawn and "rolled the whole burden of reform upon their [the Washingtonians'] shoulders." Suggesting that perhaps jealousy and misunderstanding lay behind the clergy's perception of the Washingtonian mission, the newspaper urged that they work together in a two-stage process: the Washingtonians would cure the inebriate of intoxication and prepare his will for religious conversion:

> It is utterly vain, to endeavor to bring moral motives to bear upon a mind in a state of inebriation. Consciousness must do its perfect work, reason must be on its throne. The will must be in a state of complete subjection. Until all this had been accomplished with the thousands of drunkards in our land, your office work could not begin, with them. The Washingtonians have done the work. Their subjects are ready for your influence.

Ministers who held back from working with the Washingtonians did so because they were annoyed that they had not been in charge of the entire conversion process or because the first stage had been accomplished by "*humble* instrumentalities."[58]

The Sixth Ward Washingtonians, an offshoot of the parent organization in Providence, met at the Roger Williams Free Will

57. Records of the Providence Washington Total Abstinence Society, April 26, 1842 (RIHS).
58. *The Samaritan*, March 30, 1842.

Baptist Church and adopted an even more aggressive tactic in their attempt to gain ministerial support. They appointed a committee "to invite every Clergyman in this City, to deliver before this Society, at least one Temperance Address." Should any of the ministers refuse, the committee was instructed "to ask their objection in writing, and report the same to this Society."[59]

The dangers to organized religion which were inherent in the Washingtonian leadership were multiplied as some Washingtonians began to think of their movement as "practical Christianity," a notion that provided a basis for criticizing other religious denominations. The basic ethic of practical Christianity was "doing unto others as we would have them do to us, in like circumstances." "A Teetotaler" developed this idea and criticized members of traditional denominations in light of Washingtonian ethics. The former were often "Christians . . . of the modern sort." Their Christian commitment was external rather than internal. They were "willing to be *called* Christians, so far as it may advance their reputation, and them in business, and serve as a mantle of charity to cover a multitude of sins." Such nominal Christians violated the basic laws of Christian ethics in their relationships with their fellow human beings. Barely preserving "the externals of decency," they were "ready to say to the suffering poor, Be ye warmed and fed, but do not the things that are needful." The Washingtonians, on the other hand, provided both emotional support and economic assistance to those of their brethren who needed it. The needy drunkard who signed the pledge was immediately given aid; the reformed man who was temporarily disabled was likewise offered assistance (much in the manner of a mutual benefit society). The writer concluded his criticisms of traditional Protestantism by noting, "The practical Christianity of these humble reformers may well put many of the pastors and churches of our land to blush for their cold, formal religion, and dead faith."[60]

The criticism had much in common with the antiinstitutionalism that developed within the moral reform movement gener-

59. *The Samaritan*, August 17, 1842.
60. "Teetotaler," *The New Impulse*, p. 21.

ally, as emphasis was placed on individual conversion and the compromising positions of churches and political parties were scorned. "Practical Christianity" was also the religion of many "come-outers," who felt themselves under a new dispensation, and they saw the Washingtonians as a logical extension of their movement—or rather, they saw "come-outerism" and nonresistance as a logical extension of Washingtonianism. Indeed, the *Essex County Washingtonian* became a "come-outer" newspaper under the editorship of Henry Clapp. The publisher of the newspaper, a shoe manufacturer by the name of Christopher Robinson, removed himself from the Methodist church in Lynn to become a come-outer as well. The come-outers formed a separate group of Washingtonians in Lynn and held "free meetings" both inside and outdoors, in which people could speak whenever they wanted and no one was a leader. This group was apparently separate from other Washingtonian organizations in the town, such as the newly formed Young Men's Washingtonian Total Abstinence Society, headed by William Fraser. But Fraser spoke at many of the free meetings, and the Young Men's Society may have shared in the spirit of the come-outers, for Mr. Porter, the Methodist preacher in Lynn, refused to announce meetings of the Young Men's Society.

Caroline Fraser, William's wife and president of the Young Ladies Charitable Temperance Society, would urge women to stick with the movement despite criticisms of come-outerism. "I am sorry to hear, and it is indeed painful to state, that there are young ladies who shrink from this, their duty, upon the plea, that they are afraid that it is some '*Come-Outer stuff*,'" she complained to the newspaper. She dismissed these fears as an absurd misreading of the organization at the same time she acknowledged it as a possibility. "How ridiculous, how absurd, that any reasonable person should suppose, that the young *women* wished to get up a society for discussion, under the name of 'Charitable Temperance' Society. But, supposing that there was some 'come-outer stuff,' should that deter them from doing their duty?"[61]

Henry Clapp would back up Mrs. Fraser, though he laid the

61. *Essex County Washingtonian*, March 7, 1844.

blame more squarely on the clergy than on the women. "The ministers want the poor women to stay at home and work their fingers to the bone to help pay their salaries, instead of wasting their money upon Gutter Graduates, and wasting their time at temperance meetings." Clapp would make a similar criticism of the clergy's abuse of poor women a couple of months later.[62]

In Norfolk County, similar charges of radicalism appear to have been made. "E.Q.," answering the charges of the *Temperance Journal* that nonresistants had a disproportionate influence in the movement, contended that there were only two nonresistants in the Norfolk County organization (one of whom was the very prolific Rev. John M. Spear).[63]

The threat posed by this religious orientation was immediately clear to the American Temperance Society. Their newspaper, the *Journal*, criticized the writer of the essay on practical Christianity for "a disposition, which we have noticed elsewhere, to make this wonderful reform, not merely the work of God, this we fully believe, but a religious reform in itself, and something superior to the piety found in ministers and churches." Choking particularly on the criticisms of formal religion, the writer of the article admonished: "Everything in its place; temperance in its place; philanthropy in its place; and religion in its place . . . reformation from drunkenness is not, of course, religion, nor is the most intense interest or arduous labor in reforming others."[64] Washingtonians were trying to reform not only drunkards but religion as well; theirs was a critique not of personal behavior but of religious organization.

The message inherent in this antiinstitutionalism was particularly threatening given the social position of the accusers and the accused. Many of the former were working people, and they were pointing their fingers directly at the religion of the emerging entrepreneurial class. They were also failing to show a deference to their "betters" which was obviously expected of them.

62. *Essex County Washingtonian*, May 9, 1844.
63. *Norfolk Washingtonian* (Dedham), August 11, 1843.
64. Quoted in William George Hawkins, *Life of John H. W. Hawkins* (Boston, 1859), p. 167. The antiinstitutional impulse in antebellum reform movements is analyzed by John L. Thomas in "Romantic Reform in America, 1815–1865," *American Quarterly* 17 (Winter 1965): 656–681.

In Portsmouth, New Hampshire, for example, street meetings sprang up, though not of the come-outer variety. They were simply Washingtonian meetings held in places where public drinking might be taking place. These meetings were tolerated and even condoned by the "respectable" portion of the community, as long as they took place in the working-class sections of town. But when they chose to have a meeting in front of a prestigious hotel, criticism developed: "Genteel strangers, officers and others who visited and boarded there, had been very much annoyed . . . though it might be very well to have such meetings on the Parade or at the Spring." Some Washingtonians were suitably cowed by these remonstrances and discouraged such meetings for the future, but others were not.

James L. Bufford, who was on the editorial committee of the *Portsmouth Washingtonian,* defended the practice and went straight to the heart of the social antagonisms that the meetings revealed. He noted that some had criticized the street meetings as counterproductive because they turned respectable citizens against the temperance cause since "ignorant and unlettered men, have taken the opportunity then and there under the cover of Washingtonianism to defame the characters of respectable citizens—to be personal and libelous in their remarks, thereby creating a bitter opposition among a class who have hertofore stood on neutral ground." Acknowledging that "a large proportion of those who have enlisted under our banner, make no pretensions to learning," Bufford went on to blame the problems of interaction on the wealthy of the community:

Wealth and name have created a barrier which can never be overthrown, at least until society arrives at that state when men shall be valued not according to the wealth he may represent or the name he may bear, but in proportion to his advancement in the scale of moral and intellectual worth, in proportion to the benefit he confers upon his fellow men, the good which he accomplishes in the world at large.[65]

Workingmen who participated in the Washingtonian move-

65. *Portsmouth Washingtonian,* August 24, 1843.

ment created a new kind of moral authority for themselves in their homes and in society at large. Drawing on the traditions of an evangelical religion that had previously threatened them, they created their own religion in which they were the ministers. Their gospel was a powerful one, and they carried it into other arenas as well. Their influence became most evident in the labor movement that was reemerging in the 1840s. Washingtonians had redirected the concerns of workingmen to include private issues of the home and spirituality, as well as the public questions of economic exchange. The two would be merged by labor activists. Reestablishing their moral authority within their homes, workingmen had a new cause in challenging their employers.

Chapter 6

The Petitioning of Artisans and Operatives: Means and Ends in the Struggle for a Ten-Hour Day

In November 1843, an editorial in the *Boston Daily Bee* championed the new style of labor-organizing in the region. "Time was, when a 'strike,' as it is called, was synonymous with riot and violation of the peace of society," the editor recalled. The new style, he claimed, was characterized by "temperate yet firm action. No acts of violence . . . no mobbish outbreaks." Instead, workingmen had "risen in their might, stated fearlessly their wrongs, and appealed to public opinion to sustain them in their struggle for justice." Labor reform had arrived.[1]

Labor struggles in New England were not simply conflicts within the community, but contests over who would control the community. The concern for public opinion was part of a larger effort on the part of labor activists to create community pressure on employers, particularly factory owners, who exploited working people. Labor reformers used the strategies and discourse of middle-class moral reformers in promoting their campaign, but their appropriation of these techniques represented a challenge

---

1. *Boston Daily Bee*, November 4, 1843. On the New England Labor Movement of the 1840s, see John R. Commons et al., *History of Labor in the United States*, vol. 1 (New York, 1918), pp. 536–544; Norman Ware, *The Industrial Worker, 1840–1860* (1924; reprint, New York, 1974), pp. 125–148. For a discussion of how labor reform grew following the Civil War, see David Montgomery, *Beyond Equality: Labor and the Radical Republicans, 1862–1872* (1967; reprint, New York, 1972), pp. 135–196.

rather than a capitulation to middle-class control of community morals.

As in the 1830s, the issue of time would be the predominant one, uniting artisans and operatives—men, women, and children—not in a strike but in successive petitioning campaigns aimed at state legislatures. In 1842, the Ten Hour Republican Association circulated petitions in Attleborough, Mansfield, Taunton, New Bedford, and Fall River. More were submitted again in 1843, this time from New Bedford, Lowell, Fall River, and Newburyport.[2] By 1844, the movement for a shorter workday gained momentum. The ten-hour drive of 1844 began in the spring with members of the building trades in Fall River and culminated in the creation of the New England Workingmen's Association in the fall of 1844. The Workingmen's Association drew on many aspects of the New England Association of Farmers, Mechanics, and Other Workingmen, which had preceded it a decade earlier. Local organizing took place by community rather than trade, except in the big cities. Good moral character rather than wage-earning status was the primary requirement for membership. Pledges, petitioning, and consciousness-raising about the control of culture were the strategies for change. Indeed, this time strikes were explicitly eschewed as excessively coercive, reflecting the radicalization of the moral reform impulse.

In tone as well as strategy, New England labor activism bore the mark of popular evangelicalism and the Washingtonian temperance movement. As a result, the moral-reform character of the labor movement was more personal and religious than it had been in the 1830s, dependent on spiritual progress as much as on intellectual accomplishment. Workingmen who knew the Washingtonian movement felt more comfortable with this new kind of morality, as they moved to assert it in opposition to employers. In so doing, they readjusted the boundary between the private world of salvation and moral reform, and the public world of

2. Charles Persons, "New England Workingmen's Association, 1840–1848," in *Labor Laws and Their Enforcement, with Special Reference to Massachusetts,* ed. Susan M. Kingsbury (New York, 1911), pp. 24–26. The Fall River petition came from a group known as the Association for Industry. The Lowell petitions were signed by women as well as by men.

economic relations. These new concerns also brought the formerly secular male labor movement into a sphere they could share with women and clergymen. This was particularly important because the family contract system of labor had eroded significantly during the 1830s, altering the role that household heads assumed in the relationships of many women and children with their employers in southern New England. The individual rather than the household had become the focus of contracts. Support from these women and ministers became key elements in the movement, adding another level of difference to the differences already created by occupation and locale. As a result, the dynamics of labor-organizing in the 1840s would differ significantly from those of the 1830s.

The lack of interest in striking during this period needs some comment, for the strike is generally viewed as the preeminent indicator of class conflict, or at least a recognition on the part of wage earners that their interests are opposed to those of employers. Conversely, the refusal to strike suggests deference, an identification with one's employers, or a belief in social mobility rather than class identity. Bruce Laurie, in describing working people of Philadelphia, has suggested that striking would be tantamount to acknowledging class polarities, something evangelical working people of the 1840s were reluctant to do. In a similar vein, Jama Lazerow has written of William Young's religious critique of labor conditions of New England during the 1840s, arguing that "Young and those like him tended to discourage any labor action beyond testimony and debate for fear it might lead to conflict within the community." Moreover, "Young's faith in moral power . . . hinged on a recognition of God's control over human affairs. It therefore discouraged any action against employers." By action, one presumes that Lazerow means a strike.[3]

At this point it might be worth remembering the journeymen bootmakers in Boston who won the right to a closed shop in the 1840s by pledging not to work with anyone who was not a mem-

3. Bruce Laurie, *Working People of Philadelphia, 1800–1850* (Philadelphia, 1980), pp. 140–147; Jama Lazerow, "Religion and Labor Reform in Antebellum America: The World of William Field Young," *American Quarterly* 38 (Summer 1986): 278–279.

ber of their society. The pledge was not directed against employers, but it allowed the journeymen to exercise control in their workplace and provided them with an important measure of power at the expense of their employers. The coercive aspects of their behavior are inescapable, but in the tradition of moral reform this coercion derived from control of oneself rather than from an explicit attempt to control others. Set against the practical problems of trying to organize a strike across trades and towns, an attempt that had failed miserably ten years before, the moral-reform model made better sense to these labor activists.

These were the rules of play for confrontation in New England. The pledging of the bootmakers would be picked up by the carpenters in Fall River in the struggle for a ten-hour day, but the strategy would eventually be abandoned for petitioning. Petitioning was a different form of self-assertion, which more effectively accommodated the differences of the region as the struggle for a ten-hour day moved from conflict at the workplace to conflict within the community, and as women joined with men in a broad coalition. Indeed, the strategy of petitioning and the composition of the labor movement were related.

Petitioning as a gesture meant different things to different people. The form itself had become increasingly radicalized as a result of the antislavery petitioning campaigns of the 1830s. Moreover, as a political activity, its meaning could vary, depending on whether one was petitioning for oneself or for others and whether the petitioner was a man or a woman. The labor movement of the 1840s inherited this complex perspective on petitioning as labor protest became a full-fledged wing of the reform impulse. These varying interpretations of petitioning were particularly important for labor-organizing because they provided enough flexibility to allow groups that would otherwise have been divided to work together.

In April 1844, approximately 250 carpenters and masons in Fall River agreed to work on a ten-hour system. They formed a Mechanics Association and started a labor newspaper, *The Mechanic*. Their group may have included some contractors as well as wage earners, but it seems to have been confined to the building trades in its early days. Building-trades workers in Fall River were particularly sensitive to the length of their workday that year, and they were in a position to do something about it. The town had burned down the year before, and a massive building campaign was under way. Carpenters and masons were being pushed to work more than usual, but as a result they held more bargaining power. This position of economic strength undoubtedly aided them in taking a strong position against strikes and physical coercion and arguing that they were merely honoring a pledge not to work more than ten hours a day and that they were committed to principles of moral suasion. But the commitment to moral suasion was more than a rhetorical ploy. Concern for both morality and salvation pervaded the language of labor-organizing in Fall River. Thus, when the tools of all day men recruited from Maine mysteriously ended up in Mount Hope Bay, the Mechanics Association vociferously condemned the perpetrators. One resolution stated: "We will be bold and uncompromising in advocating the cause in which we are engaged, claiming for ourselves the use of that MORAL POWER which is mighty to overturn long cherished systems of oppression and wrong, and to tumble into dust those false gods to which the rights of many are offered as sacrifice." They also went on to suggest that the destruction had come from those opposed to the Association, "in order to cast a stigma upon the upright, manly and straight forward course which we have thus far pursued."[4]

However, this moral-reform strategy provided a model for exclusion rather than for inclusion. Implicit in the organization of the Mechanics Association was the exclusion of factory workers. The wealthy mill owner, Nathaniel Borden, said as much when he criticized their demands in the pages of the local Whig newspaper, *The Monitor*. He argued that although he realized the carpenters and masons did not propose "to apply the rule to mill help," it was likely that if a ten-hour day was established in the building trades, it would soon penetrate the factory walls. "It is idle to suppose that this system can be adopted in part and have the other part remain satisfied," he pointed out. "If the rule be

4. *The Mechanic* (Fall River), June 29, 1844.

adopted at all, it must eventually be general." Distinguishing between commercial centers that depended on "traffic" for their profit, and productive centers such as Fall River, which depended on manufacturing, Borden argued that in the former case a ten-hour day might be instituted without causing financial damage but that in the latter case, cutthroat competition made such a reduction in hours unfeasible.[5] In other words, the fate of artisans in Fall River was far more intimately connected with local factory production than with conditions in the building trades of New York and Philadelphia.

In part, the reluctance of the mechanics to embrace factory workers may have been dictated by practical concerns: the need for carpenters and masons to rebuild the town gave members of the building trades a leverage that factory workers did not have. But it is also clear that the artisans regarded factory workers as a dependent population that was incapable of helping itself, the antithesis of those pursuing an "upright, manly and straight forward course." "P.," who wrote to *The Mechanic* during the summer of 1844, picked up on Borden's objection and criticized the factory owners for their recalcitrance, noting, "It is probable that the *true reason* why the mechanics' request has been so bitterly opposed in this place, is that the factory people would be next forward with their petition." However, he did not see this as a reason for mechanics and operatives to form a united opposition. Instead he asked, "Is there not some American Sadler, Oastler or Ashley who will rise and defend the factory woman and child? Among the factory owners are there no American Woods and Fieldings, who, though interested in the factory system, will come out nobly for a ten hour's rule?"[6] He was, of course, referring to the English reformers. Mechanics throughout New England had followed the British factory debates, which were reprinted in such labor newspapers as *The Mechanic*, and had

5. *The Monitor* (Fall River), April 13, 1844. Further examples of the role of mill owners in this struggle may be found in the discussion of Micah Ruggles (*The Mechanic*, May 18, 1844) and in the fictional portrayal of a mill owner (*The Mechanic*, June 15, 1844).

6. *The Mechanic*, August 10, 1844. The article also criticizes the religious pretensions of the mill owner (probably Borden) who left a church because "there was some appearance of evil in it."

cheered the benevolence of the man who had pushed to limit the workday of factory operatives. These artisans were also quite aware of the pathetic, helpless, and dependent portrait of factory workers which had emerged in these debates, and this portrait no doubt reinforced a similar vision of factory operatives in the United States.

Many mechanics in Fall River recognized that industrialists such as Nathaniel Borden controlled the building trades as well as textile production, but this did not lead them inevitably to embrace operatives as partners in the struggle for a shorter workday. In the early phases of their movement they looked to masters rather than to factory workers in attempts to build their opposition. For example, "P" claimed that the mechanics knew "their greatest enemies are the corporate companies." Rather than turning to factory workers to form a coalition, however, he claimed he "had hoped that some of the petty boss carpenters, for whom the ten hour system would have wrought real good, would have embraced the opportunity of elevating themselves. But, *slave like*, they kiss the hand that smites them."[7]

While the mechanics in Fall River did not extend their demands to include operatives, they still sought their support—unsuccessfully. Ruby Hatch, wife of Gideon Hatch, called the women of town to her house on May 7 to form an auxiliary, the Fall River Ladies Mechanic Association, "for the benefit of the Ten Hour system in this place." Placing an ad in *The Mechanic*, she urged all the women in town to join, particularly "those who work, or ever have worked."[8] Many women responded to the invitation, but not all. While family members of artisans were anxious to join, operatives were not. "Onward," who attended the first meeting, tried to garner the support of wage-earning women after the first meeting by asking, "Who . . . in this wide world, can sympathize with the ten hour man in his struggle to breathe—a *freeman*—if you cannot?"[9] Apparently it did not occur to "Onward" to ask the artisans if they could sympathize

---

7. *The Mechanic*, June 8, 1844.
8. *The Mechanic*, May 4, 1844.
9. *The Mechanic*, May 11, 1844.

with operatives who might also want to breathe; his assumption was that the movements must be carried on separately.

Although factory workers held back from the movement, other members of the community did not. Public displays of support would come throughout the spring and summer of 1844 with speeches by local clergymen and fairs organized by women. But the ultimate demonstration came with the grand Fourth of July celebration, which was meant to demonstrate the community character of the cause. The order of the procession was advertised in an extra edition of *The Mechanic*. Officers and members of the Mechanics Association would lead the way, carrying a banner of the stars and stripes. Following them would be the band and then the officers and members of the Ladies' Ten Hour Association. The committee of arrangements would have the next place, then the clergy, the Washingtonians, town officials, the fire department, and finally any citizens or strangers who cared to join in.[10] *The Mechanic* would later claim that "two thousand of the working men and working women of Fall River, who all have a common sympathy, and whose hearts all beat in unison" had formed the procession.

Several scholars have recently argued that parades were of enormous symbolic significance in the nineteenth century, and on an important holiday, such as the Fourth of July, they were meant to include and represent the entire community, right down to strangers."[11] It is not surprising that the symbolic significance of the ten-hour parade was itself contested as the Whig newspaper (*The Monitor*) which supported the mill owners in town argued there "was no general and united celebration [of Independence Day] by the people" in Fall River. As *The Mechanic* would retort, "The Editor of the *Monitor* does not recognize the working men and women of Fall River as the PEOPLE. Who then are the *people?*" *The Monitor* also attempted to undermine the idea of institutional support for the cause by suggesting that it was unclear whether the Washingtonians who marched did so on

10. *The Mechanic*, July 2, 1844.
11. Mary Ryan, *Women in Public: Between Banners and Ballots, 1825–1880* (Baltimore, 1990), pp. 30–31.

behalf of themselves or their organization. Similarly, the public nature of the cause was at issue. The editor of the *Monitor* had claimed, "The Ten Hour Association formed a procession of both ladies and gentlemen," leading *The Mechanic* to retort:

> This is true. But he aimed a deadly blow at our cause, by rendering it contemptible and private. He ought to have known, and if he had read the advertisement of the celebration, which was posted up in the streets and published in a previous No. of the Mechanic, he would have found that the arrangement was not made for any party or class of our citizens, but for all, without distinction.[12]

This had not been a parade of mechanics agitating for a ten-hour day on the Fourth of July, but a Fourth of July celebration of and for the entire community in which ten hours was meant to be a community and civic goal. This was the community as it should be constituted. In calling for community support, the mechanics had taken a significant step, beyond making pledges, toward creating a more inclusive movement.

The Mechanics Association, however, did not confine itself to Fall River in attempting to build support, but began to look toward a broader regional movement. The distance between artisans and operatives would be challenged as the mechanics began to interact with working people from other towns. In June 1844 the Mechanics Association issued a circular addressed to other artisans in New England, calling for a region-wide convention that would "point out a 'more excellent' system of labor." They hired Simon Hewitt, who was inbetween careers as a phrenologist and a Universalist minister, to promote their cause.[13] With $100 to pay for his expenses, Hewitt traveled through the Blackstone Valley and Essex County in Massachusetts into Con-

12. *The Mechanic*, July 13, 1844.
13. The circular was reprinted in *The Mechanic*, June 22, 1844. Hewitt was given money to travel throughout New England in July of that year (*The Mechanic*, July 27, 1844). His activities as a phrenologist were reported in *The Friend of Man* (Providence), March 25, 1843, when he appeared in Providence in the spring of 1843.

necticut and around Rhode Island, speaking on the importance of a ten-hour day specifically, and on the need to improve the condition of the laboring classes generally. Hewitt's background as a popular lecturer would serve him well in his speaking tour, but he may have had a broader vision of the movement than did some of the mechanics in Fall River. Hewitt was a Fourierist, and the ten-hour day was but one step toward greater world reform for Hewitt, a reform that would touch everyone.

Hewitt's reception varied tremendously from place to place. In the missives he sent back to *The Mechanic* in Fall River, Hewitt tried to make sense of the different intellectual and economic conditions he encountered while carrying the gospel of the Fall River mechanics. In the process of give-and-take which accompanied this exchange, working people throughout New England attempted to incorporate many of the ideals espoused in Fall River, while the mechanics who had sent Hewitt were forced to confront different forms of industrialization as well as different types of organizing.[14] Thus Hewitt's journey was different from that of revivalists and temperance reformers who confronted the same cycles of sin, repentance, and salvation in each town. The reform impulse would have to confront the uneven process of historical transformation explicitly.

One of the first stops Hewitt made was in Lynn. The Mutual Benefit Society of Journeymen Cordwainers in Lynn had corresponded with the Mechanics Association in Fall River and had invited representatives to attend their meeting at the beginning of August. Their initial letter had suggested that their movement had similar moral inclinations. William A. Fraser, president of the Young Men's Total Abstinence Society, as well as corresponding secretary for the Mutual Benefit Society of Journeymen Cordwainers, sent an enthusiastic response to the call for a regional meeting. "We are engaged in a highly important work, a work which recommends itself to every philanthropist," he claimed, "a work which will if carried out, help to redeem the world from poverty and all the vices now existing which arise from poverty."

14. See Philip Foner, "Journal of an Early Labor Organizer," *Labor History* 10 (Spring 1969): 205–227.

Defending the right of the shoemakers to be heard in their struggle, Fraser continued: "They claim the just and moral right, (a
right, given them by their maker,) to live, move and have a being;
a right to fair and honest compensation for their labor."[15]

What Hewitt found in Lynn, however, was a movement radically different from the one shaping up in Fall River. The cordwainers in Lynn were piece workers who had little to say about a
shorter workday. Their demands centered around higher wages,
tighter control of apprenticeship, and an end to the order system.
And far from eschewing strikes, they were in the process of trying
to organize one (an attempt that would ultimately fail).

Given both the means and the ends chosen by the shoemakers,
it is not surprising that Hewitt was a bit uncomfortable with the
movement. He reported to the mechanics in Fall River with some
concern that he had attended a convention there which had been
called "for the special purpose of securing the interests of the
craft," an approach that Hewitt implied was somewhat selfish
and retrograde. He tried to alleviate concern by speculating that
"at the same time a higher principle than mere interest seemed
to lie at the foundation of the movement."[16] Still, in regard to the
resolutions passed by the cordwainers, Hewitt was less than enthusiastic. Refusing to endorse them as "*absolute* truth or right,"
Hewitt nonetheless did find the measures "*expedient.*" Moreover,
the shoemakers were ready to do what they could to support a
region-wide movement. With this in mind, Hewitt tried to justify
the activities in Lynn to his readers back home. "When we consider the disadvantages under which this class of Humanity are,
and have for ages been laboring, we are not to feel surprised at all
if in an assemblage of men like this, much is said and done which
will not commend itself to the judgement of those who have
enjoyed greater advantages."[17] It is not clear to which disadvan-

15. *The Mechanic*, June 22, 1844. For a full discussion of the antebellum labor
movement in Lynn, see Alan Dawley, *Class and Community: The Industrial Revolution in Lynn* (Cambridge, Mass., 1976); Paul Faler, *Mechanics and Manufacturers in the Early Industrial Revolution: Lynn, Massachusetts, 1780–1860* (New
York, 1981); and Mary Blewett, *Men, Women, and Work: Class, Gender, and Protest
in the New England Shoe Industry, 1780–1910* (Urbana, Ill., 1988), pp. 3–141.
16. *The Mechanic*, August 10, 1844.
17. Ibid.

tages Hewitt was referring, although he may have been alluding to the fact that shoemakers made less money than did building-trades workers and thus had to pay more attention to wage issues.

The shoemakers would press unsuccessfully for a strike during the summer of 1844, eventually gaining the support of about one-third of the male cordwainers in Lynn. As hopes for a strike began to fade in the fall, the moral-reform rhetoric of the Fall River mechanics and the emerging New England Workingmen's Association began to assume more prominence. Yet the character of that rhetoric would never approach the religious overtones of the Fall River movement, with its concern for family prayer, church attendance, and salvation. The rhetoric in Lynn was much more consistent with the come-outerism that had begun to show up in the town's Washingtonian and antislavery movements.[18]

"Centre St.," for example, wrote an article for *The Awl* in November about how the truth and justice of their cause proceeded from God, but its religious content was quite vague. The following week, an article reprinted from the *Boston Laborer* suggested that individual thought and investigation were necessary to precede effective action, a prescription that suggested a process similar to that of conversion. "Union is necessary, combined action is necessary, but this cannot be had, without unity of thought and feeling, and this can only be brought about by individual investigation."[19] Indeed, a new history of the labor movement seemed to be in the making as one article in December argued that while men "goaded by necessity . . . banded together," their efforts had met with only "temporary success." What working people needed to succeed was more understanding. "The spirit of the age is a spirit of radical investigation," the writer claimed, for this would arm the people with the "invincible armor of truth." A contributor named Depot made a similar

18. For an excellent discussion of the importance of come-outerism in Lynn and its different strains, see Lewis Perry, *Radical Abolitionism: Anarchy and the Government of God in Antislavery Thought* (Ithaca, N.Y., 1973), pp. 97–128. The differences in the religious and reform rhetoric of these towns is explored more completely in Chapter 7.

19. *The Awl* (Lynn), November 16, 1844; November 23, 1844.

point, as he tried to turn the failure to stage a strike into a success, or at least a cloud with a silver lining:

> More than six months since, we commenced a work of reform in this town, and believing a strike was necessary, we resolved upon that measure. But finding it imbossible [*sic*] to enlist a majority in this movement, and seeing at the same time it was only acting upon the effect, while the cause remained, we have abandoned the idea and resolved to strike deeper, at the root of the evil. Our object, be it understood, is *Moral* and *Social Reform*—to show up society and its evils in all its rottenness.[20]

As part of their attempt to create a moral reform movement, the cordwainers appealed intermittently for female support, and received it—intermittently. Like the mechanics in Fall River, who wanted the support of female operatives, journeymen shoemakers encouraged female shoebinders to attend their meetings and cheer them on. They did not, however, intend to fight any of the economic inequities the women faced.[21] The jours made a couple of appeals for female support early in the summer, perhaps in imitation of the Fall River organization, but after receiving no response they ignored the women during the next couple of months as they tried to organize a strike.

As hopes for a strike faded at the end of the summer, and moral-reform rhetoric grew, so too did appeals to the women. On August 17 it was voted at the cordwainers' meeting "that each member be requested to bring a lady."[22] This move finally paid off in mid-September, when "Centre St." reported: "I was much gratified, on last Saturday evening, to see so large an attendance of *ladies* at the Town Hall. This is right; for certainly the females are as much interested in any undertaking, which has for its object the bettering of the condition of the males, as the males are themselves."[23]

As in Fall River, during the winter months women focused on

20. *The Awl*, March 1, 1845.
21. Blewett, *Men, Women, and Work*, pp. 68–96.
22. *The Awl*, August 21, 1844.
23. *The Awl*, September 18, 1844.

planning social activities to raise money and build morale. Over
the course of the year, a large number of women would give their
names and their time to planning festivities, which were well
attended by the men and women in the town. Many of the women
on the arrangements committee were probably wives, daughters, or sisters of the men in the organization, although actual
linkages are difficult to establish. Given the occupational homogeneity of Lynn during this time, however, there probably were
not too many women outside of the merchant class who did not
have a husband, father, brother, or sweetheart employed in the
shoe trade. Another tie may have come through Washingtonianism. Just as William Fraser's active involvement in the Young
Men's Charitable Temperance Society, as well as the cordwainer's society, suggests an important link between Washingtonianism and labor reform in Lynn, so does his wife Caroline's activism in the ladies' auxiliaries of both groups suggest a parallel
link for women.[24]

While women joined the labor movements in Fall River and
Lynn as auxiliary members to support a male cause, in Lowell
a very different relationship would emerge between men and
women in the labor movement. Both men and women had signed
the ten-hour petitions from Lowell which were sent to the Massachusetts legislature in 1843, but there is no evidence that they
were part of the same movement (or even that much of a movement existed). Agitation began again in the spring of 1844, when
workingmen in Lowell began meeting about the same time as
their counterparts in Fall River. Goodwin Wood was president of
a meeting held on May 16 at the Lowell City Hall, in which the
example of workingmen elsewhere in the state was declared a
model for the mechanics in Lowell in their quest for a ten-hour
day. As in Fall River, moral suasion was important here, for it
was resolved: "That we, in carrying out the 'Ten Hour System,'

24. *The Awl*, December 14, 1844; December 21, 1844. Of the 59 names of female
supporters which appeared in the *Awl*, 26 (44 percent) were married, 11 (18
percent) were unmarried, and 22 (37 percent) could not be identified either way.
Of those women who were married, 5 were married to men who signed the ten-
hour petition. The occupations of 12 husbands could be identified and 7 of them
were cordwainers.

must act with moderation, kindness and love, yet decidedly and energetically; while our object should be in all possible ways to ameliorate and elevate the condition of those who have too long been oppressed by the heartlessness and avarice of combinations and individuals, we should not forget that we are dealing with men & brethren, whose errors we are not to imitate, but to reform."[25]

It is not clear whether women were present at this meeting or not. But at a meeting held in the Anti-Slavery Hall of Lowell on July 9, women were explicitly invited to join. They were, moreover, welcomed not as family members who would be supporters of the male struggle but as workingwomen who had their own set of grievances. The idea of a household economy in which male and female workers were united in a common interest simply could not be sustained in a town where such a large part of the work force consisted of single wage-earning women unrelated to the men in the work force. One resolution passed by the men stated:

> That we regard the present system of *piece-work* as practiced in our Factories, as unjust to the Operative, uncalled for by the present good times, and high dividends; and designed cruelly to hoodwink, oppress and grind the faces of the poor. And further resolved, that as the females in the Mills are our fellow sufferers, in this respect, we hereby invite them to co-operate with us in this glorious work of reform.

Tying the issue of piecework to the ten-hour day, they further resolved: "That we seek only that which is just and right, when we ask for a reduction of laboring hours to ten per day, and a corresponding advance on, or a total abolition of, this infamous system of *piece-work*." In making this proposal, the workingmen no doubt intended to accommodate any fears that female piece workers might have had about the effect of a shorter workday on their monthly earnings. This concern for the wages of women may have had another source as well. According to *Vox Populi*,

25. *The Mechanic*, June 1, 1844.

corporations in Lowell restored wages of male operatives to the level of two years earlier in March 1844 but did not do the same for women. This attempt to split the work force along gender lines may have been part of the problem confronting workers in Lowell.[26]

When another meeting of the Lowell Association took place at City Hall on July 30, women were present. They continued to attend local meetings and soon constituted a majority of the membership. Mike Walsh would report speaking to "a full audience of factory girls and workingmen, in the large Free Will Baptist Church, on the 22nd of October."[27] "D," a correspondent from Fall River, visited Lowell in November and reported that almost 2,000 members belonged to the association, of which three-quarters were women.[28] In December the movement split; the women formed their own organization and faced a precipitous decline in membership.[29] Sarah Bagley reported in the spring of 1845:

It occurred to some few of us that such an association might be formed with a tendency to excite an interest in the cause, and perhaps ultimately result in much good. A committee was therefore chosen to draft a constitution, also one to choose officers. We had several [caucus] meetings, and the first week in January organized our association and adopted our Constitution. We then had two members besides our officers, which are thirteen in number, viz: a President, two vice-Presidents, Secretary, Treasurer and eight Directors. Since that time we have been gradually increasing and now number three hundred and four.[30]

26. *The Mechanic*, July 20, 1844. *Vox Populi* reported in *Manchester Operative*, March 30, 1844. Further discussion of this wage cut may be found in Caroline Ware, *The Early New England Cotton Manufacture: A Study in Industrial Beginnings* (New York, 1966), pp. 271–272.

27. *The Mechanic*, November 9, 1844. This may have been Hiram Stevens' church.

28. *The Mechanic*, November 30, 1844.

29. Thomas Dublin, *Women at Work: The Transformation of Work and Community in Lowell, Massachusetts, 1826–1860* (New York, 1979), p. 116, citing *The Operative*, December 28, 1844.

30. *The Mechanic*, April 2, 1845.

For reasons that are not clear, the single-sex organization had to struggle to attract a following in its early months. The members were dispirited and beleaguered, according to "Juliet," who wrote in the *Voice of Industry* a year-and-a-half later that "in Dec. 1844, a few humble individuals were seated in a badly lighted room, reviewing the past, and looking into the fearful future.—Sadness added to the gloom, and a storm raged without. . . ." Their reduced numbers may have been due less to their new form of organization than to outright intimidation by management. According to the reporter to *The Mechanic*, "the work of proscription [in Lowell] has commenced and I know not where it will end.—The first victim was their worthy President, a man highly esteemed as a man and a christian." He had been fired for talking "ten hours too much among his fellow workmen." Employers also may have directly intimidated the women, because when they met for their second meeting "the number had lessened, for threatnings and fear had taken possession of their roving minds, and altho' they saw the right, those lacking moral courage could find an excuse to desert a cause, where there was little prospect of any compensation." Apparently at this time the group adopted the motto "Try again." Although the number of women officially enrolled in the Lowell Female Labor Reform Association was small, their petitioning campaign garnered a large number of names.[31]

The different kinds of support women were willing to provide—and indeed, their very presence—provoked problems for many of the men. Simon Hewitt had to learn very quickly not to take female support for granted or to assume that women would naturally subordinate their interests to those of the men. In Pawtucket, Rhode Island, for example, he issued circulars inviting the men of the town to hear him speak at the American Hall. He was disappointed to find, however, that while a good number of men turned out to hear him speak, the women did not. Because he had seen women present at the Fall River meetings of the Mechanics Association, he was surprised to find that women elsewhere might not feel themselves included in an invitation

31. *Voice of Industry,* April 3, 1846; *The Mechanic,* December 28, 1844.

addressed to men. Hewitt was most anxious that women should attend, "for females, in general, work harder than males," and he defended his omission by arguing, "I certainly supposed the *women* would feel themselves included, inasmuch as the 'woman is of the man' and not the man of the woman, and therefore I made no allusion to them." Hewitt clearly assumed that women would occupy a subordinate position in the labor movement. Whether women in Pawtucket wanted a place that was equal to that of men, or merely different from it, is unclear, but they seem to have been making a point about Hewitt's generic use of "man" to demand separate recognition of their presence and support.[32]

The involvement of female operatives in such places as Lowell may have been one of the most important influences in the attempt that finally did develop among the Fall River Mechanics Association to try to attract mill workers. When *The Mechanic* announced that Simon Hewitt would speak in Fall River, it addressed the workingwomen as well as the workingmen and cited the example in Lowell as inspiration. "It will be seen by the doings of the meetings in Lowell, which we copy from the Lowell *Operative*, that the people of that place have commenced the work in right earnest. We trust the laborers and operatives of Fall River will not be behind them, in preparing for the great contest which is to take place between Labor and Capital."[33]

"A Ten Hour Woman" suggested that the wives of mechanics might extend their concern in this direction as well, because many might have children who worked in factories. "This is a subject in which *mothers* should feel a deep and thrilling interest," she argued, raising the specter of factory employment. "There are few mechanics in our community whose children are not obliged to engage in a species of labor as destructive to the physical as it is crushing to the intellectual energies of their nature." Making a final plea to maternal instincts, she concluded, "Where is the mother of such a family whose heart has not ached

32. *The Mechanic*, August 3 and August 24, 1844. For a different interpretation of these quotations, see David R. Roediger and Philip S. Foner, *Our Own Time: A History of American Labor and the Working Day* (Westport, Conn., 1989), p. 43.
33. *The Mechanic*, July 20, 1844.

for her little ones, as she calls them at early dawn, while they plead for a little more sleep."[34]

Asa Bronson, minister of the Baptist church, also gently nudged the Fall River mechanics to open up in July, but apparently to no avail. "Let me respectfully enquire," he began, "whether it would not be best, in order to accomplish these desirable ends, and reach these important objects, to so alter the present Constitution of the Society already formed, as to embrace all that are friendly to the *Ten Hour System* in and around this village, whether they can at present reduce that system to practice or not." If membership rules could not be bent, he suggested, a companion organization to cooperate with the Mechanics Association could be created.[35] In this vein, Simon Hewitt would also urge "upon the Mechanics and Laborers, now employed in the mills, to come together and form themselves into an Association, and help each other to better their condition."[36]

By the end of the summer, with mill workers responding elsewhere, several members of the Fall River Mechanics' Association tried to form an Industrial Association. Inviting women as well as men to join, and calling themselves the Workingmen's Reform Association, they put forward a constitution allowing anyone to join who would pay 25 cents and sign the constitution. In an address to the workingmen of Fall River the following week, supporters of the movement stressed their growing recognition of a need for unity. Bad working conditions existed, they pointed out, "because we have not, hitherto, been united; and in this has been our weakness. We have neglected to commune with each other upon the subject of our wrongs, and upon the best means of obtaining our *rights*. . . . A portion of the workingmen of Fall River have resolved to act, and to all others we would say, will you act with us?" The movement never got off the ground. While mechanics in Fall River were interested in unity, they never specifically addressed the problems that might be peculiar to

34. *The Mechanic*, June 1, 1844.
35. Asa Bronson, *An Address on the Anniversary of the Fire, Delivered in the Pearl St. Christian Chapel, July 2nd, 1844; Pursuant to Request from "Ladies' Mechanic Association"* (Fall River, Mass., 1844), p. 14.
36. *The Mechanic*, July 27, 1844.

some of the factory workers. There was no discussion of the effect
of a shorter day on those paid piece rates, for example, as there
had been in Lowell.[37]

The mechanics in Fall River were haltingly coming to terms
with the significance of factory life in shaping their artisanal experience, a significance that became more apparent as they attempted to interact with mechanics in less industrialized towns
or with different patterns of industrialization. Simon Hewitt ran
into problems in several places. In Worcester only about fifty
people showed up to hear him talk, and none of them would
speak at the meeting. In New London, Connecticut, where a ten-
hour day already prevailed, Hewitt found a great deal of apathy
among workingmen "in regard to the higher objects of our movement." Although he had written to Charles Douglass to let him
know of his arrival, no meeting hall was made available to
Hewitt. The shoemakers of Milford, Massachusetts, a farming
and shoe-making community, also showed little enthusiasm for
the cause. About 125 people attended Hewitt's lecture, but they
voted not to act. Hewitt found them far more "independent" in
their working conditions than he had supposed. They worked "by
the *job*, and pretty much as they please, as respects the *hours* of
labor," Hewitt reported, a fact that would have kept him away
had he known it.[38]

Another Fall River emissary, David Pierce, encountered similar problems in Maine when he tried to forge an alliance with
artisans at the Mechanics Convention being held in Portland,
Maine. What he found there was a group committed to education
only and opposed to the movement growing in southern New
England. Indeed, when Pierce presented the Fall River circular,
and one of the Maine delegates proposed to send representatives
to the convention in Boston, the group voted it down during their

37. *The Mechanic*, September 7, 1844; September 14, 1844.
38. *Manchester Operative*, May 18, 1844. This also may be the meeting described in *The Gleaner* (Manchester and Nashua), May 11, 1844, which described a
meeting of day laborers who worked on the canal system and who were concerned about low wages as well as long hours, and that adjourned to Wentworth
Hall for a further meeting on Thursday evening, May 9. Hewitt's activities are
reported in *The Mechanic*, August 3, August 10, August 17, September 21, 1844.

afternoon session. The question was brought up again in the evening and tabled.[39]

Pierce discovered in the course of these meetings that not only were most Maine mechanics opposed to the ten-hour movement, but some of them even doubted the truth of the grievances. Mr. Abner R. Hallowel, of Bangor, who spoke in the afternoon, "opposed ten hour associations and combinations of Laborers for the purpose of having their wages advance &c. because they had too much the appearance of monopoly and he wished to keep aloof from that great evil." The president of the convention (probably Oliver Gerrish of Portland) became quite disturbed about the "Massachusetts question" and suggested that the writer of the circular had simply had a bad day. According to Pierce, "he thought the writer of that article, at the time of writing it, had his passions very much excited, and selected all the grievances he could find and committed them to paper, while in that agitated state of mind."[40]

Pierce made a final attempt at reconciliation by stressing their shared cause, *"the elevation of the laborers,"* even though their means might be different. This calmed things down a bit, but the Maine convention remained opposed to collective action of any sort. Pierce concluded that one of the fundamental reasons for this difference in consciousness was a difference in market conditions: "The employers of Maine (in general) are not so overbearing as they are in many places, and the employed are not so overworked in that State as they are in this."[41]

No doubt it was discouraging reports such as this which led the editor of the Boston *Laborer* to urge a postponement of the fall convention.[42] The *Laborer* was overruled on this issue, in part because not all the news was bad. Although Hewitt had been unable to obtain a meeting hall in Stonington, Connecticut, he successfully organized street meetings two nights in a row. With the support of ministers in Woonsocket, Rhode Island, and Wa-

---

39. *The Mechanic*, August 31, 1844.
40. Ibid.
41. Ibid.
42. The *Laborer*, reprinted in *The Mechanic*, September 21, 1844.

terford, Massachusetts, Hewitt had been able to address large audiences. Even David Pierce found some success in Maine when he left the mechanics in Portland and moved on to the factory town of Saco. Although the initial responses in Worcester and Milford had been disappointing, word soon arrived that organizations had been formed. Meetings also took place in Andover, North Andover, Concord, Marblehead, Woburn, Haverhill, and Newton Upper Falls, inspired by word of these larger organizations. Residents from the latter town sent in sixteen subscriptions to *The Mechanic* early in September. On Friday evening, September 6, the mechanics in Newton Upper Falls held a meeting in which the hall was filled to overflowing even though no public notice of the meeting had been given.[43] A "Mechanics, Manufacturers and Laborers Association" met in Dover, New Hampshire, at the beginning of August, suggesting the presence of employers, which might not have existed elsewhere. In early September, mechanics and laborers in Manchester finally succeeded in forming a Mutual Benefit Association after being addressed by Mr. Hatch of Lowell.[44]

Many of these associations would seek female support and attempt to include women in their organizations. In Woonsocket the Mechanics Association not only encouraged workingmen to attend their meetings but extended a special invitation to women: "Ladies, to you we appeal! you, in all ages, who have ever raised your voices against oppression, come forward and join us! for you, too, suffer the pangs of unceasing toil."[45] The Milford Workingmen's Union, which openned its ranks to anyone "engaged in useful, productive industry" who would sign the constitution and pay a 25-cent initiation fee and 6 cents per

43. *The Mechanic*, September 14, 1844.

44. *Manchester Operative*, September 7, 1844, and September 21, 1844. The peculiar makeup of the Dover Association may account for the criticisms of their representative, Colby, at the fall meeting. Colby argued that laborers and employers, should set their own hours, not the legislature, objected to setting capital and labor in opposition, and believed that his constituents "did not acknowledge themselves slaves" (*The Laborer* [Boston], October 26, 1844).

45. *Woonsocket Independent*, reprinted in *Workingman's Advocate*, September 28, 1844.

month, admitted women and children for half price.[46] In Manchester, J. C. Stowell pointed to the examples of women in Fall River and Lowell and urged the "female portion" of the community to attend future meetings, arguing that no one would benefit more from these reforms than factory operatives. "The ladies of Fall River, Lowell and other places have taken hold of the work; and we see no reason why the operatives of this place should not feel more engaged in the present movement among the industrial classes." Calling for both the "influence" and "co-operation" of the women, he concluded: "Keep the fires burning upon our altars, and suffer not this heaven-born enterprise to fail its object."[47] When workingmen in Fitchburg formed an organization at the end of the year, they also invited women to join. At one of the first meetings of the Fitchburg Association it was resolved "that as the present evil state and organisation of society tends to abase & destroy the social & intellectual happiness of *woman*— we wish it to be distinctly understood that the doctrine of equality embodied in the principles of this Association extends to her the privilege of giving in her testimony in the deliberations of our meetings."[48]

Almost all of these local organizations sent delegates to the fall meeting. Wednesday, October 16, was designated as the time and Boston the place. Most of the delegates were from Massachusetts: shoemakers, carpenters, machinists, molders, and ship-workers trying to work out a way of discussing their problems beyond the craft level. In addition, they rubbed shoulders with men like George Ripley from Brook Farm and George Henry Evans, the land reformer from New York City. No women were present at the meeting, though the Ladies Association of Fall River did supply a banner that stated "Union Is Strength." As Thomas Almy, the editor of *The Mechanic* later pointed out, "We

46. *The Awl*, November 30, 1844. It was also stipulated that "all questions as to the merit of what may be called useful, productive industry shall be settled by a vote of the members present."
47. *Manchester Operative*, October 19, 1844.
48. Records of the Workingmen's Association of Fitchburg, 1844–1845, December 13, 1844 (Manuscript collection, Fitchburg Historical Society).

met with views as to the means of accomplishing our end as dissimilar as are the conditions of society."[49]

Despite their different viewpoints, the delegates managed to create the New England Workingmen's Association, to beat back the attempts of George Henry Evans to press his land reform cause, and to summon support for a petition campaign urging the legislature to reduce the hours of labor in corporations to ten. The resolution to petition the legislature was the most controversial of the fall meeting.

Before the nineteenth century, petitioning had been a deferential act, a request for the ruler of a country to intervene on a supplicant's behalf. For many white men of the nineteenth century, who had other forms of political expression available to them, petitioning carried connotations of submissiveness which rendered it distasteful. For some of the most radical reformers, it represented an interaction with a corrupt government and was thus morally unacceptable. For women, petitioning meant something different. Linda Kerber points out that in the eighteenth century this was one way in which women could approach the government and that women used the petition for a variety of personal causes, which might border on the political. By the early nineteenth century, particularly in the wake of the antislavery petitioning campaigns, petitioning had become an important political act for women. They signed their individual names in support of or in opposition to moral causes, which, particularly in the case of slavery, had significant political ramifications. As Angelina Grimké would write publicly to Catharine Beecher, it was woman's only political right.[50]

Because women were not present at this convention, their views on petitioning were not discussed, but for male delegates it raised many problems. Some of the delegates thought it useless

49. *The Mechanic*, October 26 and November 2, 1844.
50. Linda Kerber, *Women of the Republic: Intellect and Ideology in Revolutionary America* (New York, 1986), pp. 85–112; Angelina Grimké to Catharine Beecher in Alice S. Rossi, *The Feminist Papers: From Adams to de Beauvoir* (New York, 1973), p. 319; Lori Ginzberg, *Women and the Work of Benevolence: Morality, Politics, and Class in the Nineteenth-Century United States* (New Haven, Conn., 1990), pp. 67–97.

to petition, others seem to have found petitioning too submissive an act for men who were citizens. One delegate from Marblehead defended petitioning as a demand on the part of mechanics to protect the poor who had been wronged by the legislature when the corporations were originally created. Solomon Cooper of Fall River provided a more political interpretation by suggesting that petitioning could be an avenue into party politics. Both interpretations would make the activity more manly. After extensive debate, the plan was carried.[51]

Petitions from five of these towns remain: Lynn, Fall River, Worcester, Andover, and two from Lowell. In Lowell and Andover, women as well as men signed. Perhaps for different reasons, each group of petitioners made sure that they were petitioning for someone else. Men may have wanted to distance themselves from the subservient act of requesting what they believed to be their rights, and women may have wanted to demonstrate their moral benevolence while at the same time exerting a "political" right.

In Fall River, Lynn, and Andover the introductory language of the petitions was virtually identical; they focused their demands on corporations. Arguing that the legislature had a particular responsibility here, they pointed out: "You have the power to regulate all corporate bodies which you have created." They stressed the particularly taxing nature of mill work, saying that "to work more than ten hours per day, *especially in factories,* is injurious to the physical and mental power of man—thus debasing his intellect—cramping his energies, and paralyzing his strength—that it deprives him of the opportunity of cultivating his mind and of raising himself to that high rank and station in society for which God designed him." All three concluded by "respectfully" petitioning that a law be passed "constituting Ten Hours a days work in all corporations, created by the Legislature of this State," with the Lynn petition referring even more specifically to "manufacturing corporations."[52] While many of the petition-signers in

51. *Weekly Bee,* October 19, 1844.
52. *The Mechanic,* November 16, 1844; Massachusetts House Document 1604; Massachusetts House Document 1587 (MSA).

Andover worked in factories, few worked in incorporated factories. In Fall River, where factories were incorporated, few mill workers signed. And in Lynn almost all the signers were shoemakers.

In Lowell, where a large number of operatives working at incorporated factories signed the petitions, the opening language asked for a much more broadly based ten-hour law. The shorter petition, signed by about 300 men and women, asked the legislature to "enact a Law making ten hours a *day's work*—where no specific agreement is entered into between the parties interested." The longer petition referred more specifically to corporations but still sought a wide-ranging law. Noting that they sought "a redress of those evils, daily strengthening, and imposed upon us by our incorporated bodies" the petitioners asked "that no incorporated body, or any individual or individuals, either private or associated, shall be allowed, except in case of emergency, to employ one set of hands more than ten hours per day."[53] In Worcester the petitioners asked simply for a law establishing "Ten Hours per day as a day's labor for all Adult Persons."[54]

The language of these petitions and the very act of signing them continued to be debated at the local level even as they were circulated. Walter Sherrod, one of the leaders of the workingmen's movement in Lynn, found the language of the petition too submissive and inappropriate given the rights to which workingmen were entitled. Thus, at the December 7 meeting in Lynn he criticized the petition presented, saying, "He was opposed to the sovereign people's presenting themselves as petitioners, where they had the right to demand that for which they petitioned." He then distinguished between what he considered the appropriate posture for artisans to take and the appropriate posture for factory workers by noting that he "was in favor of stating that he sympathized with the operatives at work in the various incorporated mills, and demand of the Legislature, to grant them their

53. House Document 1587 (MSA).
54. Ibid. For a discussion of the language of petitions which focuses on the legal efficacy of these pleas, see Persons, "New England Workingmen's Association," pp. 23–54.

Table 1. Occupations: Male signers of 1845 ten-hour petitions

	Lowell+		Lynn		Fall River		Andover		Worcester	
	%	N	%	N	%	N	%	N	%	N
Trad artisan	14	(8)	76	(45)*	15	(24)	28	(29)	13	(8)
Bldg trades	19	(11)	3	(2)	28	(46)	9	(9)	27	(16)
Factory work	21	(12)		(0)	12	(19)	29	(30)	53	(32)
Textiles		[9]				[10]		[24]		[0]
Metal/Machine		[3]				[9]		[5]		[32]
Other								[1]		
Unskilled	18	(10)	2	(1)	15	(24)	12	(12)	3	(2)
Manufacturer	9	(5)	8	(5)*	0	(1)	7	(7)		
Cleric/prof	2	(1)		(0)	7	(12)	2	(2)	2	(1)
Retail	9	(5)	7	(4)	14	(23)	2	(2)	2	(1)
Agriculture	5	(3)	2	(1)		(0)	11	(11)		
Maritime		(0)	2	(1)	6	(10)		(0)		
Other	4	(2)		(0)	2	(3)		(0)		
Total	101%	(57)	100%	(59)	99%	(162)	100%	(102)	100%	(60)
% traced	33		59		35		37		53	

+Lowell combines two petitions.
*All traditional artisans in Lynn were cordwainers, and all manufacturers in Lynn were shoe manufacturers.
Sources: City directories of Worcester, Lowell, and Lynn in mid-1840s; Marriage records in Massachusetts State Archives; Vital Statistics published by Essex Institute; 1850 Federal Census for Lowell, Lynn, Worcester, Andover, and Fall River.

request."[55] Despite Sherrod's reservations, the petition was submitted with the names of 100 men, which were probably collected at one of the cordwainers meetings. Of those signers who could be positively identified, 76 percent were cordwainers and another 8 percent were shoe manufacturers (see table 1). Male shoemakers who shared Sherrod's reservations about petitioning may have been reassured by the knowledge that their petition was clearly meant to benefit others, particularly "dependent," female operatives.

In Fall River, petitioning was incorporated quickly into a political platform. The protective legislation for operatives repre-

55. *The Awl*, December 14, 1844.

sented a significant departure from the stand mechanics had taken the previous spring, when they attempted to rely only on their pledge not to work more than ten hours and distanced their cause from that of the operatives. By employing the strategy of petitioning, their fates would be more closely intertwined, for such legislation would no doubt benefit men in the building trades as well as factory workers. But discussion among the Fall River mechanics quickly moved to "whether the ten hour men, as such, should make an exertion to send men to the Legislature who would vote for such a law." The group decided to enter the political arena by choosing candidates from all political parties and resolved to "recommend the support of those men only who will sign the petition that has been presented to this meeting, and who will pledge themselves, if elected, to do all in their power to have such a law passed as is prayed for in said petition."[56]

The fact that petitioning was becoming a political party issue may help explain why there was such a broad occupational spread among petition-signers in Fall River: 28 percent were from the building trades, but an additional 15 percent were skilled artisans from other traditional trades, and 21 percent were shopkeepers, merchants, and professionals. Only 12 percent were industrial workers in machine-making and textiles. An additional 15 percent were unskilled workers, most of whom were designated as laborers in the census. Some of these men may have been factory workers also, since in Fall River the term "laborer" was used instead of "operative." The political edge on petitioning in Fall River may be a further reason that women there did not sign the petition.

In Andover there was also a broad spectrum of occupations among male petitioners, although in this case traditional artisans (many of whom were shoemakers), with 28 percent of the signers, and factory workers, with 29 percent, represented the largest groups, while unskilled laborers (12 percent) and farmers (11 percent) represented a significant minority. In the case of

56. *The Mechanic*, November 16, 1844. See also John Gregory's speech in *The Mechanic*, November 23, 1844.

Andover, however, this broad occupational spread may have been due less to the movement's political character than to its family orientation. Whole families in Andover signed the petition, so that some of the male farmers and shoemakers who signed may have had children working in the factories.

This family orientation in Andover was also reflected in the language of the petition. While the introduction to the petition stated that it was from the inhabitants of the town, requesting a ten-hour day for all workers employed by corporations, the cover sheet that accompanied the petition gave a different meaning. It claimed to be from the *citizens* of Andover, requesting that hours be limited for all women and minors employed in factories.[57] This suggested a different kind of document: one of men (i.e., citizens) petitioning to protect women and children.

The strategy of men petitioning to protect women and children, though all would benefit from shorter hours, was a far more common approach in Great Britain at this time than in the United States. Indeed, the different messages of the cover sheet and the petition may have been a product of the ethnic complexity of the movement in Andover. Although male petitioners from Worcester, Lynn, and Fall River were almost exclusively native-born, 24 percent of the male petitioners from Andover were foreign-born (see Table 2). Most of these men were from England, Scotland, or Ireland, and most were factory workers.[58] They may have carried the ideology of Great Britain's ten-hour movement

57. Massachusetts House Document 1587/2 (MSA).
58. Of the 23 foreign-born men who signed, 21 (91 percent) were born in Ireland, Scotland, or England. Of the 30 factory workers who signed the petition, birthplaces for 22 could be determined: 16 were foreign-born, 15 (94 percent) of those were from those three countries. Of the 6 factory workers from the United States signing the petition, 4 were machinists. For a discussion of the attitudes of male workingmen in England toward the regulation of female labor during this period, see Marianna Valverde, "'Giving the Female a Domestic Turn': The Social, Legal, and Moral Regulation of Women's Work in British Cotton Mills, 1820–1850," *Journal of Social History* 21 (Summer 1988): 619–634. For a discussion of how the struggle for a shorter workday in the United States differed from that in England, see Kathryn Kish Sklar, "'The Greater Part of the Petitioners Are Female': The Reduction of Women's Working Hours in the Paid Labor Force, 1840–1917," in *Worktime and Industrialization: An International History,* ed. Gary Cross (Philadelphia: Temple University Press, 1988), pp. 106–107.

Table 2. Nativity of 1845 ten-hour petition signers

	United States		Foreign		
	%	N	%	N	% traced
Lowell					
Women	90	(90)	10	(10)	14
Men	67	(21)	33	(10)	18
Andover					
Women	88	(44)	12	(6)	29
Men	76	(72)	24	(23)	34
Lynn (Men)	100	(53)	—	(0)	53
Fall River (Men)	95	(137)	5	(7)	31
Worcester (Men)	94	(32)	6	(2)	30

Sources: Marriage records, Massachusetts State Archives; Vital Statistics of Lowell, Lynn and Andover, published by the Essex Institute; 1850 Federal Census for Lowell, Lynn, Worcester, Andover, and Fall River.

with them, fusing it with the ten-hour agitation in the United States.

As an occupational analysis of male petitioners makes clear, traditional artisans, such as shoemakers and members of the building trades, made a common cause with factory workers in their petitioning campaigns. But as an analysis of their real property makes clear, this was not exclusively a movement of propertyless wage earners. The ten-hour petitions were signed by a significant minority of men whose wealth would have provided them with a comfortable independence (see Table 3). In Lynn, by 1850, some 37 percent of the men had amassed real property valued between $501 and $5,000. Most of them listed their occupation as cordwainer, so many might have been masters rather than journeymen. In Worcester, 53 percent of the signers had more than $500 in real property, including six out of eight of the iron molders who signed the petition. In Fall River, 30 percent of the signers fit into this category, as did 35 percent in Andover. As a moral reform rather than a trade-union movement, ten-hour agitation had clearly reached beyond wage earners living on a subsistence income in garnering support.

The movement also drew female support, though of different kinds. Women who signed petitions in Lowell and Andover prob-

Table 3. Real Property: Male signers of 1845 ten-hour petitions

	Lowell+		Lynn		Fall River		Andover		Worcester	
	%	N	%	N	%	N	%	N	%	N
$0	80	(4)	61	(28)	67	(87)	58	(38)	44	(14)
$1–500	—	(0)	2	(1)	3	(4)	6	(4)	3	(1)
$501–1,000	—	(0)	15	(7)	5	(6)	14	(9)	13	(4)
$1,001–5,000	20	(1)	22	(10)	22	(29)	15	(10)	34	(11)
$5,001–	—	(0)	—	(0)	3	(4)	6	(4)	6	(2)
Total	100	(46)	100	(130)	99	(65)	99	(65)	100	(32)
% traced		3		46		28		23		28

+Actual numbers from Lowell are too small to be meaningful.
Source: 1850 Federal Census for Lowell, Lynn, Worcester, Andover, and Fall River.

ably did so for very different reasons. Those in Lowell who signed were almost all single wage-earning women, and virtually none of them were related to the men who signed the petitions. As might be expected, where occupations could be determined, the female signers were usually factory operatives (81 percent).[59] The occupational homogeneity of the women who signed stands in sharp contrast to the occupational diversity of the men from Lowell who signed.

In Andover, however, many of the women who signed were related to male petition signers. Thirty-six percent of the petition-signers in Andover could be clearly identified as women, and of that number some 25 percent could be clearly identified as married when they signed. This in itself presents a very different profile from that of the women in Lowell who signed, almost all of whom were single. Even more striking, however, is the fact that 81 percent of the married women who signed the petition in Andover were married to men who also signed the petition. Marriage was clearly a more significant factor for the women in Andover who signed than for the men. Thirty-three percent of the

59. The numbers here are very small: occupations could be identified for only 6 percent (43 out of 725) of the female signatures on the large petition submitted from Lowell. Given the newspaper accounts of female participation emanating from factory operatives, however, this small sample probably represents an accurate picture of the women who signed this petition.

men who signed could be clearly identified as married, but only 41 percent had wives who signed the petition. Among the unmarried petition-signers were many of the children of these married couples.

It is difficult to know what to make of the women who signed the petition in Andover because it is impossible to determine their occupational status and we have no other record of their participation in the New England Workingmen's Association. They do not appear to have formed their own organization, which may explain their absence from the workingmen's regional meetings. But when they signed the petition, they used their own first names rather than their husbands', an act of independence that reinforced their assertiveness in signing a petition to the government.

The most important similarity they shared with the women of Lowell was their age. Both groups of female signers were significantly younger than the men who signed. The median age of women from Lowell who signed the ten-hour petition was 20, and the median age of women from Andover was 22 (see Table 4). The men were considerably older: in Lowell the median age was 26, in Andover it was 31; in Fall River, 30 and in Lynn, 33. The younger age of the women from Lowell is compatible with their status as factory workers, for it reflects the shorter-life-cycle nature of factory work for women at this time, as opposed to the longer time span of artisanal (or factory) activity for men. The median age of the Andover women, then, suggests that the unmarried women who signed might have been engaged in factory work also.

The fact that in both Andover and Fall River female petition signers were younger than the men who were signing should remind us of an additional complication in the organizing activities of men and women, artisans, and operatives at this time. Further expectations of deference would be built into their relationship based on age, particularly as the struggle for a ten-hour day assumed regional rather than local dimensions and young women from Lowell asserted their demands publicly along with men from such towns as Lynn and Fall River. These older male artisans might view their petitioning as a way of protecting these young women, while female operatives used the petitions as a

Table 4. Median ages: Signers of 1845 ten-hour petitions

	Male	(N)	% traced	Female	(N)	% traced
Lowell	26	(39)	22	20	(158)	22
Andover	31	(91)	33	22	(53)	30
Lynn	33	(52)	52	NA		
Fall River	30	(162)	35	NA		
Worcester	28	(37)	32	NA		

Sources: Marriage Records, Massachusetts State Archives; Vital Statistics of Lynn, Lowell, and Andover published by the Essex Institute; 1850 Federal Census for Lowell, Lynn, Worcester, Andover, and Fall River.

way to assert themselves in the labor movement without threatening the men with whom they were forming an alliance.

The conflicts between male artisans and female wage earners has been well documented in recent years, making the activities and alliances of the New England Workingmen's Association all the more curious.[60] The organization did not unite all wage earners or all men and women in the struggle for a ten-hour day. But as the petitions reveal, it did unite many who had different social and economic experiences. Petitioning was one way these differences could be accommodated, though not eradicated. Indeed, the petitions would draw women into more active participation in the labor movement as they were called on to justify themselves to the legislature. From that point of public speaking these women moved on to positions of leadership in the New England Workingmen's Association, spearheading even more extensive petitioning campaigns in the next few years. Petitions did not bring about a legislative solution to long work days, and when the petitions failed so did the coalition. But while petitioning flourished, it provided an important means for artisans and operatives to work together.

60. In addition to Blewett, *Men, Women, and Work,* see Christine Stansell, *City of Women: Sex and Class in New York, 1789–1860* (New York, 1982); and Ava Baron, "Women and the Making of the American Working Class: A Study of the Proletarianization of Printers," *Review of Radical Political Economics* 14 (1982): 23–42.

Chapter 7

The Dilemmas of Moral Reform

At one of the earliest ten-hour meetings in 1844, "the choir" at a labor-reform meeting concluded the evening's activities by adapting the tune of "The Gospel Banner" to the new words of the labor movement:

> Now be the "*ten hour*" banner,
> In every land unfurl'd;
>   And be the shout hosanna,
> Re-echo'd through the world.
>   Till ev'ry isle and nation,
> Till ev'ry tribe and tongue,
>   Receive the great salvation,
> And join the happy throng.[1]

The singing made clear that the ten-hour campaign of the 1840s was not just a labor movement; it was also an important manifestation of the reform impulse. The influence of the antislavery and temperance movements and of revivalism were unmistakable. But though labor reform drew on these other movements, it also presented a basic challenge to them and the world they had structured. As several historians have pointed out, middle-class moral reform and evangelical religion legitimated

1. *The Mechanic,* June 8, 1844.

164

the economic relationships of wage labor by demarcating a private world that was suitable for moral principles from a public world that was not.[2] Stories of salvation and personal reform focused on transcending a corrupt world, not changing it. The ahistorical, autonomous, and cyclical world of conscience and family was the appropriate arena for moral reform; the historical and progressive world of industrial development was not. Popular evangelicalism and the Washingtonians had left this boundary intact. So had radical antislavery advocates who focused on the exchange of slavery but shielded free wage labor from criticism. Labor activists, however, did not. They argued that the boundary was permeable and that standards of personal morality could be applied to the public world of exchange. They imaginatively structured a new world of economic and social relations with the rhetoric of moral reform.

When Simon Hewitt reported to the readers of *The Mechanic* about his experiences in other towns, his "progress" narrative was very historically grounded in his accounts of the uneven process of industrialization throughout the region. His was not a pilgrim's progress, a private tale of redemption, though the idiom was surely familiar to him. It was instead a story firmly rooted in the differences of time and place, and as such it set the stage for adapting religious and moral critiques to the problems of industrial change. The autonomous response of personal reform was inappropriate in light of these differences.

Religious Hypocrisy Unmasked

Labor activists attempted to challenge the line between spiritual progress and economic activity with a variety of approaches. They began by confronting the arguments that manufacturers were advancing in the 1840s to defend long hours, arguments in which the traditional claims of paternalism coexisted (uncom-

2. John Ashworth, "The Relationship between Capitalism and Humanitarianism," *American Historical Review* 92 (October 1987): 823–824; Ann Fabian, *Card Sharps, Dream Books, and Bucket Shops* (Ithaca, N.Y., 1990), pp. 75–76.

fortably) with the emerging bourgeois distinction between the amorality of the marketplace and the moral universe of private behavior. Nathaniel Borden, the mill owner from Fall River, combined both arguments when he defended long hours. He argued on the one hand that business was subject to the laws of nature, and on the other hand he stoutly maintained the connection between a fourteen- or fifteen-hour workday and the virtue of his employees. "The best men I have ever known," he contended in defense of long hours, "were among the most industrious."[3] Others would argue that working people who were given extra leisure would use the time for vicious purposes. This argument about a vicious factory population was not only confined to the mills of southern New England. The president of the Lowell Association reported a conversation with a factory overseer who "thought it a great blessing to the city of Lowell" that factory operatives were overworked, "since giving them leisure would be but to increase their viciousness, immorality and degradation."[4]

The proponents of a ten-hour day who confronted these arguments faced the difficult task of arguing that long workdays degraded them morally *and* that they were virtuous enough to use the increased leisure time that came with shorter workdays to good advantage. The contradictions inherent in this position were obvious: everytime working people claimed they were virtuous enough to control their own leisure, employers could claim that long workdays were the source of virtue.

One of the most important lines of attack in escaping this contradiction was to focus on the moral and spiritual failings of the men who claimed to be creating this virtuous work force. If popular religion had offered an arena to attack the authority of elites in traditional religious settings, undermining the deference of common people to their betters, the labor movement offered an opportunity to attack the religious pretensions of employers in the workplace.

As "A Working Man" wrote, the calling of merchants and manufacturers challenged the laws of God by stealing his time. These employers claimed they could not reform individually because

3. *The Monitor* (Fall River), April 27, 1844.
4. *The Mechanic* (Fall River), August 10, 1844.

they would be unable to compete with the unregenerate. The writer replied by citing the natural abundance provided for men and animals in this country by their heavenly father. "[H]as it come to this," he demanded, "that men are obliged to do violence to their consciences, injustice to their fellow men, and to sin in the face of high heaven, in order to obtain a living and avoid ruin. It cannot be." The way an individual earned his bread had to be determined first of all by whether or not it gave glory to God by contributing to the well-being of his creatures. Thus "A Working Man" concluded, "Let that man who attempts to justify the exercise of his vocation whatever it may be, on a plan neither sanctioned by the word of God, nor his own convictions, merely on a plea of necessity: I say, let that man ponder well on what he is doing, for his is truly a critical position."[5]

The hypocrisy of the "respectable," a staple theme in popular evangelicalism, would be expanded on by labor reformers. "Ada" of Fitchburg asked, "Do we not find many professing Christians in the community who are the *authors* and *supporters*, of systems of oppression and wrong?"[6] The relationship between overwork and hypocrisy was particularly played out in criticisms of work on the Sabbath. An article on Lowell would take up this point in the *Middlesex Standard*. The reporter was horrified to observe one Sunday, "a group of laborers—coats off—sleeves rolled up—heaving at levers—smiting with sledge-hammers—in full view of the street, on the margin of the canal, just above Central Street Bridge." The hypocrisy was clear to the observer if to no one else. "Around me were solemn go-to-meeting faces—smileless and awful; and close at hand were the delving, toiling, mud-begrimed laborers. . . . And this, too, in a city where the Sabbath proprieties are sternly insisted upon; where some twenty pulpits deal out anathemas upon all who 'desecrate the Lord's day.'" The hypocrisy was rooted in different kinds of morality: "What would be sin past repentance in an individual becomes quite proper in a manufacturing corporation."[7]

5. *The Mechanic*, June 22, 1844.
6. *Voice of Industry* (Fitchburg, Lowell, and Boston), October 9, 1845. For another example, see "Concord" in *Voice of Industry*, December 5, 1845.
7. *The Mechanic*, October 12, 1844.

When *The Mechanic* ran this article it commented that the same situation applied in Fall River: "On Saturday night the overseer says to his men—'Such a job must be done to-morrow; unless you come and work upon it we shall have no more employment for you.' Thus the laborer has no alternative—he must either work without respite from one month to another, or by losing his situation deprive his family of bread." While working people were forced to desecrate the Sabbath, employers could piously attend church. Such owners could "be seen riding with their families, in gilded coaches, to the house of prayer, so called, and listening to the 'droppings of the sanctuary,' as they fall from the lips of the fat salaried priest, who takes particular care that his '*droppings*' are not offensive to the delicate ears of his money loving hearers."[8]

As critics pushed forward their arguments about the moral failings and hypocrisy of employers, they expanded these arguments into a critique of the emerging bourgeois distinction between private and public morality. In essence, they questioned whether the public world of business could be amoral and the personal world moral. This is what Sarah Bagley meant when she claimed "the *real, actual, practical* religion of the corporations [was] a very different thing from profession."[9] Practical religion, pregnant with the antiinstitutional connotations that had been emerging in the antislavery and temperance movements, was expanded to include all social and economic relationships.

A front-page article in the *Voice of Industry* entitled "Who Are the Infidels?" would pick up on this issue of practical religion. The writer pointed out that many professing Christians were quick to brand social reformers as infidels because they tried to bring "about equitable relations between man and man—the individual and society—capital and labor." These Christians might pray for the kingdom of God but were loath to think it might be instituted on earth.

8. Ibid. Further criticisms of work on Sundays may be found in *The All Sorts* (Fall River), January 1843. See also complaints about men being fired from the carpet factory in Lowell for refusing to work on Sunday in *Voice of Industry*, October 23, 1846.

9. *Voice of Industry*, September 18, 1846.

They seem to think religion consists more in going to meeting on the Sabbath, and giving in their adherence to established creeds and forms of worship, than in obeying the "weightier matters of the law, faith, justice, and mercy." It seems to be part of their religious belief, that if they take good care of themselves and families, they need have but very little concern for the welfare of others—they are not their "brother's keeper."[10]

It is in the context of this critique that we need to place the ensuing attack on competition. Ten-hour advocates were unanimous in their condemnation of competition. Asa Bronson stated that he viewed it "as a species of idolatry, as hateful to a Holy God, as the idolatry of China or Hindustan." Bronson went on to claim that he "would as soon worship Juggernaut as Competition."[11] There was nothing natural about competition; it was a false god created by greedy individuals.

The Workingmen's Association of Fitchburg was equally adamant in condemning the moral implications of competition. In one resolution passed in November 1844 it stated: "That the God of nature designed mankind to live as a band of brothers for the mutual good of all but the Laws & customs of men have rendered them a gang of Ishmaelites." Their next resolution made a similar point in claiming: "That while the spirit of the New Testament teaches us to pray for each other the customs of men require us to *prey upon each other*."[12]

There were, of course, economic criticisms of the competitive system as well. An article from the *Christian Citizen* noted that "the working man receives no benefit from such excessive competition, for while it adds to the severity of his toil, it decreases the price of the article which he produces."[13] However, the strongest criticisms came on moral grounds. Competition was not a natural law of the economic world beyond human control, but the result of human greed. And as a result of this greed on the part of

10. *Voice of Industry,* April 3, 1846.
11. *The Monitor,* June 15, 1844.
12. Minutes, Workingmen's Association of Fitchburg, November 29, 1844, Fitchburg Historical Society.
13. *The Christian Citizen,* reprinted in *Voice of Industry,* March 19, 1844.

employers, their employees were forced to work the longest hours possible so that no other employer could possibly manufacture any products for a cheaper price. Thus Sarah Bagley indignantly demanded in one of her editorials, "Think you the *benevolence* of 'the powers that be' ordained the 'all day system' of labor? was it not rather their avarice?" As Bagley leveled her charges of avarice, she was not simply analyzing the economic problems of industrialization in terms of individual moral failings. Instead, she was using this charge of moral failure to attack claims of benevolence and to suggest that an alternative system was both possible and desirable. The contention of many employers that long hours were not only a necessary by-product of a competitive market system but also a source of virtue in the working population was simply not sustainable, and neither was the paternalism that stood behind it.

Arguments such as these also explicitly revealed the tensions that were inherent in the relationship between religion and work. If nineteenth-century religion was characterized by a growing acceptance of the concept of free moral-agency, labor activists made it clear how extensively employers limited the moral agency of working people. Ten-hour activists were only too aware of the way in which the will could be coerced, despite all claims to the contrary. Abraham Bowen, for example, criticized the attempts of the Quaker preacher Jacob Vining to import all day workers from Maine into Fall River to subvert the plans of the ten-hour mechanics. He described Vining's activities as a form of compulsion that undercut the workingman's ability to freely exercise his will. "Now we ask, if the Elder's doing all he can to prevent a system from going into operation for the reduction of the hours of labor, is [he] not, in effect, *compelling men to work on the long hour's system.*" Bowen went on to liken the minister's role in the ten-hour movement to that of Paul, who "held the clothes of the young men who stoned the Martyr Stephen."[14]

Employers might claim that work was morally elevating, but labor activists responded with a picture of labor that suggested

14. *The All Sorts*, August 2, 1844.

mindless as well as soulless animation. Thus Asa Bronson would argue that while he was an "unfaltering advocate of industry," he believed that "a man to be industrious need not lower himself down to the veriest drudge—need not sink himself into a mere laboring animal—a pack horse."[15]

As arguments were advanced against the mind-numbing nature of wage work, labor activists staked out an alternative arena of spiritual autonomy. When paternalist mill owners took responsibility for the moral condition of their employees, they appropriated part of their employees' moral self. The religious imperatives that provided the means for working people to renegotiate their relationships with their families would also be important in their attempts to renegotiate their relationships with their employers. Religion provided a competing authority strong enough to challenge a parent, whether it be a metaphorical or biological one, and in the 1840s activists used it.

One Fall River activist, "W," was adamant in defending each individual's obligations before God: "The light of modern truth has shown us that notwithstanding all our modern preaching . . . we must remain in sin and ignorance and perish, unless we become servants of Christ, and according to his precepts, renovate ourselves in his own righteous way."[16] Another workingman in Fall River argued that extra time was necessary so that he could perform the various duties required to save his soul. The responsibilities of workingmen were numerous, including family prayer, religious devotion, reading of the scriptures and attendance at church services. *"I cannot devote more than ten hours per day to physical labor,"* "H" wrote, *"and appropriate sufficient time to the regular, faithful and solemn discharge of the religious duties binding upon me."* How was family prayer possible when children and parents collapsed with exhaustion upon returning home from work? And each day that passed without family devotion would bring each member of the household closer to backsliding. Maintenance of the Christian faith required constant watchfulness. Searching the scriptures, a fundamental respon-

15. *The Monitor*, April 18, 1844.
16. *The Mechanic*, June 8, 1844.

sibility of Protestant faith, required even more time. "How can the poor mechanic, and operative in the mill, search the scriptures daily and faithfully," he demanded to know, "and at the same time be compelled to labor 'fourteen hours' per day?"[17]

Factory time conflicted with religious time, not only on a daily basis but during revivals as well. Asa Bronson addressed these issues in his argument with Nathaniel Borden when he demanded:

> If at any time, and especially when God is pouring out his spirit and reviving his work and building up Zion and awakening sinners and converting souls, our operatives cannot have a little time to serve God and seek the kingdom of heaven between the hours of *five* and *seven* in the morning, nor through all the day, until eight in the evening, will not christians perceive that we have a need for reform?[18]

An artisan in Fall River also reported to *The Mechanic* a case of a factory overseer who had quit his job and moved to New Bedford to work, where a ten-hour day prevailed, because the length of his workday interfered with the portion of time God had given him for tending to his spiritual well-being. He told his employer he "could not in conscience any longer resist God, and set at naught the divine and holy laws given man for the protection of his life, the health of his body and mind, and for his moral, mental and social culture." Particularly offensive to this workingman were the dismissals of tardy employees who "might have been detained by offering up a short petition, to the father of all our mercies, for a continuance of his blessing, and returning thanks for the past, or reading a portion of his word, to know his will, in order to perform it better."[19]

Without a willingness to commit oneself to the necessary amount of time for religion, backsliding was the only possibility. As "H" pointed out in a letter to *The Mechanic:* "We must either be like the New Hampshire deacon, who in order to save time,

17. *The Mechanic*, May 25, 1844.
18. *The Monitor*, May 18, 1844.
19. *The Mechanic*, May 25, 1844.

.

and to keep his men in the field, during the haying season always made the shortest prayers, and in his haste, lost his fervency and devotion, or we must neglect it altogether, which of necessity is too often the case."[20]

While questions of religion permeated the debate over hours in antebellum New England, the emphasis and intensity of this religious orientation varied from town to town. It was in Fall River, where a majority of the town's ministers actively supported a ten-hour day, that questions of individual salvation and personal prayer were most vividly evoked. Asa Bronson, the popular reform-minded minister of the First Baptist Church, lectured and wrote in defense of the cause. It was Bronson who took on Nathaniel Borden in *The Monitor* to argue the moral and spiritual benefits of a shorter workday. Bronson was joined by John Gregory of the Universalists, George Randall of the Episcopalians, H. P. Guilford and A. M. Averell of the two Christian Churches, and Benjamin Phelon of the Freewill Baptists. Ministers from the Unitarian, Congregational, and Quaker congregations opposed the workingmen.

This was not an opposition of evangelical versus rationalist ministers, but rather a division of mill-owning versus non-mill-owning congregations. The Congregationalist, Unitarian, and Quaker congregations had been founded by the mill owners in town and tended to be better heeled than Baptists, Christians, Universalists, Freewill Baptists, and even the Episcopalians. Although the Episcopal churches in other towns might appeal to a wealthier constituency, the one in Fall River seems to have catered to a growing class of English factory workers.[21]

The social background of these ministers was also an important factor as ministers stressed their affinity with men in the community. Most of the ministers in support of a ten-hour day had been mechanics themselves, and they used this background to establish a rapport with workingmen. John Gregory made this point when he addressed a Fourth of July crowd, saying, "I be-

20. Ibid.
21. Teresa Murphy, "Labor, Religion, and Moral Reform in Fall River, Massachusetts, 1800–1845" (Ph.D. diss., Yale University, 1982), pp. 50–55.

lieve the ministers in this place, who have espoused the ten hour system, have been mechanics." Mr. Phelon offered similar personal testimony in another speech when he said, "My sympathies are with the laborer—I am of you—I labored until they made a parson of me, and not a parson broad brim either." Although currently called to be a minister, he would always be a mechanic, as he made clear by claiming, "If I cannot be sustained by speaking the word of God, I shall not refuse to return to labor again."[22]

Most of the clergy supporting the mechanics (with the exception of Russell from the Episcopal church) were probably not trained in theological schools. Drawing on the traditions of popular religion which challenged the authority of respectable middle-class clergy in the spiritual arena, these ministers carried that challenge into labor relations as well. As a result, the clergy were invested with dual authority in the labor movement: they represented the word of God, yet they understood the experience of workingmen. Their opponents could not tell them that they did not understand the problems of the productive process. John Gregory, a former painter, thus challenged the "manufacturers, and lawyers and Doctors and Storekeepers and Priests, who have raised a cry against us for doing what we conceived to be our duty . . . [to] condescend to come down and try us—and ascertain whether we know whereof we affirm." Gregory promised that if their opponents could prove them incompetent judges of social conditions they would abandon their ministries, roll up their sleeves, and return to their former occupations. "I will take up my brush," Gregory claimed, "and these brethren will take their respective implements of trade, and we will work with them side by side—and show them that we are not ignorant of the mechanic arts."[23]

Ministerial support was not as widespread in other towns, nor were the religious arguments central to labor-reform rhetoric. But the clergy who did champion the cause were an important means for transmitting the ten-hour gospel and giving legiti-

22. *The Mechanic*, July 13, 1844. According to an article in *The Argus* (Fall River), January 12, 1843, Phelon had just arrived from Nashua, New Hampshire, to begin preaching in Fall River.
23. *The Mechanic*, July 13, 1844.

macy to the demands of its advocates. Simon Hewitt, who would go on to become a Universalist minister in Salem, Massachusetts, received support from ministers in several mill towns he attempted to organize. Maxey Burlingame, an elder of the Freewill Baptist church in Blackstone (and formerly on the company payroll of the Blackstone mill) defended the ten-hour day from the pulpit, helped Hewitt post advertisements for his speaking, and allowed Hewitt to use his church to speak out on shorter hours. William Henry Fish, a Unitarian minister with close ties to the Hopedale community, opened the doors of his church in Millville, as did John Boyden, the reform-minded Universalist minister in Woonsocket. John Davis, the Congregational minister in Woonsocket, wrote a series of articles in 1846 defending the ten-hour day.[24]

Philo Pettibone, the Congregational minister in Fitchburg, who led the recently formed, radical Trinitarian Church, provided similar inspiration. Labor exploitation was part of a long list of inequities that included slavery, intemperance, war and "licentiousness in all its loathesome, destructive influences."[25] Perhaps because these radical reform impulses were kept within an evangelical congregation, rather than moving without, a more spiritually oriented posture could be maintained.

Hiram Stevens also proved to be an important apostle of ten-hour enthusiasm. Stevens left his Freewill Baptist congregation in Dover, New Hampshire, after having been caught up in Millerite teachings there. In the summer of 1844 he took over the Free Will Baptist Church in Lowell, where he allowed his church to be used as ten-hour meeting hall. Upon returning to his old congregation in Dover a couple of years later, he became a leader in the ten-hour agitation in that town.[26]

In Lowell, except for Hiram Stevens, ministerial support was

24. *The Mechanic*, August 24, 1844; *Voice of Industry*, June 10, 1846.
25. Philo C. Pettibone, *"Thy Kingdom Come": A Sermon, Preached October 16, 1844, at the Dedication of the Trinitarian Church* (Fitchburg, 1845), p. 31.
26. Information on Hiram Stevens and the Millerites is in the Dover Freewill Baptist Church Records, vol. 1, December 4, 1843–August 22, 1844 (NHHS) as well as in "First Free Will Baptist Church" (typescript), Records of the Freewill Baptist Church, Dover, N.H. The *Dover Gazette* noted Stevens's leadership at ten-hour meetings in the issue of March 27, 1847.

slight. Finally, in 1846, the Rev. Lemuel Porter would speak in favor of a ten-hour day, but he did so as street meetings began to spring up in town to protest work on Sundays. The Sabbath-Day Christians, who had the demeanor and tactics of "true Washingtonians," come-outers, and free speech radicals, were holding meetings in the street near places where wage work was mandated on the Sabbath. Their sermons were bitter denunciations of the clergy for failing to treat the working people in their congregations in a true Christian spirit. Jama Lazerow suggests that labor reform in Lowell had become a type of religion, but it might be more accurate to say that religion had become labor reform as the personal world of religious salvation was historicized by Sabbath-Day Christians.[27] Labor radicals drew on the imagery of religion even as they challenged the institutional authority of churches, but they focused on changing the material conditions of work.

In Lynn the radical reform impulse moved about as far beyond institutional churches as it would go in any town in the nation. In a variety of forms, come-outerism structured reform activity in Lynn and marginalized clergy who might have otherwise participated in that town's reform activity. This may account for the lack of discussion about issues of religion or salvation in Lynn.[28]

Where such discussion did occur, however, the line between religious aspiration and economic activity was purposely blurred. Narratives focused less on the triumphs of salvation than on the physical and economic constraints of salvific progress, less on the spiritual independence of true believers than on their dependence on workplace conditions. If evangelical religion encouraged working people to become agents of their own destiny, that agency now became problematized, as the cyclical and performative nature of religious conversion narratives was transformed into an instrumental language of change. A similar transformation was apparent in the adaptation of Washingtonianism.

27. *Voice of Industry*, June 10, 1846; October 9, 1846; October 23, 1846; Jama Lazerow, "Religion and the New England Mill Girl: A New Perspective on an Old Theme," *The New England Quarterly* 60 (September 1987): 442.

28. For a discussion of come-outerism in Lynn, see Lewis Perry, *Radical Abolitionism: Anarchy and the Government of God in Antislavery Thought* (Ithaca, N.Y., 1973), pp. 97–128.

Temperance Transformed

As working people tried to establish an image of moral assertiveness in a morally degraded atmosphere, Washingtonianism would provide them with a model equally as important as religion. And just as religious leaders had provided support, so would Washingtonian speakers. In Fall River the Washingtonians marched in the ten-hour parade on the Fourth of July in 1844, and many of the leading Washingtonians supported the ten-hour men in the pages of *The All Sorts*. As *The Mechanic* would claim in trumpeting this support, "the Ten Hour men are Washingtonians in principle."[29] Leaders among the Lynn Washingtonians were also leaders among the cordwainers and the ten-hour advocates. When David Pierce came from Fall River to offer support to the journeymen of Lynn in their labor struggles, he was also dragged by William Fraser to Mechanics Hall to address the Washingtonian Society. While the impact of institutional religion in Lynn was limited, that of temperance reform was not.[30]

The ideal Washingtonian was particularly suited to providing a solution to the dilemma of representing a man who could be morally degraded yet virtuous, for both coexisted in the reformed drunk as it might in the reformed worker, at least the reformed male worker. Workingwomen were still bound by expectations of moral purity. But Washingtonianism provided an excellent model for the workingman to assert his moral superiority over the employer. Thus labor reform and Washingtonianism shared a dual strategy of conversion and subversion. Working people and the community at large might be converted by the example and rhetoric of labor activists while the moral authority of mill owners was undermined.

Temperance was often discussed in the ten-hour newspapers as part of the personal reformation associated with the ten-hour movement. One unsigned article in *The Awl*, for example, spoke

29. *The Mechanic*, July 13, 1844.
30. David Pierce's name figured prominently in the Record of the Fall River Washington Total Abstinence Society (Manuscript Collection, First Baptist Church of Fall River).

of the need to combat alcohol with renewed vigor. To those readers who might argue that "temperance has nothing to do with the laboring man's interest," the author replied that "in order to remove the oppression under which we labor, we have got to come out from moral degradation."[31]

Because ten-hour advocates perceived important parallels between temperance and labor reform, they also believed they could profit by examining the progress of the fight against alcohol. Goodwin Wood of Lowell argued that the temperance movement was progressing haltingly toward its goals through a tacking process of trial and error. He suggested that the labor movement might make more rapid and direct progress if members "investigated the matter thoroughly at the onset."[32]

Analogies were developed about the enslavement of the will in the context of both work and drinking. As ten-hour advocates explored the failings of both capitalists and workers in attempts to create a ten-hour day, comparisons were often made to drunkenness and drunkards. When Wood addressed the workingmen and workingwomen of Lowell on July 30, 1844, he put forward a resolution that working people should investigate the causes of their laboring problems, just as temperance advocates had investigated the causes of drunkenness. He was particularly interested in pursuing the "striking likeness between the rum-drinker and the capitalist," because neither was able to control his baser urges. The drunkard began his career of debauchery by drinking only a few glasses of alcohol a day, but he increased his intake with the passage of time, craving ever-larger amounts. The willpower of the capitalist was corrupted in a similar manner: "At first he is pretty well satisfied with six per cent for his money— soon he wants 12½ percent—and then 20 and 25—and finally he was not satisfied with fifty per cent." Just as Washingtonianism had inverted the relationships of moral authority between the elite and the common people, the labor-reform movement inverted relationships of moral authority between working people and capitalists.[33]

31. *The Awl*, August 9, 1845.
32. *The New England Operative*, reprinted in *The Mechanic*, August 10, 1844.
33. Ibid.

The mechanics in Fall River used a similar sort of logic when several members of their association returned to work on the all-day system in the spring. The efforts to reclaim these lost souls, the editors of *The Mechanic* argued, should conform to the principles developed by the Washingtonian Temperance Society, principles of moral suasion. For "those who have fallen from the noble stand which they have taken," the newspaper recommended:

> They should be looked upon more in pitty [*sic*] than in anger, and like good Washingtonians we must endeavor to raise them from their degraded state, and make them feel once more that they are MEN—MEN capable of achieving a vast amount of good, of delving in the paths of science and Literature, and of becoming ornaments to themselves and to society. We must make them feel too, (which we verily believe is the case[)] that the men who now employ them more than 10 hours a day, look upon them with contempt, and feel to despise them for their want of manly courage and independence.[34]

The "workaholic," like the alcoholic, was morally paralyzed by the acquisitive economic system surrounding him. It degraded his human condition and isolated him from the companionship of those who truly cared about him. He was exploited by those whose only concern for him was the financial gain he brought them. But all was not lost. Companionship and support would provide the strength to withstand the temptations offered him by greedy employers.

In talking about the way in which the will was paralyzed, however, ten-hour advocates provided some important revisions to Washingtonian ideology. They agreed with temperance reformers that "grog shops are the passageways to poverty, wretchedness, and ruin," but pointed out these were not the ultimate causes of intemperance—and neither was the use of tobacco, as Orin Fowler, minister of the Congregational church of Fall River, contended. The problem was rooted in the workplace, not in the tavern, *The Mechanic* said:

34. *The Mechanic*, May 4, 1844.

> Hard labor, and long hours have produced the use of tobacco, in order to "wile away the day" and to furnish an artificial feeling, to fill the place of the natural one exhausted by overworking. . . . The antecedent cause of drinking is the use of tobacco, and the antecedent cause of using tobacco is long hours of labor.

As a result, the newspaper shifted the blame for these social ills from storeowners to masters and manufacturers: "Upon the employers, principally, not upon the grog seller and druggist, we charge the increase of intemperance in Fall River." *The Mechanic* went on to criticize Fowler, who would "strain at a gnat and swallow a camel." Suggesting somewhat cowardly and venal motives, the newspaper asked if the ministers did not hesitate to "condemn a legitimate fruit of oppression, why do they not denounce the system, the cruel, the crushing system of long hours[?] Are they afraid of *interests*, or popularity[?]"[35]

This point of view was echoed in the *Voice of Industry* when "D.J.H." argued that the "temporary forgetfulness" of intoxication was the only alternative open to men burdened by overwork and denied all other "sources of enjoyment." Alcohol, in his opinion, was "used as a substitute for rest and as a stimulant to enable man to perform over-work."[36] Another article in the newspaper made the same point, claiming, "Our present tedious system of half paid labor, is a generator of intemperance, men who exhaust too large a portion of their physical powers require a stimulus, and many of them will have it; others being deprived of suitable associates, shut out the whole long day from congenial companions; will seek some source of gratification, though it be the haunts of dissipation."[37]

This sort of environmentalist critique was also useful in explaining the failures of the temperance movement. Thomas Almy, editor of *The Mechanic*, argued that the Young Men's Temperance Society, which he had joined at its formation in 1842, had failed because young men had not had the time to attend meetings:

35. *The Mechanic*, June 8, 1844.
36. *Voice of Industry*, May 8, 1846. D.J.H. would speak approvingly of "True Washingtonianism" in this article.
37. *Voice of Industry*, June 5, 1845.

"TIME *was needed for rest and repose from labor,* in order to fully appreciate its importance, and give *opportunity* to attend the meetings." According to Almy, much excitement was generated for participating in the Fourth of July parade with the Washingtonians, "but as soon as the *excitement* of the *parade and show* had died away, nothing more could be effected."[38]

The ten-hour movement had moved far beyond temperance critiques in assessing the causes of poverty, degradation, and inequality. Yet consistent with the Washingtonians, the labor movement was looking to those who controlled the system for moral responsibility, not to the individual victimized by it. D. C. Hazen professed amazement at the temperance advocates who remained unsympathetic or oblivious to labor reform. "This going to the temperance meeting in the evening," he argued, "and there pledging for the reclaimation of the drunkard, and on the day following to return to a grinding mill, and there practice as evil upon the poor laborer, which if looked at in its right light, would be considered equally as bad as rum-selling, is not to my mind the work of true reformers."[39]

The performative efficacy of Washingtonian narratives was questioned by labor reformers who reoriented their discursive strategies to a more instrumental language of change, a language which recognized that change would require more than performance and the face-to-face encounters of Washingtonians with each other and their audiences. This reorientation did not mean a total repudiation of the Washingtonian speaking style, only that speaking was no longer the focus of reform, but rather a waystation, a means to achieving change. The structure of society had to be changed as much as the individual.

The rhetorical style of the Washingtonians was still used to great effect by labor activists, however. The Boston labor meetings, in line with Washingtonian practice, set a limit of ten minutes on each speaker.[40] In the street theater of labor organizing, Washingtonian dramas were adapted and a "true workingman's style" echoed a "true Washingtonian style." In the summer of

38. *The Mechanic,* June 15, 1844.
39. *Voice of Industry,* May 8, 1846.
40. *The Mechanic,* December 7, 1844.

1845, for example, the Lynn workingmen began holding outdoor labor meetings. The speaker at several of these meetings was the shoemaker and sometime shoe manufacturer John Gibson, who alternated speaking engagements between the cordwainers and the Washingtonians. In June, when he spoke, the newspaper reported that he "went to work on this occasion in workingman's style":

> having mounted the rostrum, which by the way, was a common light wagon drawn up on the square and a flower barrel placed in it for a desk on which to place the documents and lamps; then, with coat off, and sleaves rolled up above the elbows, and with a stentorian voice, he proclaimed in emphatic language such incidents and facts as in the language of the *bill*, would be likely to make the *Quakers* of Broad street *stare*.[41]

The outdoor meetings in Lynn were held in strategic places where business and commerce were carried on, just as taverns had been a popular location for temperance rallies. With large numbers of people gathered around, labor activists not only spoke of the injustices of laboring conditions, enjoining their listeners to action, they also confronted representatives of their employers who were taunted by the crowd.

On July 11, 1845 Gibson spoke in Washington Square, where, according to "Sutrina," he urged laborers to "open their eyes and see their melancholy situation, surrounded as they were by such crying evils." Gibson described the "calculating strides of the monster capital, who was gorging himself on their lifeblood and that of countless widows and orphans." But he also urged the journeymen to strike, suggesting that dramatic oratory was not enough and that working people needed to move beyond his performances. Otherwise sympathetic listeners were a bit unnerved by Gibson's call for coercion. "Sutrina" had reservations about the means but was impressed by his heroic stance. "I heard truths enough to satisfy me," Sutrina claimed, "that, however exaggerated some of his points might be, he was thoroughly

41. *The Awl*, June 28, 1845.

aware of the existence of the hydra-headed monster, Oppression; and that wherever he saw a head he would fearlessly strike at it." Gibson did not confine himself to stories about the woes of others, however. Noting Gibson's authority to address these issues, Sutrina also pointed out, "He has evidently suffered from the evils of which he complains, and consequently speaks of them in *earnest.*"[42]

The crowd participated in the performances, particularly when opponents showed up. One defender of the shoe bosses was "interrupted with questions in a real 'free meeting' style, until having exhausted himself he stepped down."[43] Another critic of the workingmen, described by *The Awl* as "a slovenly fellow [who] came forward in vindication of the oppressor, and against the oppressed," received similar treatment. The audience taunted him until he "finally left the stand amidst a universal shout of indignation."[44]

These kinds of interactions, combined with the rowdiness of young boys who also attended and caused trouble, disturbed some in the community, for the newspaper commented in August, "Much is said of the propriety, or *im*-propriety of holding out door meetings. We believe that none are opposed to this movement but our oppressors and their *tools.*—For our own part, we believe much truth is spoken at these meetings, although, perhaps, the proper spirit is not always manifested. At any rate, it seems to agitate the extortioners of 'grinders row' and vicinity." The newspaper went on to endorse such meetings in the future, saying:

> Let the workingmen agitate the question of their wrongs. Let them hold out-door meetings and in-door meetings, until the oppression which we feel, and the wrongs under which we suffer, no longer exist;—until "right shall triumph over might,"— until all kinds of slavery, both black and white, are buried deep and forever.[45]

42. *The Awl*, July 19, 1845.
43. Ibid.
44. *The Awl*, July 26, 1845.
45. *The Awl*, August 2, 1845.

These were not personal stories so much as explicit social critiques. Washingtonian narratives focused the attention of the audience on the speaker, the reformed drunkard, as he held his fate in his own hands. His personal reformation was the endpoint, the goal. But labor speakers directed attention away from themselves, to the enemies who were oppressing them.

John Cluer provided the most effective transformation of temperance diatribes into labor strategies. Cluer was a reformed drunkard and Chartist from England who drew huge crowds throughout New England factory towns in the mid-1840s. Cluer did not attempt to separate his temperance and labor oratory, combining both into a story of oppression against working people. One report to the *Boston Weekly Bee* described Cluer as "that notorious Scotch fanatic, J. C. M'Clure." The newspaper went on to describe his activities in New Bedford as a "'stump orator,' abusing and insulting every body and every thing that differs from his opinion of things in general, and endeavoring to create ill feelings among the operatives and their employers." The reporter found Cluer's temperance oratory to be a mere pretense for more radical activity, "doing more injury to the cause than the true friends of temperance are aware of." Not everyone was so dismayed, however. A writer for *The Awl* would retort, "He is just the man we want in the field."[46]

Cluer's own description suggests how his temperance preaching was quickly transformed into labor activism. In writing to the shoemakers of Lynn about his performance in New Bedford, he first depicted the forces of good against the forces of evil by noting "that every *aristocrat, parson rum-seller, land-shark, brothel-keeper, bigot* and *fool* in New Bedford are united to put me down! But a few of the *workies* are with me, and we succeeded in arousing a spirit of enquiry." Cluer focused his sights on the clergy in this case, and he held them up as models of immorality against the noble behavior of his supporters. Cluer had set up a street meeting outside the liquor-dispensing Parker House, where one of the town's clergymen boarded, and he had been pelted with stones. "I preserved three of them as specimens of

46. *The Awl*, September 20, 1845.

pious arguments in favor of rum and regeneration!" he claimed. Worse yet, "These holy blacklegs . . . had recourse to another 'move.' $500 was subscribed to hire the victims of their avarice and sanctimonious juggling to mob me; but the warm-hearted workingmen were too dignified to sell themselves to do such cowardly work."

Cluer did more than simply recruit the working people in his struggle against evil and intemperance. The problems of the laborer and the problems of the drunk were one and the same. In speaking of the need for labor agitation, Cluer would argue:

> The great difficulty seems to be to get a sufficient number of the sons of toil to *think for themselves.* The Heathenish doctrine of you "are in the situation that God has placed you in," must be scattered to the winds; the whole brotherhood of man must be taught that "a man's a man for a' that." The world must understand the philosophy of doing unto others as they would that men should do unto them. The people, the whole people, must rise in intellectual greatness against the united monopoly of Capital-craft and Priest-craft.[47]

During the next several years, Cluer traveled throughout the industrial towns of New England agitating for a ten-hour day and laying out strategies for achieving that goal which went far beyond his own temperance narratives. In the fall of 1845 he laid out a three-stage plan: first a general convention, then a petitioning campaign, and if those two strategies failed, he urged that the workingmen and workingwomen consider a general strike. His competition with the clergy also continued when he spoke on a Sunday at City Hall in Lowell on *"practical christianity."* The *Voice of Industry* would comment, "The services are spoken of by those present, as well worthy the noble and christian object, of *elevating humanity* by dealing justly with all men and ceasing to oppress the unfortunate."[48]

Cluer's reputation and morals would be attacked by the Whig

47. *The Awl*, September 27, 1845.
48. *Voice of Industry*, December 5, 1845.

newspaper in Lowell and defended by the *Voice of Industry*, but he continued to be a popular speaker, combining his message of temperance with that of labor reform in a style that outraged many of his opponents. While visiting Dover, New Hampshire, in the spring of 1847, his speeches at both a labor-reform picnic and a temperance meeting caused extensive controversy.[49]

Despite the activities of such men as Gibson and Cluer, the relationship between Washingtonianism and labor reform was neither one way nor unambiguous. The sensationalist language of Washingtonian speakers need not be aimed against "respectable" members of society. Indeed, it might be used in just the opposite way, as a voyeuristic lens for the middle class to view working-class degradation, a path that seems to have been adopted by another Washingtonian lecturer, John Gough.

Gough's moral suasionist approach to temperance received early support from William Young and the *Voice of Industry*. When Gough spoke at a temperance picnic sponsored by the Martha Washingtonians, the *Voice of Industry* spoke approvingly of his views, which were "large and liberal, philosophical and strictly Washingtonian." Gough's belief in moral action meant that he "loves the drunkard and extends to him a helping hand— which restores him to friendship's manhood, instead of sending him to the house of Correction and infamy. He loves the Rumseller as a *man*, but '*abhors*' the traffic."[50]

But Gough stuck to temperance narratives and stayed clear of labor reform. Public speaking on his former drunkenness was a path of upward mobility for him, and his reliance on middle-class sponsors and a middle-class audience became clear. When William Young gave notice of John B. Gough's speaking engagement in Fitchburg, the newspaper was critical of the admission charged to his lecture (12½ cents), enough to keep the poor drunkard away from the lecture hall, merely to fatten the purse

49. For further discussion of the controversy over Cluer's morals, see Norman Ware, *The Industrial Worker, 1840–1860* (1924; rpt. New York, 1974), pp. 139–141. On the controversy in New Hampshire, see *Dover Enquirer*, April 6, April 13, April 20, and April 27, 1847; *Dover Gazette*, April 3, April 10, April 17, April 24, and May 8, 1847.

50. *Voice of Industry*, August 21, 1845.

of temperance societies already composed of wealthy people. "What consistency! A virtual prohibition put upon the poor inebriate, from hearing the sad experience of his brother's degradation, and his glorious return to the path of sobriety and happiness."[51]

The following year a writer to the *Voice of Industry* pushed the criticism of Gough to extend to reformed inebriates in general, who seemed to be making a fortune on the lecture circuit. The writer, "W.R.," was particularly indignant that Gough was to earn $100 per week for a lecture tour in the South. These improper lecturers, the writer believed, had hindered the temperance movement in recent years, not helped it, by encouraging men to become drunks with the certain assurance they would be forgiven and even achieve upward mobility. "I am one who would give *all credit* due to reformed inebriates," he claimed, "and restore to them *all* the privileges and respect of society which they deserve, (which I think cannot be more than those who have lived honest temperance lives)."[52] These were exactly the sort of criticisms middle-class reformers had begun to level at Washingtonians, but in this case it may have been rooted in a somewhat different perspective, where Gough's upward mobility was viewed as a betrayal to working people. Gough embraced the middle class while such men as Cluer criticized it.

Thus when the *Courier* of Lowell waged its smear campaign against Cluer, the *Voice of Industry* compared these revelations to those about Gough's backsliding and noted that the *Courier* was willing to defend Gough, but not Cluer, for his mistakes. Noting that Cluer had never broken his pledge or lived for days in "drunken and licentious debauchery," the *Voice* pointed out: "This *christian, virtuous* Courier is crying out to the utmost of his ability against Cluer, while the 'mantle of charity' which covers the *sins of our party,* is thrown over Mr. Gough." The editors of the *Voice of Industry* went on to reiterate that they did not mean to cast aspersions on Gough's character "as it remains yet to be proved to us, that he fell voluntarily," and that they were only

51. *Voice of Industry,* May 29, 1845.
52. *Voice of Industry,* December 11, 1846.

bringing his name up as a point of comparison. The implication, however, was clearly that Gough, to some extent, had ties to the other side.[53]

Intertwined with Gough's embrace of the middle class, though, was a parallel commitment to the performative efficacy of his speaking, which focused concern for change in his very person. This became clear in an incident when his critics lampooned his piety as hypocritical. An article reprinted in the *Voice of Industry* from the *Chronotype* noted that Gough was "very much shocked because Mary Taylor played the 'Devil in Pari' one day, and sung sacred music at St. Peter's church another." As the newspaper would suggest somewhat scornfully, "This reminds us of a worthy deacon who abruptly left one of the Handel and Hayden Society's concerts, on being informed that one of the horns had 'Fisher's Hornpipe' blown through it the day previous."[54] When labor reformers spoke, they were instruments of change rather than constitutive of it, something Gough did not understand.

Even among labor activists, Washingtonianism could work at purposes contrary to the overall direction of the movement. In Lynn, Washingtonianism may have drained off some of the leadership it originally provided the labor movement. By the summer of 1845, for example, William Fraser had returned to leading temperance battles and his name disappeared from the cause of labor. As an active participant in the Reformed Men's Charitable Washingtonian Society, of which Henry Clapp was president, Fraser was moving increasingly toward a free-speech, come-outer position.[55] John Gibson, whose own vitriolic speaking style and street organizing was a prominent feature of attempts among cordwainers to organize that summer, would condemn the "Clapp come-outers" as he set up a newspaper in Lynn at the end of 1845 called *The True Workingman*. He planned to drive Clapp-ism "from the town, across the mountains, to the Pacific Ocean, and there buried at low water mark, so deep that it can

53. *The Mechanic*, September 7, 1844.
54. *Voice of Industry*, April 30, 1847.
55. *Pebble against the Tide* (Lynn), April 12, 1845.

never have a resurrection, or its stinking carcass ever again be smelt by man or beast."[56]

Washingtonianism could divide the labor movement in another way as well. To Washingtonians who relied strictly on moral suasion and opposed all legal intervention, unity with operatives in petitioning campaigns may have been problematic. This was clear when mechanics in Fall River expected operatives to act the same way as carpenters in achieving a ten-hour day. One speaker to the Workingmen's Reform Association in Fall River noted: "The *friends* of temperance and of the poor inebriate, had toiled on year after year with but little success. But when the *drunkard* took hold of the work himself, a mighty revolution was effected." Adapting their approach to the ten-hour movement, he argued: "So it must be with the laboring classes. If they wish to be raised, to the elevation God had made them to fill, they must raise themselves."[57]

William Young also looked at labor and liquor problems in the same terms. He saw legislation for a ten-hour day, for example, as a stopgap measure. It would apply only to corporations (because they were licensed by the state), and the problem of oppression would simply crop up in another way. Thus Young urged the formation of mutual labor organizations. "The laborers should till their own soil; work their own stock; make their own industry, instead of supporting such hords of useless exchangers and mercenary speculations as are now consuming and luxuriating upon their hard earnings."[58]

Young was right about the limited impact of ten-hour legislation, but in the end his strategy suggested more a withdrawal from the world than a transformation of it. His view, however, did not necessarily reflect the attitudes of others, who had prob-

56. *The True Workingman* (Lynn), December 20, 1845. The preceding week, Gibson reported with approval that some of the original Washingtonian leaders, such as Edward Carroll and Benjamin Mudge, were starting a new Washingtonian Society to compete with the come-outers, and they were doing so with support of some of the clergy (*The True Workingman*, December 13, 1845).

57. *The Mechanic*, September 7, 1844.

58. *Voice of Industry*, June 5, 1845.

lematized the issue of self-reform and reoriented the focus of reformers toward economic and social conditions, undermining the rigidity of the boundary between the world of personal choice and public exchange. Labor reformers were ultraists who pushed moral reform beyond the limits of other reform radicals as they tried to accommodate reform to industrial difference.[59]

The fact that labor reformers introduced the language of personal morality into the discourse of labor conflict and economic relationships may suggest a backward-lookingness, an attempt to reestablish the moral economy of a "traditional" world still remembered. The classic formulation of this view comes from Norman Ware, who described "the protests of the forties . . . [as] conservative, defensive in temper and purpose . . . struggles to return to a past that had gone."[60] It is a reading of these labor protests which fails to comprehend the contested nature of religion and reform in the early nineteenth century as well as the importance of these cultural arenas in the creation of a modern industrial world. Labor reformers suffered from no such illusions. They were not interested in recreating a world that had been lost, but in pointing out the contradictions of the religious and material world being constructed. Illuminating the ways in which the agency of working people was limited by these conditions, they cast themselves as agents of a new social order. They looked to the future, not to the past, as they transformed the discourse of personal reform into an instrumental language of labor activism.

59. Jama Lazerow, in "Religion and Labor Reform in Antebellum America: The World of William Field Young," *American Quarterly* 38 (Summer 1986): 267, sees Young as representative of the New England labor movement in the 1840s and emblematic of the inability of a religious and moral critique to effect any change. For a discussion of the limits of the way in which ultraist antislavery advocates viewed the wage labor question, see Jonathan Glickstein, " 'Poverty Is Not Slavery': American Abolitionists and the Competitive Labor Market," in *Antislavery Reconsidered: New Perspectives on the Abolitionists* (Baton Rouge, La., 1979), pp. 195–218.

60. Ware, *The Industrial Worker*, xvi; Thomas Dublin shows how the women in Lowell were aggressive, not defensive, in their ten-hour goals (*Women at Work: The Transformation of Work and Community in Lowell, Massachusetts, 1826–1860* (New York, 1979), pp. 108–131).

Chapter 8

Women, Gender, and
the Ten-Hour Movement

When Simon Hewitt spoke in Millville, Massachusetts, on his organizing tour in the summer of 1844, he reported proudly that his talk had been "honored by a *fair* number of the *FAIR.*" Hewitt had learned in Pawtucket not to take the presence of women for granted, and he demonstrated his newfound sensitivity to gender by adding: "The *fair* ones however would be *fairer* still, if the present *un*-fair system of labor were superceded by one we may most properly term the *FAIREST.*"[1] Nothing could better symbolize the importance of women in labor reform than the imagery of this statement that juxtaposed female virtue with labor exploitation.

Men and women worked together in the petitioning campaigns of the 1840s, but they did not necessarily share the same perspective on their activities. For many men in the ten-hour movement, the corruption of women, and the need to protect them, were important symbols in the critique of industrial relations. The permeability of the boundary between workshop activities and private morality meant that the public world of economic exchange could violate the inner sanctum of the home as well as vice versa. Thus, male artisans in such towns as Fall River and Lynn constructed a discourse about women and morality which focused on separate spheres: domesticity, female purity, and def-

1. *The Mechanic* (Fall River), August 24, 1844.

191

erence to men. Workingmen were interested in asserting their moral authority within their families as well as in the workplace and sought the approval of women in this endeavor.

The discourse of female morality which these workingmen shaped certainly failed to comprehend the realities of wage work in the lives of many women, at the same time that it restricted the nature of the participation and leadership of women in the labor movement. However, it did not defeat them. As working-women from Lowell would make clear, this was a discourse that could be manipulated to sanction female activism. Just as work-ingmen had asserted and problematized their agency, so too did workingwomen, though not in quite the same way.

Female Auxiliaries

For male artisans in such towns as Fall River and Lynn, the presence of women legitimated their labor activities as under-takings in moral reform. One editorial in *The Mechanic*, of Fall River, spoke of the critical nature of the moral support that women offered, pointing out, "When defeat seemed to stare us in the face, the wives, and mothers, and daughters and sisters, of the mechanics, came forward to our aid, and bade us persevere in our work of reform.—Mechanics, may we never forget their works of beneficence." "Centre St.," writing for *The Awl* to en-courage female support, claimed that women should attend the workingmen's meetings because it "is as righteous to do so as to go to church; for if the salvation of our souls does not depend upon this enterprize, that of our minds and bodies does, which together forms no very small consideration."[2] An editorial in *The Awl* a few weeks later expressed relief that their undertaking was not a political one that would exclude women. "As it is strictly a moral enterprise, it opens to her willing heart a wide field of usefulness. . . . Her enthusiasm will give a glow to our cause which will attract to its advocacy many who else would freeze us with their icy indifference, or stab us with their cold blooded

2. *The Awl* (Lynn), September 18, 1844.

criticism."[3] In both cases here, the presence of women was used by the workingmen to signal that theirs was a moral movement. Morality, by this time, had become not only privatized but feminized as well.[4] But precisely because the feminine side of this morality was associated with the private world of the home, the participation of independent wage-earning women in the labor movement constituted a particular threat.

In towns like Lynn and Fall River, both women and family were important symbols in the attack on industrial exploitation as artisans argued that factory work degraded women and subverted the family. "N.N.," a frequent contributor to *The Mechanic*, consistently offended the factory workers in town even as he rushed to their defense. Although he was supposed to be addressing the issue of hours, and writing for a ten-hour day, in fact it was the social and economic organization of factory work which he condemned, with the issue of hours tacked on here and there. Describing the evils of the factory system, N.N. argued that the factory system made operatives immoral. Recognizing that his comments would "draw the fire of the women," he drew on examples from "the old country people":

> They tell me that the factories in their land are called "THE HOT BEDS OF VICE." . . . A person from Lancashire told me, that the factory districts abound with illegitimate children. A mother, said he, will apologize for the impurity of her daughter by saying, "she could na' keep." Others have told me, that the females employed in the factories of the old country, have a boldness in their speech and manners, by which they are distinguished from other females.[5]

N.N. would not directly ascribe the same sexual improprieties to factory girls in the United States, but he saw the potential for immorality: "By bringing together in a mixed state, male and female—by placing females so much under the control of over-

3. *The Awl*, December 21, 1844.
4. Ruth H. Bloch, "The Gendered Meanings of Virtue in Revolutionary America," *Signs* 13 (Autumn 1987): 37–58.
5. *The Mechanic*, October 12, 1844.

seers, agents and millocrats—and by impoverishing and oppressing the operatives there, it is a positive moral evil."[6] N.N. felt no better about the way factory operatives used their wages. "A thorough factory girl is a wasteful, tawdry, slatternly person. They buy a good many clothes. These are of a kind generally as befiting a person, as paper shoes in a thaw." As a result "factory labor *disqualifies a woman for being a* HELP IN A FAMILY." He would apply similar criticisms to other wage-earning women, noting, "The bonnet and dressmakers are notoriously deficient in the qualifications of the kitchen."[7] But factory girls received the bulk of his criticism, and while N.N. was focusing on a factory girl's presumed lack of household skills, the character implications of his assessment were obvious. A bad housekeeper and an immoral woman were one and the same.

N.N.'s articles caused quite a stir in town, though no written responses from factory operatives were ever printed. But, N.N. assumed a defensive posture in his next article, suggesting that factory girls were usually pious and that he was referring to domestic training as an apprenticeship issue only. Yet his moral reservations about females doing factory work persisted. In a later essay he condemned factories for disqualifying women from being fit mothers. Among other things, mills injured "*the gentle passions of women.*" As N.N. went on to explain:

> From some cause or another, either from the despotism exercised over them, or from a too great familiarity with males, which the factory system promotes, the factory girls exchange some of their feminine qualities for the masculine—she becomes too *bold.* Her naturally fine tones of voice are from loud speaking made coarser. There are various causes which produce this *manly* appearance, and which spoils their manners.[8]

With arguments such as this, it is not surprising that factory girls in Fall River avoided the movement. The fact that there was

6. Ibid.
7. *The Mechanic*, November 23, 1844.
8. Ibid; November 30, 1844.

an uproar suggests that N.N.'s views were not shared by everyone. Thus N.N. noted that his articles had "recently excited the indignant feelings, of quite a number of girls, against me." He continued, "As women always claim the victory, as honorable a retreat as can be made is intended in this communication. If I live I intend not to battle the women but the factory system." Quickly forgetting he was in retreat, however, N.N. attacked the factory girls even more directly, challenging them "not to demand proofs of the defects in their education; these are too obvious to be denied." He concluded his attack on the domestic skills of factory girls by invoking motherhood: "Against factory women I have no animosity, though I could find fault with many of you. This is omitted. . . . 'My mother' is too hallowed a title to be disgraced, to be dishonored by ignorance and by coldness of affection."[9]

The fact that these articles continued to run in *The Mechanic* suggests they did have a constituency, probably for two different reasons. For mechanics who were trying to undermine the paternalistic arguments of employers, or arguments that economic exchange had nothing to do with personal morality, family degradation was a potent symbol. Family organization and female virtue had become tropes for debating the effects of industrialization in England; artisans in New England duplicated the pattern. Factories, which used the metaphor of family organization to legitimate their control over their employees, were thus attacked for undermining the actual—or, more accurately, idealized—families of those they employed.[10]

This argument would resonate not only as an attack on factory paternalism but also as a defense of the artisanal household in which the adult male was supposed to be the head and in which adult men faced the challenge of industrialization as a challenge to their family authority. In their Washingtonian temperance movement and the labor-reform movement, men were rebuild-

9. *The Mechanic*, November 30, 1844.
10. See Lord Russell's speech on factory girls as mothers reprinted in the *Voice of Industry* (Fitchburg, Lowell, and Boston), June 4, 1847. For an excellent discussion of how this trope functioned in British debates, see Catherine Gallagher, *The Industrial Reformation of English Fiction* (Chicago, 1985), pp. 113–126.

ing their moral authority within their households. Their loss of jobs while women and children were finding them, and the economic reorganization that accompanied this shift, were attacks on male authority, and so also was the social and sexual autonomy of women. As Christine Stansell cogently argues, the supposed immorality of the factory girl in New York was constructed at least in part around the challenge her independence posed to the role women were supposed to assume within the home.[11] Workingmen were not only applying standards of private morality to public activities, they were publicly asserting their rights to privately control their families.

The Awl would also run an article taken from the *Boston Laborer* at about the same time as the series in Fall River was being published. Here, however, the metaphor of family disruption was even more potent. The author laid out the divine order, in which women remained at home to care for their children while men labored. The factory subverted this design not only by drawing women and children into the work force but also by creating a system in which they would outperform men. "The highest inducement is offered for the labor of the female and the child, while the man and the father is actually denied labor. The female operative can perform the labor as well or better than the male and human avarice looks not at the design of being, or the consequences of a violation of the Creator's laws."[12]

Ideal womanly virtues portrayed in the mechanics' press focused on traits that suited a girl to motherhood. Thus one article argued: "Woman should be acquainted that no beauty hath any charms but the inward one of the mind and that gracefullness in manners is more engaging than any of person; that modesty and meekness are the true and lasting ornaments." These qualities would prepare a young woman "for the management of a family, for the education of children, for an effection to her husband, and

11. Christine Stansell, *City of Women: Sex and Class in New York, 1789–1860* (Urbana, Ill., 1987), p. 127.

12. *The Boston Laborer*, reprinted in *The Awl*, October 9, 1844. Referring to a ruckus among teenage boys at one of the woolen factories in Fall River, "Fearnobody" argued: "The boys, like most boys, are troublesome. No better can be expected as men were put out of their places to save money for the benefit of whom? The owner knows. Better had they employ men and give adequate wages and have peace." (*The Mechanic*, November 22, 1844.)

submitting to a prudent way of living. These only are the charms that render wives amiable, and give them the best title to our respect."[13]

The only sort of workingwoman to receive sympathetic treatment in the workingmen's press was the seamstress, working at home, starving and helpless. The image of the starving seamstress may have resonated at this time, in particular, because the seamstresses in Boston had been engaged in a continuing battle, along with journeymen tailors and tailoresses, to receive higher wages. In public meetings during 1843 and 1844, they had testified to their meager weekly wages, which were not enough to sustain a family even when both parents worked. Middle-class moral reformers, such as Walter Channing and Deacon Moses Grant, men who were active in the temperance movement, had championed the cause of workers in the sewing trades. The tailoresses and seamstresses, even more than the tailors, were having difficulty establishing a bill of prices that would be acceptable and had garnered public sympathy for their plight. As a reporter for the *Essex County Washingtonian* would report, "No class of people in this part of the country perhaps have been treated so shamefully as the poor females who are driven to the necessity of seeking employment and getting a living by the needle."[14]

The seamstress would reappear as a literary figure in the labor press. Thomas Hood's "Song of the Shirt," which was so widely known in England, found its way into *The Mechanic* as well.

> O! men! with sisters dear!
>   O! men! with mothers and wives
> It is not linen you're wearing out,
>   But human creatures lives!
> Stitch—stitch—stitch,
>   In poverty, hunger, and dirt,
> Sewing at once with a double thread,
>   A shroud as well as a shirt.[15]

13. *The Mechanic*, August 10, 1844.
14. *Essex County Washingtonian* (Lynn), October 12, 1843; *Workingman's Advocate* (N.Y.), August 3, 1844; *The Boston Daily Bee*, November 16, 1843.
15. *The Mechanic*, November 30, 1844. Both Christine Stansell, writing about

The poem was meant to inspire middle-class reform in England and the United States, but when it was printed by the workingmen in their newspaper, degraded womanhood became not so much a spur to middle-class reform as further ammunition in the workingmen's attack on middle-class hypocrisy. A similar tone would be sounded in the poem "Female Labor," which both *The Awl* and *The Mechanic* reprinted from the *Portland Tribune*. In part, it read:

> Poor women—see them tug and strive—
>   No moment they can call their own;
> 'Tis wonderful they thus survive,
>   Since all the bliss of life has flown.
> They try to smile and pass away
>   The time as pleasant as they can;
> O God of might! to thee we pray
>   For truth to melt the heart of man. . . .
>
> Yet uncomplaining they pursue
>   Their labors day by day,
> With no bright future in their view,
>   To chase the shades of gloom away.
> O, let the tear of pity fall,
>   Ye men of wealth and power; O list
> Unto the wasting mother's call,
>   And in the work of death desist. . . .[16]

The plight of the seamstress brought melodrama into the workingmen's movement, with stock images of the helpless female and the wicked villain employing her. This was particularly true in Lynn, where the shoemakers transformed the pitiful

---

New York City, and Catharine Gallagher, writing about English fiction, note that the seamstress was a workingwoman with whom the middle class could sympathize because her occupation was both feminine and genteel. But as the labor press in Fall River and Lynn make clear, this was a version of wage-earning women that appealed to mechanics as well. See Stansell, *City of Women*, pp. 128–129; and Gallagher, *Industrial Reformation*, pp. 130–132.

16. *The Mechanic*, July 13, 1844.

seamstress into the pitiful shoebinder. An editorial in *The Awl* quoted directly from "Song of the Shirt" and then addressed "the thoughtless child of wealth who 'trips the light fantastic toe' so glibly across the brilliant ballroom," with lines refashioned from Hood's poem:

> It isn't leather your're treading out
> But human people's hearts,—[17]

"Centre St." would urge the women in Lynn:

> Tell to us and the world whether there are not some that will cheat a *woman* or not . . . or whether there are not some that will make cash contracts with widows who have families to support, and pay them off in orders, or shave the cash debt at the rate of ten per cent. If these stories are true, let the sufferers make them known; tell the men's names, if they can be called men, and where they live; let them be published to the world.[18]

Later another article in *The Awl* would describe female involvement in the workingmen's campaign in similarly melodramatic and improbable terms. "The story of her wrongs is full of bitterness, and the guilty wretch who caused them, trembles in his shoes lest she will expose him. Hitherto he has found her tame, submissive, at times almost crouching—but now she dares look him in the eye, and every such glance is a dagger to his soul."[19] As Mary Blewett has astutely noted, these stories were completely unrealistic scenarios of female participation in the labor movement; the most likely result of directly confronting an employer in this fashion would be dismissal and economic catastrophe.[20] These melodramatic vignettes, however, although ostensibly addressed to the women in Lynn, were probably meant more for the men. What was absent, but implied, in these news-

17. *The Awl*, January 4, 1845.
18. *The Awl*, September 18, 1844.
19. *The Awl*, December 21, 1844.
20. Mary Blewett, *Men, Women, and Work: Class, Gender, and Protest in the New England Shoe Industry, 1780–1910* (Urbana, Ill., 1990), pp. 85–87.

paper articles was a male hero whose job it would be to confront the villain and save the helpless heroine.

Women would spur men into action if not by eliciting heroics then perhaps by provoking desire. Early in the spring of 1844, *The Mechanic* announced: "MECHANICS! come out to meeting This Evening at the Town House, and you will hear something that will well repay you for your time and trouble. The Ladies will be on hand, and probably we shall be favored with a word of encouragement from them."[21] "Centre St." in Lynn was even more explicit about this enticement in September when he addressed young women: "Your attendance, of course, will cause a larger attendance of the young men, . . . this will nerve them to action, and they eventually will act." After the women in Lynn organized a social event, Noggs would remark humorously on the women who were present, "Instead of being reformers, they were absolute destructionist, tearing hearts to pieces," and conclude: "Long live the Cordwainers Society say I. United may they be not only to one another but to the 'high *binders*' present there that night." One of the toasts made at the evening's entertainment was even more explicit: "*Ladies*—may the enemies of the working classes be embargo'd from your embraces—cursed with a perpetual non-intercourse, and blockaded from all ports of matrimony."[22]

If desire failed, there was still humiliation. When "Centre St." urged the women in Lynn to "learn our songs, and help us to sing them; make speeches if the men won't," he probably intended to shame men into action rather than encourage women to take over leadership. In a similar vein, the Rev. Benjamin Phelon told the women of Fall River at their Fourth of July picnic, "Be sure you back up the mechanics, and if you observe any one cowardly turning away from the right, drive him to his post. Or if he will desert, loan him a dress and put him in the kitchen."[23]

This was a man's movement, and the assertiveness that came with public organizing was portrayed in terms of manliness. In

21. *The Mechanic*, May 18, 1844.
22. *The Awl*, September 18, 1844; January 4, 1845.
23. *The Mechanic*, July 13, 1844.

Lynn one writer to *The Awl* argued: "The truth is, many of the laborers themselves do not fully appreciate their rights, as *men*." "Centre St." would urge workingmen to come to the regional convention and "bring your neighbor working man."[24] In Fall River, mechanics referred constantly to the manliness of their activities. Their moral behavior was manly. Thus "P" noted in the pages of *The Mechanic:* "There is nothing manly in these men who remain and labor long hours after they see what the mechanic has to contend with." Thomas Almy hoped that carpenters brought in from Maine would "have the manliness to let their employers know that they are not to be used as *tools*." Elsewhere he noted, "The People are forming themselves into Associations—buckling on their moral armor, and preparing to fight manfully for their rights."[25] Men were the major actors on the public stage, and their moral reform was to be carried out in a gender-hierarchical fashion. Although men were drawing on standards of private morality which had been gendered female, they were regendering it as male when applied to public problems.

Within this framework, sporadic references to women's rights would emerge. A toast at one of the first Cordwainers' Tea Parties was made to the women: "With hearts ever merry and free, may your banners ever wave proudly over the heads of your oppressors, bearing the motto Virtue, Industry, and Woman's Rights!" Another toast at a later party celebrated the female intellect: "Woman—May slavery be the lot of him who would enchain the female mind with inferiority of intellect, or seek to crush the kindling flame of enthusiasm which animates their actions."[26] These allusions to women's rights, while intriguing, did not assume a prominent place in the labor movement of these towns.

The women in such towns as Lynn and Fall River who did

24. *The Awl*, September 11, 1844.
25. *The Mechanic*, June 29, 1844; July 20, 1844.
26. *The Awl*, January 11, 1845; April 26, 1845. When Cluer wrote to the shoemakers in Lynn about his activities in New Bedford, he pointed out that women as well as men attended his talks. "As I am an advocate for *equal* rights the *ladies* take part in all our debates, &c. It is truly pleasing to see them seated in the lecture room aiding us in our struggles for self emancipation" (*The Awl*, September 27, 1845).

participate in the ten-hour movement accepted the gender-hier-archy of labor reform and legitimated their presence as family members, primarily with reference to the duties of motherhood. After the women in Fall River sent their banner to the first meeting of the Workingmen's Association, Ruby Hatch, presi-dent of the ladies' auxiliary, responded to the thanks the men extended to them for their banner by invoking the example of the Spartan women. "I find hardly an instance of heroic daring in the male sex, but what was prompted by some fair daughter of Eve," she claimed, "and in the history of the Spartans, we find the mother telling her son, if his sword was too short, he must take one step nearer his enemy. Woman's influence is ever felt and ours is needed now."[27] "A Ten Hour Woman" would write of the need for women to get involved in the ten-hour movement in Fall River to protect their children from working long hours in the factories. She also would argue, "Are the rights of our husbands, fathers and brothers to be wrested from them so easily, if we can prevent it?"[28]

From Lynn similar sentiments emerged from women writing to the newspaper in support of the jours. "Girtrude" would call the women in town to "this toil of mercy" so that "your sons and daughters no longer wear the oppressor's yoke; peace, comfort, education, and all that is desirable, shall be theirs." They would be rewarded by a new social order with "the darkening cloud of oppression dispersing, and the noon-day of equality shedding its peaceful rays, around our hallowed associations and quiet homes."[29]

Ruby Hatch's reference to the Spartans as well as "Girtrude's" vision of impending equality were allusions to the civic role of nurturing, the place of domesticity in the creation of the republic Linda Kerber has named republican motherhood. It gave women a civic and political role, though their relationship to the re-

27. *The Mechanic*, November 16, 1844. John Quincy Adams also used this example of the Spartan women when defending a woman's right to petition. John Quincy Adams, *Speech of John Quincy Adams, of Massachusetts, Upon the Right of the People, Men and Women, to Petition* . . . (Washington, D.C., 1838), p. 67.

28. *The Mechanic*, June 1, 1844.

29. *The Awl*, September 11, 1844.

public was indirect, through their male family members.[30] A woman's intellect and education would be valued, but circumscribed within the world of domesticity.

Female Leadership

This was the context in which women from Lowell would begin to assert themselves in the New England Workingmen's Association during the spring of 1845. They had joined with the men in Lowell as fellow wage earners rather than family members, they had circulated and signed petitions, and by this time a few of them had testified before the state legislature defending their petitions for a ten-hour day. But in the spring of 1845 they officially entered the regional labor movement when the New England Workingmen's Association agreed to seat the female delegation from Lowell, voting, "The Ladies of Lowell having formed an association auxiliary, to the Mechanics' and Laborers' Association, the convention voted that they be invited to take seats with us and participate in the proceedings."[31] This was the first ladies' auxiliary to do so. The ladies' auxiliary from Fall River was seated at the next meeting, and their president, Ruby Hatch, even sat on one of the committees.[32]

The women from Lowell were far more assertive. They not only attended the meetings of the New England Workingmen's Association, they soon began to speak at them. Sarah Bagley must have been aware of the controversy that had been engendered in the antislavery movement by the public speaking of women such as the Grimké sisters and Abby Kelley. She was no doubt equally aware of how the woman question had split the antislavery movement a few years earlier. So in her maiden

30. Linda K. Kerber, *Women of the Republic: Intellect and Ideology in Revolutionary America* (New York, 1986), pp. 283–288.

31. *The Mechanic*, April 2, 1844.

32. Mary Reed, a factory girl from Fall River, would speak to the NEWA in the fall of 1845 (when the association met there), but she was the only factory girl from Fall River to speak to the group (*Voice of Industry*, September 18, 1845).

speech before the Workingmen's Convention she dealt carefully with the issue of separate spheres.

The occasion of her first speech was to present a banner that read "UNION FOR POWER—POWER TO BLESS HUMANITY." The banner was a refashioning of the factory girls' slogan during the 1830s which had been "Union Is Power."[33] By adding the phrase "Power to Bless Humanity," they invested their slogan with ideals of benevolence, particularly feminine benevolence. The action also evoked memories of the banner sent by the Fall River ladies a few months earlier with the slogan "Union is Strength." William Young would report in the *Voice of Industry,* both the presentation of the banner and the address "were transactions of no small moment and importance, and doubtless will long be remembered by all present on that occasion."[34]

As Bagley entered into the public discourse on labor reform, she used history, a distinctly female history, to denature women's sphere at the same time she accepted its existence. "For the last half a century, it has been deemed a violation of woman's sphere to appear before the public as a speaker," she claimed. Bagley did not explain her reference to activities fifty years earlier, though perhaps she was alluding to the end of the revolutionary period in the United States and France. But she had most emphatically given "woman's sphere" a historical character. She would also go on to describe the ten-hour day as a political right. "When our rights are trampled upon and we appeal in vain to the legislators, what shall we do but appeal to the people?" she asked the workingmen. "Shall not our voice be heard and our rights acknowledged here; shall it be said again to the daughters of New England, that they have no political rights and are not subject to legislative action?"[35] As Bagley described it, legislation for a ten-hour day did not suggest protection so much as it suggested a direct relationship with the state. But it was men who had access to the political arena through their votes, and women needed their support.

33. *The Man* (New York), February 22, 1834.
34. *Voice of Industry,* June 5, 1844.
35. Ibid.

"Will ye not be the recording angel who shall write on the walls of those who refuse to protect your daughters and sisters, as the angel did on the walls of Belshazer?" Bagley asked the men in the audience. She was careful to articulate a female sphere of labor activism distinct from the men's. "We do not expect to enter the field as soldiers in this great warfare," she reassured them, "but we would like the heroines of the Revolution, be permitted to furnish the soldiers with a blanket or replenish their knapsacks from our pantries."[36] The example of female patriotism in the Revolution was particularly complex, for while it suggested domestic activity, that action was not simply assimilated to a moral category; it also involved instrumental political activism. The latter interpretation had been given particular prominence in debates about women's political rights to petition against slavery. Men like John Quincy Adams had argued that women's acts of patriotism had granted them greater rights as citizens than they currently had.[37]

Yet Bagley spoke to the men as the primary actors in this drama, urging them, "Let your future action be peaceful, but firm and decided." She also admonished them: "We do not expect this banner to be borne away by the enemy as a trophy of our defeat."[38] Women would be subordinates in the labor movement, standing on the sidelines to support the men who did battle. Like the women in Lynn and Fall River, Bagley accepted the gender-hierarchy of labor reform; she claimed to be acting within women's sphere. At the same time, she undermined the authority of its restrictions both through her historical allusions and through her public speaking to a mixed audience. The ability of wage-earning women to establish a voice in the labor movement would be particularly important to them as they dealt with the relationship of woman's proper sphere to the moral degradation of factory work. To speak rather than to be spoken of constituted a dramatic change in the language of the ten-hour movement. The

36. Ibid.
37. Adams, *Speech on Right to Petition*, p. 75.
38. *Voice of Industry*, June 5, 1845.

words and images might be the same, but the dramatic performance changed their meaning.[39]

The Lowell women were young and single, and thus they used
the image of daughters to great advantage, to describe themselves as future mothers who needed time to prepare for that
important activity. Later on, as Bagley became a regular contributor to the *Voice of Industry*, she would underscore the hypocrisy
of mill owners by pointing to their attack on female virtue. "At
one time, they tell us that our 'free institutions' are based upon
the *virtue* and *intelligence* of the American people, and the influence of the mother, form and mold the man—and the next
breath, that the way to make the mothers of the next generations
virtuous, is to enclose them within the brick walls of a cotton mill
from twelve and a half to thirteen and a half hours per day."[40]

A female writer of one of the Factory Tracts would make a
similar argument, claiming that factory girls who marry "become a curse instead of a helpmeet to their husbands" and that
"It has been remarked by some writers that the mother educates
the man. Now if this be a truth, as we believe it is, to a very great
extent, what, we would ask, are we to expect . . . ?"[41] E.S., a
female operative from Manchester, argued that a shorter day
would lead "to the elevation of our race in general," but more
specifically "to the improvement of the condition of women in
particular." The time a woman spent improving her mind would
benefit her children, for "if we would have a good government,
we must have intelligent mothers."[42]

The concerns factory girls expressed were not so different from
those that "N.N." had raised in Fall River. But because factory
girls were making these comments, rather than having them
made about them, they were expressing a moral sensibility that
N.N. denied them. Indeed, Lowell women would use their experience in the factories as a peculiar basis for their authority to

39. For an excellent discussion of female speaking in the antislavery movement, see Jean Fagan Yellin, *Women and Sisters: The Antislavery Feminists in
American Culture* (New Haven, Conn., 1989), pp. 35–42.

40. *Voice of Industry*, January 16, 1846.

41. "An Operative," *Factory Tract One* (Lowell, 1845), p. 4.

42. *Voice of Industry*, November 13, 1846.

speak on issues of factory degradation just as the Grimké sisters had used their experience as slaveholders to speak out on slavery. The Washingtonians had done something similar in speaking of their struggles with alcohol, though as men they could admit to having been debased and redeemed; women had to present moral degeneration as a pressing but unrealized threat in the lives of other women. In part they did so because social conventions denied them the right to acknowledge personal degradation, but this convention had the effect of directing attention away from the experience of the speakers toward the larger social issues of family and society.

Mehitable Eastman, when she spoke publicly to the Manchester Industrial Reform Association, described how she had been employed in the factories for eight years and been "subject to its increasing heartlessness and cruelty." She claimed authority to speak about this not because she had been degraded but because she had witnessed first-hand degradation: "Who can speak the truth on this subject, if the operative cannot, who has dragged out a miserable existence within the prison walls of a factory? We have witnessed from time to time the cruelties practiced by brutal overseers and selfish agents upon defenceless operatives, while they dare not speak in self defence lest they should be deprived of the means of earning their daily bread." She would go on to encourage operatives to agitate for a ten-hour day, reminding them that "the children of Israel did not arrive at the promised land, save through a journey of forty years in the wilderness."[43]

The young women from Lowell and Manchester spoke as virtuous young women whose fellow workers were being led down the path to degradation. As Huldah Stone would suggest, they were trying to prevent a morally corrupt factory population from being created: "The factory system as now existing is the greatest curse of our country! And if suffered to go on as it has done, without a check, poverty, degradation and misery, will be the

---

43. *Voice of Industry*, September 4, 1846. See also Lise Vogel, "Hearts to Feel and Tongues to Speak: New England Mill Women in the Early Nineteenth Century," in *Class, Sex, and the Woman Worker*, ed. Milton Cantor and Bruce Laurie (Westport, Conn., 1977), for a discussion of this quotation.

inevitable lot of the laboring and producing classes!"[44] When they agitated to eradicate these problems they presented themselves as defenders of female virtue and domesticity as well as workers.

Eastman explicitly stressed their activities as a response to the pleas of others rather than the product of their own initiative, saying, "Since in this reform movement our aid has been solicited, and our influence is so much needed, shall they be withheld from the side of truth and right? No, never while we have hearts to feel and tongues to speak will we silently and passively witness so much that is opposed to justice and benevolence." Almost as if she had forgotten that she was a factory operative seeking to improve her own lot, the author wrote as someone who acted for others: "Never, while a wretched being is crying to us for succor, from the alleys and dens of our cities—from our crammed manufactories, and work-shops, from poverty stricken garrets and cellars. . . . Never shall we hold ourselves exempt from responsibility."[45]

The problem of Sunday labor was, in particular, one where female operatives could act as benevolent ladies assisting others, for it was men, not women, who were required to work on Sundays. Sarah Bagley thus attacked newspaper publisher William Schouler's claim that religion was flourishing in Lowell. Regardless of the number of churches in Lowell, Bagley pointed out that "the *practical* religion of the manufacturers" was something different. Were he to visit Lowell on a Sunday he might see "workmen employed by the hundreds, in shops and canals" or "teams moving gravel, and building materials into the factory yards to be used in the erection of new mills." Bagley would also argue, "It is true you might have seen a by-law making it obligatory on the *females* employed by the company to attend church and pay five dollars a year for a seat, but it would cost you no more pains to find 14 men who were employed by one company, where you

44. *Voice of Industry*, September 23, 1846. Sarah Bagley would make a similar argument in an open letter to William Schouler (*Voice of Industry*, September 18, 1846).

45. *Voice of Industry*, September 4, 1846.

visited, who were discharged from their employ for refusing to work on the Sabbath."[46]

Middle-class women of the nineteenth century were considered to be moral beings who then extended their sphere of influence into the broader public arena. Lowell women, in contrast, used their concern for the morality of "the public" to prove their own personal virtue as well. Oliva, in an article for the *Voice of Industry* entitled "Woman's Sphere of Influence," would ask, "Is there any good work or benevolent enterprise to be carried forward where she may not labor? . . . Let her not wait until society is prepared to appreciate her labors of love—but be vigilant in preparing them."[47] When the Ladies' Labor Reform Association of Lowell appointed Huldah Stone as their correspondent to the *Voice of Industry*, they wrote: "God speed thee in thy holy mission gentle '*voice*,' mayest thou speak comfort to the despairing— whisper *Hope* to the ear, and pour balm into the heart lacerated and festering with the cankering cares of life—reclaim the wandering, sin enslaved, wretched and lost ones of Our Father's family."[48]

As the factory girls attacked the religious hypocrisy and immorality they found around them in Lowell, they held up their earlier home-life as an oppositional ideal and a source of virtue. Ada, for example, wrote from Fitchburg: "Do we not find many professing Christians in the community who are the *authors* and *supporters*, of systems of oppression and wrong?" In a blistering attack on the religious bankruptcy of employers, Ada asked, "And what think you, will not their heaps of shining gold rise mountain high, between these worldlings and a righteous God?"[49] Following this bitter denunciation, Ada published a poem, "My

46. *Voice of Industry*, September 18, 1846. Bagley was referring to fourteen men dismissed from the Lowell Carpet Mills. Similar criticisms were made of the Amoskeag mill in Manchester. See *Manchester Operative*, May 18, 1844; *The Gleaner* (Manchester and Nashua), February 22, 1845; *Voice of Industry*, October 23, 1846.

47. *Voice of Industry*, December 5, 1845.

48. *Voice of Industry*, July 31, 1845.

49. *Voice of Industry*, October 9, 1845.

Childhood's Home," two issues later in which the domestic
source of her virtue would be elaborated:

> But where'er my pilgrimage in future shall be,
> My vision, favorite home, shall oft turn to thee;
> Early friends, by-gone days and precepts given,
> Shall sweetly soothe my pathway to heaven.[50]

Huldah Stone would make a similar point when she argued
that the intelligence attributed to factory operatives was not the
product of long days at a clattering power loom. Rather, "They
gathered their intellectual treasures among the green hills and
fertile vales, of their own loved mountain homes, where the pure
air of heaven, gave life and animation to the whole being."[51]

In speaking the language of morality and pastoral virtue,
wage-earning women appropriated and transformed a discourse
that in other contexts condemned them. Whether they fully subscribed to all its tenets is more difficult to determine. After all,
what other language could they speak with propriety? Yet the
differences between the perspectives of workingmen and those of
the women in Lowell with respect to this discourse seemed especially clear in the way in that female leaders of the labor movement discussed religion.

Sarah Bagley, for example, indicted mill owners as religious
hypocrites who undermined the religious inclinations of mill
operatives. She admitted that many operatives in Lowell were
not as religious as they should be, but she believed that mill
owners should bear much of the responsibility for this situation.
Many operatives, she pointed out, failed to attend church either
because of exhaustion or because they did not have time to kindle
a sense of religious devotion. Neither did churches themselves
inspire the confidence of operatives by kowtowing to their op-

---

50. *Voice of Industry*, November 14, 1845.

51. *Voice of Industry*, September 25, 1846. Further comments in *Voice of Industry*, October 16, 1846. Jama Lazerow, "Religion and the New England Mill Girl: A
New Perspective on an Old Theme," *New England Quarterly* 60 (September 1987):
430–431, argues that quotations such as these suggest that mill girls constructed
a romanticized view of their past consistent with their religious sentiments.

pressors. "Is it strange that operatives should stay away from the churches," Bagley asked, "where they see the men filling the 'chief seats,' who are taking every means to grind them into the very dust, and have no sympathy with them, and look upon them only as inanimate machines, made to subserve their interests?"[52] In another article, she criticized the ministers who supported the corporations and long hours for the operatives, pointing out that a ten-hour day might be viewed as a "means of grace":

> Now if attending church is necessary for the spiritual growth and perfection of the operative we put the question, whether the clergy of our city are doing all their duty, by removing *all* obstacles, in the way of spiritual improvement and perfection.
>
> We do not appear as an apologizer for a neglect of attending church, and yet we doubt whether those who would condemn them would give any better examples, if they were in like circumstances; especially if we take into the account, the constant violation of the Sabbath, by the corporations for whom they work.[53]

As women in Lowell discussed religious issues, they did so in a way that was quite distinctive from the religious rhetoric of men in Fall River. Workingmen in Fall River expressed repeated concern for their own salvation and about the need for time to pray. Religion for Lowell operatives revolved around issues of propriety and social relations, such as the desirability of attending church with mill owners. Lowell operatives complained about the way an agent who might attend religious services with them would never receive them in his parlor, and of how little time they had to prepare the clothing they needed to wear to church.[54] These women evoked religion to justify their social protest, but they did not circumscribe themselves within it.

This concern with the propriety of religious activities rather than more spiritual matters is surprising, given that religion in

52. *Voice of Industry,* May 1, 1845.
53. *Voice of Industry,* January 23, 1846.
54. *Voice of Industry,* May 8, 1846; January 23, 1846.

the early nineteenth century was disproportionately supported by women and that Lowell at this time was home to a large number of churches. It may be that issues of propriety were more important in Lowell than in other towns precisely because religion in Lowell was so clearly defined by these terms. Young women in Lowell, unlike workingmen elsewhere, were *required* to attend church services as an outward display of their moral virtue. Their attendance was a central feature in the public relations activities of mill corporations. This is not to say that young women in Lowell did not harbor sincere religious beliefs, but that religion had an added and clearly significant social dimension that affected the way they drew on their religious experience.

It may also be that female leaders of the labor movement in Lowell were more radical than the rank and file and that issues of salvation were more important to the masses of women who signed the ten-hour petitions than they were to such militants as Bagley and Stone. By simply evoking religion, female leaders could gain legitimate access to a labor movement dominated by men and rally a large number of women to their support.

The language of female morality and domesticity was not inherently radical. Indeed, as Christine Stansell shows, when middle-class women in New York City pressed the virtues of true womanhood on the wage-earning women in the Ladies' Industrial Association, they undercut the militancy and self-reliance of the workingwomen's protests.[55] The case was quite different, however, in Lowell. As reformers like Bagley and Stone demonstrated, the language of female morality need not turn women into passive and apolitical victims. Quite the opposite, it could energize their collective struggle to assert their rights as laborers.

Women's Rights

Women in Lowell not only used the idea of separate spheres to assert their rights as laborers; they also problematized the con-

55. Stansell, *City of Women*, pp. 147–149.

cept to assert their rights as women. As their involvement in labor reform continued, women in Lowell stressed the constructed nature of separate spheres in critiques that were increasingly directed at male domination in general as well as at labor exploitation.

For female activists in Lowell, intellectual parity was the most important issue. When Oliva wrote of extending woman's sphere to such activities as temperance, she also stressed the importance of women gaining an understanding of politics and recent history. "The good mother might allow her daughter to read the history of Greece or Rome, but to read the political history of our own country would be another affair, and would subject them to ridicule at once."[56] Huldah Stone wrote often on the importance of improving the minds of women (and the human mind generally), though she was also careful to add that intellectual improvement made woman "a fit *companion* and *friend* of man—not a *slave*." The gender relationship she was suggesting here must have resonated in the arena of labor relations as well as domestic arrangements, for it came up in the context of Stone's announcement that the Female Labor Reform Association (FLRA) was purchasing the *Voice of Industry*.[57]

Hard on the heels of this purchase would come some of the most radical prose from women. The week after the FLRA purchased the *Voice*, they ran a letter copied from the *Boston Bee*. Ellen Munroe had written to the editor of the newspaper to complain about the habit of editors "to fill their papers with advice to women, and not infrequently with ill concealed taunts of women's weakness." She went on to complain that this weakness was largely a social construction rather than a natural condition, and that—worse yet—men, who had all the advantages of being male in this society, used their position to abuse women, not protect them: "You boast of the protection you afford to women," she argued.

Protection from what? from the rude and disorderly of your own sex—reform them and women will no longer need the

56. *Voice of Industry,* December 5, 1845.
57. *Voice of Industry,* March 5, 1846.

protection you make such a parade of giving. Protect them, do you? let me point you to the thousands of women, doomed to lives of miserable drudgery, and receiving "a compensation which if quadrupled, would be rejected by the man laborer with scorn"; are they less worthy protection because they are trying to help themselves?

Munroe ridiculed the manliness of men who would not help workingwomen. "Prate no more of your manliness," she warned them. "Why the very boys at play in the street will laugh at you." It was not the protection of men which mattered for women, but help from "the strong and resolute of their own sex." She would back into the issue of women's rights when she noted:

> It has been said that men and women are "natural enemies," which I do not believe; but if a running fight must be kept up between the two, let women have half the battle-field and fair play. The time may come when both parties will learn that they can be much better friends, when they have more equal rights.[58]

A couple of months later, "Martha" would lay out the most explicit platform for women's rights which showed up in the *Voice*. She did so after blasting the effects of Christianity on woman's condition: "It is on the *degree of civilization and refinement*, and not on the virtues of any *religion*, that female privileges depend." Martha repeated this assertion and then continued her attack on Christianity by observing: "If the christian faith were carried out, it, of all others would subject the female sex to the lowest point of subjection in servile dependence on man, and implicit obedience to what he conceives his lawful commands." Martha drew on examples from Europe of the subjection of women and cited examples of female monarchs to prove that women were better rulers than men. She was content that the domestic would remain woman's sphere, but she argued for women's equality with and superiority to men. "In mind, we affirm the female is not inferior to the males and in delicacy and

58. *Voice of Industry,* March 13, 1846.

corectness of taste she transcends him." Thus Martha would argue that women should have the "indefensible and inalienable right" to have greater educational opportunities, the right to have their judgment respected equally with men's, the right to "buy and sell, solicit and refuse, choose and reject" and the right to speak freely, "freedom of intercourse, and unrestrainedness of expression in language and address."[59] Workingwomen who penned these articles assumed a far more assertive (and antagonistic) position in the labor movement than had women a year or two earlier.

Perhaps the most pointed exchange came in a series of articles written by "A Spectator" and "An Operative" in which Spectator (who was described as a "liberal minded physician" in Lowell) argued that factory girls needed to reform themselves rather than the system. He recommended that young men and women adopt a sensible uniform, devote their time to study, and save their money so that in five years they could buy land and move west. He devoted more specific advice to factory girls, however, arguing that if men were immoral it was women's fault. "Man, without moral faculties, is a selfish and brutish being; and if woman suffers from his bad acts, she must reflect that it was she who neglected to suppress his propensities or exercise those moral faculties that would alone guide and govern them." He suggested also that women in trying to tickle the fancy of men led men to use them "as a plaything." Spectator also suggested this sort of woman "knows as little as the wild Arab, and has far less simplicity and gentleness of disposition, totally unfit to take charge of the household affairs that belong to her."[60]

These charges echoed those of "N.N." in Fall River, but this time, with women controlling the newspaper, operatives responded. "An Operative" would acknowledge women's role as

59. Martha's comparative perspective overlaps with that of Lydia Maria Child's *History of Women in Various Ages and Nations* (Boston, 1835) and Sarah Grimké's *Letters on the Equality of the Sexes and the Condition of Woman* (Boston, 1838). The parallels are particularly striking because the Garrisonians were meeting in Lowell the same week Martha wrote this essay (*Voice of Industry*, May 8, 1846).

60. *Voice of Industry*, January 15, 1847.

moral influence but argued that men constrained female development:

> I know she has been called the great transgressor, since the time of our poor old mother Eve, when Adam fell asleep and left her to fight the adversary alone; but methinks if we look behind the screen, we shall find the wirepullers that make woman what she is, and prevents her being what her own energy of character would enable her to be. Our laws are framed for us, and we are required to yield obedience—and woman is just what man makes her, or rather allows her to be.[61]

After Spectator ridiculed the nature of female education which was available to privileged young ladies who did have the time to study, Operative asked him how factory workers were to get the time and opportunity to pursue the course of study he proposed, a course of study she agreed would be desirable.[62] "We must make the same request of the male portion of community as Diogenes of the conqueror," she added. "When asked what he could do to benefit him, he replied, 'just stand out of my sunshine.'"[63] Spectator suggested turning Sunday over to study by ignoring mill requirements to attend church and that women should study early in married life. Their education should make them "intellectual, artless and virtuous" to influence men—a condition found among the uneducated "who are in a state of nature" and among those highly educated.[64] Operative, reiterating the concern of Lowell women with religious propriety, replied that failure to attend church would result in social ostracism, though she added that "man forms our customs, our laws, our opinions for us." A woman who tried to step outside her sphere, whether it be in the factory or the kitchen, to "plead the cause of right and humanity" would be shouted down. Men formed the laws that the women had to obey, controlled the education

61. *Voice of Industry*, January 22, 1847.
62. *Voice of Industry*, February 19, 1847; March 5, 1847.
63. *Voice of Industry*, March 19, 1847.
64. The context of this remark made it clear that Spectator conflated the highly educated with the highly born. *Voice of Industry*, March 19, 1847.

women would receive, and made sure to appropriate all the highest honors for themselves, leaving women with a few crumbs for their "sphere."[65] Men were, in short, the villainous architects of women's sphere.

Clearly there were class differences between Operative and Spectator, but Operative ignored those to focus instead on differences organized around gender, even to the extent of collapsing the factory and the kitchen into the same sphere. Another female correspondent did note the differences of class, however. Martha Hollingworth, writing from Pennsylvania, referred to Spectator's argument that women would have time for education when first married. "Perhaps his minds eye when he penned the paragraph, might be wandering into the abodes of the wealthy, who have others to wait upon them," she suggested, "but go into the abodes of the mechanic and workingman, where a woman has all to do and ask each one how much time she can spare to cultivate her mind." And as to Spectator's suggestion of a uniform for factory girls, she suggested: "I suppose it wounds the vanity of those who get their living by the labor of others, to see those who produce all the wealth to dress as well as themselves. . . . Has it come to this, in this boasted land of liberty, that female operatives must wear a badge by which to be known?"[66]

As female activists stepped beyond the bounds of propriety not only to organize men but also to challenge their authority, they short-circuited criticisms that might emerge from fellow workingmen by writing about the issue and identifying such criticisms with employers and overseers. The attempt of one of the women to sell the *Voice* in Nashua was reported in several columns. She had been turned away by Mr. Hill, overseer in the old machine shop: "He would not allow a female to present a paper advocating the cause of labor."[67] Huldah Stone treated the problem even more dramatically the following year. In Methuen the

65. *Voice of Industry,* April 16, 1847. Operative would also argue here that women were more fit to govern than men, as the example of a women quelling mobs demonstrated. She would refer particularly to Mary Needles, who quelled the antislavery riot in Philadelphia a few years earlier.
66. *Voice of Industry,* June 18, 1847.
67. *Voice of Industry,* October 16, 1846.

agent permitted her to take her paper only into the cloth room, an act she considered tyrannical, but in the Essex Corporation machine shop in Lawrence the "Bossee" refused to subscribe, saying, "Females are out of *their place* while soliciting names to a working man's paper." Stone invoked the image of Mary bringing tidings of Christ's resurrection to justify her activities and claimed to pity "such a man—one who holds the female sex in such low estimation. . . . I suppose he is one of those who would wish to have 'the *woman*' a domestic animal, that is, know just enough to cook his victuals, mend his feetings, rock the cradle and keep the house in order; and if she wished for any further information, why she must ask her Lord and Master!" It is interesting that she closed by describing the *Voice* as "devoted entirely to the interests of the thousands of females who are toiling beyond anything which their physical nature can endure."[68]

In their petitioning and public speaking, Lowell women had more in common with ultraist women of the antislavery movement, who moved into the struggle for women's rights, than they had with women involved in the temperance movement and female moral reform societies, whose activities were more clearly limited to benevolence and the protection of their homes. Yet while the discourse was shared the networks were not, so that actual solidarity among antislavery women and labor activists should not necessarily be assumed.[69]

When Martha laid out her arguments on the condition and rights of women, she may have been influenced by women attending the antislavery convention in Lowell that week, for the labor reformers and Garrisonians had exchanged speakers. But that very exchange also exposed the limits of overlap. The Garrisonians had accused the labor reformers of being too limited in their objectives, and the *Voice* had leveled a similar charge at the antislavery activists.[70]

68. *Voice of Industry,* July 9, 1847.

69. For a discussion of how different social networks could result in different kinds of activism, see Nancy A. Hewitt, *Women's Activism and Social Change: Rochester, New York, 1822–1872* (Ithaca, N.Y., 1984), and Joan Jensen, *Loosening the Bonds: Mid-Atlantic Farm Women, 1750–1850* (New Haven, Conn., 1986).

70. *Voice of Industry,* May 8, 1846. For a discussion of the relationship between labor and antislavery, see Jonathan A. Glickstein, " 'Poverty Is Not Slavery':

After this exchange, "D.J.H." proposed that preparatory to try-ing to unite these groups, a social meeting might be a good idea, in order to promote "a more intimate acquaintance between the members of the different groups of the reform movement."[71] Such a meeting did take place during the summer, though D.J.H. would complain: "For a time the unmeaning conventionalities of society and the fear of transgressing the rules of the world's etiquette, made our meetings seem cold and formal."[72]

Ultraist ladies of the antislavery movement were not always sensitive to the ways in which differences of class structured their relationship with wage-earning women. This had been clear in 1843, when Maria Weston Chapman contacted Harriett Farley to gain support from factory operatives for a fair in Lowell to be sponsored by the Boston Female Anti-Slavery Society. Farley warned Chapman that the Boston society must neither assume a high level of affluence among Lowell operatives nor insult them with leftovers from activities in Boston. "These are *hard times*," Farley reminded Chapman, and wages of operatives had been cut. "Lowell people are poor compared with inhabitants of Bos-ton, and our clergymen keep up a continual drain upon their purses." At the same time, operatives were "somewhat sensitive with regard to a second hand fair, as they would consider it; though it might be far more splendid than anything of the kind they have hitherto witnessed."[73]

The distance between the Lowell women and better-heeled supporters of women's rights also became clear in an exchange

American Abolitionists and the Competitive Labor Market," *Antislavery Recon-sidered: New Perspectives on the Abolitionists*, ed. Lewis Perry and Michael Fell-man (Baton Rouge, 1979), pp. 195–218; Eric Foner, "Abolitionism and the Labor Movement in Ante-bellum America," in his *Politics and Ideology in the Age of the Civil War* (New York, 1980); John Jentz, "The Antislavery Constituency in Jackso-nian New York City," *Civil War History* 27 (June 1981): 101–122; and Edward Magdol, *The Antislavery Rank and File: A Social Profile of the Abolitionists' Constit-uency* (Westport, Conn., 1986).

71. *Voice of Industry*, May 15, 1846.
72. *Voice of Industry*, September 11, 1846.
73. Harriett Farley to Maria Weston Chapman, Lowell, March 10, 1843 (Anti-Slavery Collections, Department of Rare Books and Manuscripts, Boston Public Library). Farley was editor of the *Lowell Offering* and was considered a company pawn by such female labor activists as Bagley and Stone.

with Mary Townshend of Providence at a meeting of the New England Labor Reform League in March 1847. Mrs. Townshend, a Garrisonian abolitionist, delivered a speech on the right of women to speak, among other things, though she did not wish the right to vote, and "she would ask whether those who advocate the abolishing of negroes, are in favor of the intellectual emancipation of females. Why the North was full of slavery of every kind." At a later point she also pointedly asked the operatives "why they liked to work here better than elsewhere," reflecting a conclusion she had reached after talking with some of the operatives in the city.[74]

It appears that Mrs. Townshend suggested domestic service as an alternative to factory work, for William Young, in replying to her question, "said it was because the domestic encountered so much of the spirit of aristocracy; here, at least, among themselves, they can have an equality." Several operatives present agreed with him.[75] The following day the written response of "An Operative," which drew on a comparison with slavery that would resonate with Mrs. Townshend, was read to the convention. Slaves, the operative pointed out, would often speak well of their masters to strangers out of suspicion. "It is not only by observation, but by *years* of actual experience in these mills, that all the blessings of the factory system are to be seen and understood."[76] In the tradition of the Washingtonians and antislavery advocates, the writer deftly undercut the aristocratic assumptions of her questioners and assumed the authority to speak for herself on labor issues.

Women who participated in the labor-reform movement in Lynn and Fall River may have also constituted reform networks distinct from the antislavery movements in their towns. No linkages could be established between women who participated in the Lynn Workingmen's Association and women in the Lynn Female Anti-Slavery Society, for example.[77] For Fall River there

74. *Voice of Industry*, April 9, 1847.
75. Ibid.
76. *Voice of Industry*, April 23, 1847.
77. Given that two leaders of the shoebinders of Lynn in the early 1830s did go on to join the Female Anti-Slavery Society in Lynn, this distinction is particularly interesting. It would be interesting to know, however, if any of the female sup-

are no lists of names to provide a similar point of comparison, but when one of the female writers described the Ladies' Mechanic Association there she commented, "We have few, if any, of the wives and daughters of the rich and noble among our number." Indeed, the Ladies' Mechanic Association may have been viewed as a pretentious upstart by women in some of the more established causes, for the writer of this letter went on to comment about the response of more affluent women: "We will not upbraid them for their contemptuous sneers at our efforts; but hope that they may never be engaged in a worse cause."[78] And when *The Mechanic* ran an ad for the Ladies' Antislavery Fair in December 1844, the Ladies' Mechanic Association moved quickly to have a fair at the same time.[79]

It may also be that the place to look for an overlap in Lynn and Fall River would be with the ladies' auxiliaries to the Washingtonians. Caroline Fraser's name shows up in both organizations in Lynn, but beyond that there are few names available for comparison. The domestic orientation of the female labor organizations in these towns, however, was certainly more in keeping with the spirit of the temperance movement than with the antislavery movement.

Different patterns of industrialization separated the women of Lowell from those in Lynn and Fall River, just as these differences separated working people from one another generally. Yet all of these women shared a discourse of female morality which allowed them to cooperate with each other and the men in the labor movement. At the same time, they used this language in different ways. While female labor activists in Fall River and Lynn accepted the boundaries of separate spheres, those in Lowell challenged them in their public performances and eventually in their critiques which emphasized the socially constructed rather than natural character of their position.

---

porters of the cordwainers in the 1840s belonged to the Independent Antislavery Sewing Circle, which had been set up in Lynn in 1843 and after a couple of years had grown to about thirty members. The women seem to have spent most of their time binding shoes (about 2,000) for slaves.

78. *The Mechanic*, June 1, 1844.

79. *The Mechanic*, November 30, 1844; December 28, 1844.

Conclusion

In the fall of 1846 the Mechanics & Manufacturers Steam Shop opened in Manchester, New Hampshire, with much ado as it granted its mechanics a ten-hour day in exchange for a 10 percent reduction in wages. Employees "turned out" in a procession led by a band with banners reading "New Machine Shop, No Lighting Up!"[1] Shorter work hours for the men at the new machine shop no doubt emboldened female operatives in town to attempt a turnout when their factory lit up, but management prevented them from leaving the yard.[2] Several participants lost their jobs and were blacklisted, while one boardinghouse keeper lost her tenement.[3]

Perhaps sensing an end to the fragile coalition of men and women in the ten-hour struggle, "E.S.," a female operative from Manchester would write: "It remains with the 'young men' to say how long we shall be in bondage to the present system of labor; or will they abandon the field and leave us to the tender mercy of him who never earned his food by the sweat of his brow?"[4] When the New England Labor Reform League met in Dover,

1. *Voice of Industry*, September 25, 1846.
2. *Nashua Oasis*, reprinted in *Factory Girls Album and Operatives Advocate*, October 3, 1846; *Voice of Industry*, October 2, 1846.
3. *Voice of Industry*, October 16, 1846. When machinists in the old machine shop in Manchester made similar demands, they too were fired.
4. *Voice of Industry*, November 13, 1846.

222

New Hampshire, a female factory operative expressed the hope that "the principles of the League would extend to the amelioration of Factory girls directly, for the men would sometimes seek redress from the ballot-Box."[5]

Their trepidation as well founded, for meaningful ten-hour legislation in New England was still several decades away. New Hampshire would pass a ten-hour law in 1847, but it was generally acknowledged to be ineffective. So was the 1853 ten-hour bill passed in Rhode Island. Instead, shorter hours were instituted in a more piecemeal fashion during the 1840s and 1850s, by trade, by town, and, as a result, by gender. Machinists in Boston won a ten-hour day in 1851, as did mechanics in Worcester. Ten hours became the norm in the new shoe factories being built in Lynn and staffed by young single women from the New England countryside, and an eleven-hour day was introduced into the Lowell mills in the 1850s.[6]

Petitioning was nudged aside by political party activity, which, as Thomas Dublin has noted, marginalized women in labor struggles because they did not have the vote. This move to the ballot box, however, was by no means confined to the labor movement. Lori Ginzberg argues that by 1850 moral suasion had lost its promise in all areas of reform while political party participation grew. Women were pushed out of many causes that had previously included them, as activists in the 1850s viewed the transforming potential of religion and reform with increasing disdain.[7]

Although politics displaced culture in the struggle for reform in the 1850s, the concerns raised by antebellum labor reformers were hardly dead. Questions of culture and conflicting interpretations of Protestant religion would resurface in labor and

5. *Voice of Industry*, July 30, 1847.
6. Norman Ware, *The Industrial Worker, 1840–1860* (1924; reprint, New York, 1974), pp. 144–148, 160–161; Mary Blewett, *Men, Women, and Work: Class, Gender, and Protest in the New England Shoe Industry, 1780–1920* (Urbana, Ill., 1988), p. 106; Thomas Dublin, *Women at Work: The Transformation of Work and Community in Lowell, Massachusetts, 1826–1860* (New York, 1979), p. 202.
7. Dublin, *Women at Work*, p. 201; Lori Ginzberg, *Women and the Work of Benevolence: Morality, Politics, and Class in the Nineteenth-Century United States* (New Haven, Conn., 1990), pp. 116–132.

community struggles after the Civil War. As Herbert Gutman notes in his landmark essay on Protestantism and the labor movement in the Gilded Age, Christianity suffused the rhetoric of labor activists in a variety of ways as they challenged labor exploitation in the late nineteenth century. Indeed, Gutman sees direct links between the religious critiques of the post–Civil War era and those of pre–Civil War reform, arguing that the working people who drew on this language late in the century were still tied to the traditions of earlier years, that "perfectionist Christianity . . . offered the uprooted but discontented Protestant worker ties with the certainties of his past and reasons for his disaffection with the present."[8]

Working people of the late nineteenth century were far more ethnically heterogeneous than were those in New England during the 1830s and early 1840s. Thus, when labor activists at the end of the century appealed to evangelical Protestantism, the different demographic context may have given their appeals a more conservative and nostalgic character than was the case in the antebellum period. Yet the fact that Protestantism continued to inform entrepreneurial ethics in the years after the Civil War, when men such as Andrew Carnegie legitimated their exploitative labor practices with the gospel of stewardship, suggest the continuing importance of religion as a site of nineteenth-century industrial conflict.

The ten-hour movement in the antebellum period was not oriented not so much to the control of work as to the control of leisure. As historians including Roy Rosenzweig have shown, those struggles continued in later years. In his study of late-nineteenth-century Worcester, Rosenzweig argues that demands for an eight-hour day grew out of a defense of working-class leisure activities such as the culture of the saloon, which represented an "alternative culture." Drawing on the categories of Raymond Williams, Rosenzweig argues that such an alternative culture rejected but did not challenge the values of the dominant culture. In large part, this particular kind of response reflected

8. Herbert Gutman, "Protestantism and the American Labor Movement: The Christian Spirit in the Gilded Age," *American Historical Review* 72 (October 1966): 96.

ethnic differences that not only distinguished workers from employers but divided workers among themselves.[9]

Workers in New England during the 1830s and 1840s were in a different position. They were well aware of the cultural heritage they shared with their employers; the question was one of control. Many working people and employers shared a discourse of religion and reform, but operated as competing discourse communities fighting for different interpretations. Despite their shared cultural heritage, or rather, because of it, these workers demonstrated in their labor movements a growing awareness of the way in which control of that culture had broad implications for power relations in their society. That lesson would not be forgotten.

9. Roy Rosenzweig, *Eight Hours for What We Will: Workers and Leisure in an Industrial City, 1870–1920* (New York, 1983).

Index

227

Library of Congress Cataloging-in-Publication Data

Murphy, Teresa Anne.
  Ten hours' labor : religion, reform, and gender in early New England / Teresa
Anne Murphy.
    p. cm.
  Includes bibliographical references and index.
  ISBN 0-8014-2683-9 (alk. paper)
  1. Labor movement—New England—History—19th century. 2. Labor
leaders—New England—History—19th century. 3. Hours of labor—New
England—History—19th century. 4. Women—Employment—New
England—History—19th century. 5. New England—Popular culture—
History—19th century. I. Title.
HD8083.A11M87 1992
331'.0974'09034—dc20   91-55534